HINDU-CATHOLIC ENCOUNTERS IN GOA

HINDU-CATHOLIC ENCOUNTERS IN GOA

Religion, Colonialism, and Modernity

Alexander Henn

Indiana University Press

Bloomington & Indianapolis

This book is a publication of

Indiana University Press
Office of Scholarly Publishing
Herman B Wells Library 350
1320 East 10th Street
Bloomington, Indiana 47405 USA

iupress.indiana.edu

Telephone   800-842-6796
Fax   812-855-7931

Library of Congress Cataloging-in-Publication Data

Henn, Alexander, [date]
   Hindu-Catholic encounters in Goa : religion,
colonialism, and modernity / Alexander Henn.
   pages cm
   Includes bibliographical references and index.
   ISBN 978-0-253-01287-6 (hardback) — ISBN 978-0-253-01294-4
(paperback) — ISBN 978-0-253-01300-2 (e-book) 1. Syncretism (Religion)—
India—Goa (State) 2. Hinduism—Relations—Christianity. 3. Christianity
and other religions—Hinduism. 4. Catholic Church—Relations—
Hinduism. 5. Postcolonialism—India—Goa (State) 6. Goa (India : State)—
Religion. 7. Goa (India : State)—Religious life and customs. I. Title.
   BL2016.G6H46 2014
   261.2'45095478—dc23
                                                      2013050142

1 2 3 4 5   19 18 17 16 15 14

In Memory of Rosel and Theodor

Contents

Acknowledgments

THIS BOOK HAS a long history. Many people, friends, and colleagues helped me in the process of its research and writing; a number of academic institutions supported me while working on it.

In Heidelberg, the late Richard Burghart and Klaus-Peter Köpping gave me valuable advice and support during the period 1990–2000 in which I did most of the fieldwork. An initial grant by the German Academic Exchange Service (DAAD) and the University Grants Commission Delhi (UGC) helped me to start the project. Grants and fellowships by the German Research Council (DFG), the Ministerium für Wissenschaft, Forschung und Kunst Baden Württemberg, and the German Volkswagen Foundation helped me to continue my research and write a first set of publications that eventually led to this book.

In India, my special gratitude goes to Alito Siqueira at Goa University and Milan Khanolkar for their immense support, hospitality, and friendship at all stages of my research, as well as their academic and artistic inspiration and help with regard to archival work, fieldwork, and translation. We jointly produced two ethnographic films, *Kakra Jagar* (1994) and *Staying Awake for God* (2010), and I thank Gauri Patwardhan and P. M. Sateesh (1994) and Gasper D'Souza (2010) for the shooting, sound-recording, and editing of the films. I would like to acknowledge Narayan Desai and the late Kasturi Desai for their continuous support and hospitality during my fieldwork in Goa. My special thanks goes to the late Pai and Mai Siqueira, and Celia, Savio, Fatima, and Edith, as well as Appa and Kaki, Millin, Apoorva, Kishor, Ketki, and Mira and all "the kids" for making Gabriele and me their family and Goa our second home.

Among the people who allowed me to do research in their villages, including the filming and recording of their Jagar ceremonies, I owe special thanks to the Fatorpekar family, in particular Ramchandra, Nanu, and the late Deniz, and the Pednekar family, in particular Suresh, Mahadev, Chandranath, and Ramesh in Kakra (Tiswadi). In Siolim, Guddem Vado (Bardez), my special thanks go to Vital Devraj "Dadi" Shirodkar and his son Kanhaiya Shirodkar. In Siolim, Marna, I thank the late Sebastian D'Cruz for helping with church archives. Family Fernandes, that is the late Mr. and Mrs. Fernandes, and Jessica, Dr. Das, James, Joseph, and Vaila, made our stays in their house in Igroz Vado for many years a completely "homely experience." In Malkarne (Quepem), I thank Mhadu Shane Malkarnekar, and in Vaghurme (Quepem), Babel Bhimar for showing us the Perni masks and sharing with us the fading memories of their Perni Jagar.

For permission to participate in, photograph, film, and record their Jagar ceremonies in 1994, I thank the organizers and performers in the villages of Keri, Veling, Magilvado, and Apeval, all in Ponda Taluka. The people of Naushe (Tiswadi) allowed me to film their Jagar in 2009.

Bob Newman, Rico Noronha, Pamela D'Melo, Bernadette Gomez, Y. S. Prahalad, Salil Konkar, and Cartoonist Alexy all helped me and inspired my research in Goa in distinct ways for which I am grateful to them. I also thank Vinayak Volvoykar, Freda Tavares, and Manuel Magelhães for help with transcriptions and translations and the men from Arambol for helping me to understand the *Kristapurana*.

Narayana Jayaram, William Robert Da Silva, and Peter Ronald De Souza at Goa University; Teotonio De Souza, Charles Borghes, and Mrs. De Souza at Xavier's Center of Historical Research; Maria de Lourdes Bravo da Costa Rodrigues at Panjim Public Library; Vinayak Khedekar at Kala Academy; and Mathew Almeida and Pratap Naik at Thomas Stephens's Konkani Kendr in Goa all helped me at different stages of my research and learning. Shubha Chaudhuri from the American Institute of Indian Studies in New Delhi helped generously with the digitization of the video material.

In Lisbon, I owe special thanks to Rosa Maria Perez for her continuous support and for inspiring me to look at the *Livro do Pai dos Cristãos*.

Fellowships from the Cluster of Excellence "Asia and Europe in a Global Context" at Heidelberg University and from the Käte Hamburger Kolleg "Dynamics in the History of Religions" at Bochum University provided valuable frameworks for research and discussion, and allowed me to finalize the manuscript of the book. In Heidelberg, I thank especially Bo Sax, Axel Michael, and Christiane Brosius for their persistent support. In Bochum, I owe special thanks to Volkhard Krech, Marion Eggert, and Lucian Hölscher.

At the Indiana University Press, I wish to thank Rebecca Tolen, June Silay, and Margaret Hogan for their most professional help in the process of turning my manuscript into a book.

Joel Gereboff at Arizona State University in Tempe, Veena Das at Johns Hopkins University in Baltimore, and Ines Županov at the École des Hautes Études en Sciences Sociales in Paris read through parts or earlier drafts of the manuscript and gave me their valuable comments. David Foster at Arizona State University helped with the translation of early-modern Portuguese chronicles. Anne Feldhaus, Steve Mackinnon, James and Miko Foard, Juliane Schober, Shahla Talebi, and Miguel Aguilera greatly supported me with advice and their friendship and made my transfer to Arizona State University a most pleasant affair. I thank them all. My greatest gratitude for her continuous support and for providing most of the photographs for the book goes to Gabriele.

Note on Transliteration

For readers' convenience the use of diacritical signs is limited in this book. In particular, all names of places, languages, Hindu gods, and festivities are given in their Anglicized form, except where phonetic specification helps to illustrate archival contexts and highlights special historical or cultural circumstances.

Some chapters of this book feature scholarship that has been published previously and subsequently reworked. Parts of chapter 2 have been published in *Transcultural Turbulences: Interdisciplinary Explorations of Flows of Images and Media,* edited by Christiane Brosius and Roland Wenzlhuemer (Vienna: Springer, 2011). Chapter 3 is a significantly revised and expanded version of "Jesuit Rhetorics: Translation and Conversion in Early-Modern Goa," published in *The Constitutive Interplay Between Rhetoric and Culture,* edited by Ivo Strecker, Christian Meyer, and Felix Girke (Oxford: Berghahn, 2011). Some parts of chapter 5 appeared in *Rituals in an Unstable World: Contingency—Embodiment—Hybridity,* edited by Alexander Henn and Klaus-Peter Koepping (Frankfurt: Peter Lang, 2008). Chapter 6 is a revised version of an article first published in *International Journal for Urban and Regional Research* (2008) 32.3.

HINDU-CATHOLIC ENCOUNTERS IN GOA

Introduction

Goa is a special place. A narrow stretch of lowlands along the Arabian Sea on India's western coast, it is the smallest of India's states. Linguistically, it belongs to the Konkan, the Konkani-speaking region that reaches from Thane in Maharashtra in the north to Mangalore in Karnataka in the south. To the east, Goa and the Konkan are separated from the Deccan highlands of Karnataka by the mountain ridge of the western Ghats. Goa's population comprises little more than 1.2 million people today of whom 65 percent are Hindus, 27 percent Christians, and 6 percent Muslims (Government of India 2011). Goa is thus thoroughly embedded into the Indian nation and yet stands out from its neighbors' culture by what conspicuously looks like "European," that is, Portuguese, features in its architecture, folklore, cuisine, and the everyday life of many of its people. The historical background for this particularity is Goa's early and long-lasting colonial domination, which subdued the region for almost half a millennium, from 1510 to 1961, under Portuguese rule and Catholic hegemony. Along with Daman and Diu, the two other enduring Portuguese enclaves further north on India's coast, Goa marks today the territory of the longest-held European colony on the South Asian subcontinent.

The export of tropical spices and exotic goods made Goa's early-modern capital, Cidade de Goa, into a rich, cosmopolitan, and well-connected city that is glorified in the historical literature as *Goa Dourada* or "Golden Goa." Its port became an important trading post in the mercantile network that connected China, Japan, the Moluccas, and India with Europe. In the mid-sixteenth century, Goa became the political and religious capital of the Estado da Índia, the Portuguese Asian empire and the Catholic archdiocese of Asia and Africa, which, by the end of the century, embraced Portuguese possessions from Cape Verde in the west to Mozambique in the south and Macao in the east. At the same time, mass conversion campaigns, conducted by missionaries of various Catholic orders and accompanied by the extensive destruction of temples and mosques, led to a massive exodus of Hindus and Muslims from Goa and a steady growth in the number of Catholics who eventually became the overwhelming majority. The adoption of the Portuguese language, Portuguese dress and food habits, and Portuguese styles of architecture, music, arts, and sports by upper-caste converts gave Goa distinctly European features.

Religious oppression and cultural hegemony were ameliorated, if only partially, by the mid-eighteenth century, when new territorial acquisitions and political changes gradually allowed the influence of Hindus to grow. The changes divided the Portuguese colony into two geographical regions, which became known as the *Velhas Conquistas* or Old Conquests and *Novas Conquistas* or New Conquests (see figure I.1). The areas are marked to this day by notable differences in the demographic distribution, political influence, and cultural visibility of Hindus and Christians. The territories of the Old Conquests had come under Portuguese control in the initial wave of the military conquest that followed the celebrated first naval passage from Europe to India by the Portuguese captain Vasco da Gama in 1497–1499.[1] They comprised at first only the Islands of Goa, the four islands located in the delta of the river Mandovi, which Afonso de Albuquerque (1462–1515), the first governor of the Estado da Índia, conquered in 1510. Integrated today in the province of Tiswadi, this first stronghold of the Portuguese conquest was expanded in a second military operation in 1543, which added the provinces of Bardez and Salcete. Subdivided into two "mission fields," one in the north that was looked after by Franciscans and one in the south that was controlled by Jesuits, the Old Conquests experienced the full onslaught of the early-modern Catholic conversion campaigns and were—albeit with significant local compromises, as recent historical research points out—transformed into a region that was, in terms of religion, predominantly Catholic and, in terms of culture, significantly Portuguese.

The territories of the New Conquests came under Portuguese control only in 1763 and 1788 through political negotiations with the weakened Adil Shah dynasty of Bijapur (Karnataka), which ruled over one of the successor states of the Muslim Bahmani sultanate that had conquered the Hindu kingdom of Vijayanagara in 1632.[2] These regions complemented the Old Conquests with seven new provinces—Ponda, Sanguem, Quepem, Canacona, Pernem, Bicholim, and Satari—and embedded the Portuguese-Catholic core colony of the Old Conquests in a perfect semicircle into a composite Hindu-Muslim rural society and culture.[3] Although henceforth under Portuguese control as well, liberal tendencies in Portugal and strengthening Hindu polities in India prevented the New Conquests from being exposed to the same enforced religious conversion and iconoclastic violence that had so drastically transformed the Old Conquests in the sixteenth and seventeenth centuries. As a consequence, the incorporation of the New Conquests marked the beginning of an increase in number and influence—Hindu nationalists today like to call it a "revival"—of Hindu population and culture in Goa. Fostered in the nineteenth and twentieth centuries by serious economic decline and massive labor emigration of Goan Catholics, this strengthening of Hin-

GOA: THE OLD AND NEW CONQUESTS

Figure I.1. Map of Goa: Old and New Conquests. From Hall 1992: 14.

duism eventually also affected the Old Conquests and allowed, if only gradually and with various setbacks, Hindus and Hindu culture to again gain a foothold in Tiswadi, Bardez, and Salcete. In 1961, Goa was liberated from Portuguese rule by military intervention of the Indian army, which eventually brought a secular constitution and religious freedom and pluralism to the new Indian state.

It is the extraordinarily early beginning and long duration of Portuguese domination and Catholic hegemony that make Goa an ideal subject for a study on religion, colonialism, and modernity. Far-reaching transformations marked this extended period of foreign rule and missionary impact. These included not only the complex changes in society, technology, and the nature of knowledge to which we refer today as the transition from the medieval to the modern era. Dramatic revolutions were also shattering the contemporary Christian worldview, when Europe encountered until then largely unknown and unexpectedly rich religious cultures in Asia and America and was shaken by the religious divisions and reorientations that accompanied the Protestant Reformation and Catholic renewal at home. The domain most critically involved in these early-modern upheavals and encounters was religion. The spread of Christian doctrine—in particular as an attempt to politically contain Islam and as a theological mission to eradicate paganism—was second only to the global trade in exotic products as the motive and justification for Europe's colonial expansion, led by Portugal and Spain. Preceding notions of race and nationality, religion was also part of the transformation of old and the emergence of new discourses and practices that marked the cultural differences at the colonial frontier and in the Christian "mission field" (Seth 2010; Anderson 1991). In fact, Christianity was the only identity and value that still unified the European nations as they competed over the colonial distribution of the world's lands and riches vis-à-vis the Jews, Muslims, and people variously designated as gentiles, idolaters, or pagans. For this reason, religion figures prominently in postcolonial studies and theories, and is identified as a major element in the Orientalist discourses and colonial technologies that created the distances and marked the oppositions that distinguished the European Self from the Oriental Other (Said 1985; Inden 1986, 1990; Chatterji 1993; Dirks 1995; King 1999; Cohn 1996).

One of my primary aims in this book is therefore to scrutinize the encounter between Hindus and Catholics in Goa and other parts of India as a way of understanding the role that religion played in the transformation of old and the emergence of new cultural differences at the historical beginning of colonialism and modernity. In the first section of the book, I pursue this goal by looking at archival sources, predominantly travel literature, chronicles, and missionary works, that shed light on the sixteenth- and seventeenth-century Portuguese conquest and the beginning of Christian proselytization in India. This will include the celebrated "first contact" of Vasco da Gama (1469–1524) with Indians upon his arrival at the Malabar (Kerala) Coast in 1498, as well as the unfortunate period in the middle of the sixteenth century when the Portuguese-Catholic regime set out on an atrocious iconoclastic campaign against Hindu and Muslim culture in Goa and other parts of India. A third chapter is dedicated to the work of Jesuit missionaries who, around the same time yet seemingly at odds with the violence surrounding them, began to actively study Indian languages and Hindu literature in order to produce Indian-language Christian texts, such as the famous *Kristapurana* composed by the English Jesuit Thomas Stephens (1549–1619), which seem to transmit a distinctly hermeneutic spirit of cultural understanding and empathy.

The rather ambiguous role that religion thus played for the transformation and emergence of cultural differences in the early-modern period continues to resonate in the encounters of Hindus and Catholics in Goa today. This comes to the fore in particular in the manifold syncretistic expressions and practices that bring Goan Hindus and Catholics together in jointly performed rituals. Based on ethnographic fieldwork in Goa and the adjacent states of Maharashtra and Karnataka, I explore this intersection of Hindu and Catholic practices and expressions in contemporary popular religion in the second section of the book. An important focus of this analysis is the connection and affinity between Hindu village gods and Catholic patron saints, which illustrates the significance of the Goan *ganv,* or village, for the religious coexistence and interaction of Hindus and Catholics. Two other chapters deal with the ludic night ritual Jagar that simultaneously honors the Christian Trinity and an array of Hindu gods, and wayside shrines in Goa's cities that display Hindu and Catholic images side by side or under one roof. Not surprisingly, the Jagar ritual and the Hindu-Catholic twin-shrines attract regular worship from both Hindus and Catholics.

Arguably, the syncretistic practices today have their background in the fact that the early-modern Portuguese conquerors and Catholic missionaries did not at first have a clear idea about the religious identity of the Indian people, to whom they generally referred as *gentios* or gentiles. In fact, unlike the Orientalists of later ages, early-modern Europeans did not even view the Indians in polarized terms as the radical Other of the European or Christian Self. Instead, the Portuguese were impressed by what they considered similarities between Indians' religious expressions and their own Christian culture. Notably, some were so enthralled by the apparent resemblances that they confused gentiles and Christians on first sight. An instructive instance of this uncertainty was reported from Vasco da Gama's first voyage to India. Relying on the novel geophysical knowledge that had been established by Christopher Columbus's voyage to America not long before, Da Gama's dangerous trip around the Cape of Africa to the far shore of India was considered a journey to another unknown frontier of the globe. Nevertheless, the Portuguese captain was inclined to see the familiar in things and people he encountered when he landed at the Malabar Coast near the town of Calicut in 1498. In particular, he persistently mistook the Hindus he met there for

Christians. Hence, we can reconstruct from the report of his first voyage that Da Gama went to a Hindu temple in Calicut that he mistook for a Christian church and prayed there in front of a Hindu image that, he believed, portrayed the most Catholic figure of "Our Lady." Modern historiography is uncertain as to what made the Portuguese captain fall prey to such a gross error. Was it just a short-lived "gaffe" triggered by the hope of finding Christian allies against the notorious Muslim enemies in the East, as Sanjay Subrahmanyam (2001: 26) insinuates? Or was the error instigated by old European rumors about an "Eastern Christianity," that had lost contact with its Western origins long ago, as Charles Boxer believes ([1969] 1991: 37)? Or were still other presuppositions and considerations at stake with regard to the unexpectedly rich and sophisticated religious culture that the early-modern seafarers "discovered" in India and which revealed to some of them striking similarities with their own Christian beliefs and practices?

There are indications that, at least in some circles, the confusion between gentiles and Christians was soon resolved. At the same time, though, the curious "search for the similar" (Pearson 1987: 116) in the religion and culture of the foreign land long continued among the early-modern Europeans who traveled to India or wrote about it. Hence, the European chroniclers and missionaries of the time mention apparent similarities between the Christian Trinity and the Hindu *trimūrti*,[4] the Mother of God and the Devi,[5] Holy Water and the *thīrta*,[6] and other alleged affinities. The curious "similarities" triggered many debates regarding their interpretation. Was there a genuine theological affinity between gentile and Christian beliefs and practices, or were the two even related by genealogical ties? Did the "blind heathens" have prior knowledge of the Christian Truth, which they had ignored or lost? Had the influence of the "Mahometans" destroyed earlier Christian traces among the gentiles, or were even the infamous deceptions of the devil at work here? As mentioned before, modern scholars have gone in other directions and discuss, for instance, whether wishful thinking with regard to the hope of finding Christian allies against Muslims in the East played a role in the search for similarities (Subrahmanyam 2001), or ponder the role of old legends about a powerful Christian kingdom, ruled by the mysterious priest-king John, somewhere in the vast territories of the "Indies" that in contemporary perception reached from Ethiopia in the West to Cathay (China) in the East (Boxer [1969] 1991). Michael Pearson considers yet other possible circumstances and discusses whether the conspicuous interest in the apparent similarities between gentiles and Christians might have been the expression of a distinctly "liberal attitude" prevailing among some of the Portuguese explorers and Catholic missionaries (1987: 116; [1992] 2005b: 156). This theory also resonates with historians who see harbingers of modern pluralism and cultural relativism sprouting in the early-modern religious encounter at the colonial frontier in Asia (Stroumsa 2010; Rubiés 2000; Županov 2001).

Uncertainties and unintended consequences in the handling of the gentiles continued and prevailed even after the encounter between Hindus and Catholics had turned by the middle of the sixteenth century into a hostile, violent affair. By that time, the combined forces of the Portuguese-Catholic regime had started a ruthless campaign to eradicate and destroy all traces of Hindu and Muslim culture in the three Goan provinces of the Islands of Goa, Bardez, and Salcete. Public displays of Hindu symbols had been banned and performance of Hindu rites, including temple festivals, marriage ceremonies, and cremation rituals, was prohibited under serious penalty. Even harsher was the Portuguese king's command, at the instigation of the local archbishop, that all Hindu monuments and images be demolished and replaced with Catholic churches, chapels, crosses, and images. Ironically, though, precisely the iconoclastic nature of this atrocious onslaught contributed, if only indirectly, to the partial survival of the memory of what it destroyed. This became possible because, in many cases, the destruction and replacement of the Hindu monuments and images were seen by the local population as corroboration of the sacred significance of the Hindu material culture. This reconfirmation frequently took iconographic or ritual forms that helped to memorialize what had been destroyed and replaced. An example is the image of St. Anthony killing a snake in the village of Siolim (Bardez; see figure 2.1), which to this day is widely associated with the local Hindu god Vetal, whose temple had been replaced by St. Anthony's church. The systematic replacement policy of the early-modern attack, moreover, ensured that after the late eighteenth century, when Hindus gradually started to come back to the Old Conquests areas and to build temples and shrines there again, Hindu monuments and shrines came up in close proximity to Catholic churches, chapels, and crosses. Both these effects—the remembering of Hindu material culture in its Catholic replacement and the emerging territorial proximity of Hindu and Catholic monuments and images—were particularly important in facilitating syncretistic expressions and practices.

Uncertainties with regard to the treatment of gentiles also come to the fore in clerical controversies and inconsistencies regarding missionary methods and policies. One controversy, discussed in detail in chapter 3, was triggered by the Italian Jesuit Roberto Nobili (1577–1659), who introduced a method of conversion in his mission in Madurai in Tamil Nadu that became known and notorious as *accommodatio*. This allowed converts to Catholicism, especially Brahmans, to continue with a number of significant local customs such as wearing a cotton thread and hair tuft, keeping a vegetarian diet, or applying sandal-paste symbols on the forehead as signs of high-caste ranking, even after they had become Christians. Nobili and his supporters argued that all these practices were merely social customs, but his critics countered that they had a religious meaning and thus continued pagan superstitions that were meant to be eradicated. The controversy over what became known as the "Malabar Rites" dragged on for more than a century and involved local missionaries as well as high-ranking clerics including several popes. In its initial phase, church rulings were decided in favor of Nobili, but later attitudes turned against him, and *accommodatio* was strictly prohibited in 1703 (Županov 2001; Catholic Encyclopedia n.d.: s.v. Malabar Rites).

In Goa, similar assimilative initiatives were started earlier. One was the incorporation of certain elements of ludic religiosity, such as the Jagar night ritual—after replacing its Hindu meanings with Catholic ones—into the liturgy and entertainment of Catholic church feasts. Another form of assimilation came into practice when Jesuit missionaries, around the middle of the sixteenth century, began to study Indian languages and make artful use of literary models of Hindu *bhakti* literature[7] in order to produce Indian-language Christian literature, such as Bible adaptations, catechisms, and hagiographies, something that modern scholarship celebrates today as the historical initiation of intercultural translation and hermeneutics (Tulpule 1979; Van Skyhawk 1999; Falcao 2003). Like Nobili's *accommodatio* in Tamil Nadu, all these assimilative methods and initiatives in Goa met with serious clerical objections, however, in the late seventeenth and eighteenth centuries and were eventually abandoned and banned, though never fully given up by local people. What becomes interesting here however is not only the clerical controversies and shift of strategies but also the apparent inconsistencies in the missionary policies in the alleged assimilations. The sources indicate that the major work of the Jesuit linguists and literary scholars began in exactly the same period in which the Portuguese-Catholic regime enforced the demolition of Hindu monuments and ordered the violent suppression of Hindu expression in Goa and other areas under its control. More disturbingly, the iconoclastic violence most likely also included the destruction of precisely those Hindu books that the missionaries were using in their production of Indian-language Christian works. Two questions thus are most puzzling: What does translation mean in a context in which the literary sources of those with whom communication and understanding is allegedly facilitated are actually destroyed? And does hermeneutics indeed capture the principles of the early-modern missionary activities in the fields of linguistics and translation if the primary goal was actually conversion, not communication, let alone dialogue?

This study shows that religion played an ambiguous role in the early-modern onset of Portuguese colonialism and Catholic mission in India, and in the encounter of Hindus and Catholics in Goa. In this sense, the material from Goa presents an intriguing discrepancy when compared with prevailing theories of Orientalism and postcolonialism. While these approaches highlight religion as a strong marker and maker of cultural difference, the material from India and Goa reveals religion to be an inherently ambiguous and intriguingly hybrid dimension of the early-modern encounter. Certainties about the role of religion in marking Orientalist polarities and constituting ideological distances between the European Self and the Oriental Other, we learn, are challenged by the uncertainties on the part of the Portuguese regarding the religious identity of the gentiles and their relationship with the Christians. Similar ambiguities appear in the unintended consequences of the iconoclastic attack on Hindu culture, and the controversies and inconsistencies between assimilation and confrontation, hermeneutics and violence, in the proselytizing policies. Notably, these critical questions are not only raised with regard to historical and theoretical positions that see religion at the core of the Orientalist discourse and praxis. Critical questions are also emerging with regard to scholarly positions that see religion in the early-modern encounter involved in "liberal attitudes," the beginning of intercultural "hermeneutics," and, in general, the "emergence of modern religious pluralism." In other words, the role of religion in the transformation of old and the emergence of new cultural differences in the early-modern colonial encounter must be conditioned and framed by questions regarding its role in the complex transformations that we conveniently summarize as the emergence of modernity.

There are strong indications that the historical circumstances that conditioned the early-modern colonial encounter still resonate in the life of Hindus and Catholics in Goa today. What becomes of particular interest in the second section of the book is therefore recent scholarship that characterizes Goa by reference to what is variously called its Luso-Indian (Thomaz 1981–1982), Indo-Portuguese (De Souza 1985; Kamat 2001), Hindu-Christian (Dias 1980), or, more generally, "composite," "acculturated," "hybrid," "*métisse*," or "syncretistic" culture (Couto 2010; Pearson 1987, [1984] 2005a; Newman 2001; Robinson 1998; Axelrod and Fuerch 1996; Chandeigne 1996; Henn 2003). Specifically, I present here my ethnographic research that scrutinizes the multitude of religious expressions and practices through which both Hindus and Catholics in Goa ritually honor and express trust in the sacred forces and principles of the respective other religious community. I describe Goan Hindus who regularly worship Saiba St. Francis Xavier, the Catholic patron saint of Goa, whose mummified body is preserved in the cathedral of Old Goa, as well as Goan Catholics who, for their part, venerate Saibini Sateri–Shanta Durga, the Goan manifestation of the goddess Durga who is worshipped in countless temples and whose iconic body is believed to embody the earth of Goa. Saiba and Saibini stand vicariously for hundreds of Catholic patron saints and Hindu village gods who are closely identified with their villages or towns and are trusted to be *jāgṛit*, as Hindus say, that is, alert and responsive to their devotees' needs and requests, or to work miracles, as Catholics assert, that is, to interfere in the mundane world in order to take care of the health and well-being of the people who invoke them. Syncretistic expressions and practices, it turns out, are widespread in Goa and can be found among Hindus and Catholics of all castes and classes in the traditional settings of the villages and in the modern environment of the cities. One can observe syncretism in intimate private contexts, such as the devotional gesture a Hindu may make when passing a Catholic wayside cross, or the devotion presented to the image of a local Hindu god displayed in a taxi driven and owned by a Catholic. It finds vast public expression in hundreds of wayside shrines that present icons and tokens of Hindu gods and Catholic saints side by side and, not rarely, under one and the same roof, thereby attracting worship from people of both communities. And syncretism is articulated in big public ceremonies such as the cross-religious worship that is quite regularly paid to Catholic patron saints and Hindu village gods at church and temple festivals, or the simultaneous invocation of the Christian Trinity and Hindu deities in the Jagar.

Various historical and theoretical perspectives become of interest when trying to account for this peculiar syncretistic feature of Goan culture. Historians emphasize the notorious inefficiency of the early-modern Portuguese empire in India, something they relate to multiple factors: the limited military and demographic presence of the Portuguese in their Asian colonies, their insufficient land base and general aloofness from the local society, undue delays and discipline in the local implementation of decrees and orders coming from Portugal, and, in general, a continuous dependence on local middlemen for major political and economic issues.[8] Arguably, all of these deficiencies explain not only the early and fast decline of Portuguese mercantilism in Asia but also the notable hybridity of the society and culture it produced. Another attempt to understand Goa's culture focuses on the postcolonial reappraisal of Antonio Gramsci's theory of hegemony and subalternity. This approach essentially draws from Gramsci's argument that hegemony, due to its far-reaching cultural aspirations, can never be complete and uncontested, and thus—notwithstanding its totalitarian character and readiness for coercion—always faces opposition and is forced to make compromises with subaltern forces. Subalternity, on the other hand, has a distinct admiration for the hegemonic regime and thus—despite its inherent resistance—is never completely free from self-alignment and complicity (Guha 1989; Comaroff and Comaroff 1991). Directly or indirectly, this postcolonial theory has inspired historians and anthropologists studying Goa, who present its hybridity as the result of a regime that constantly struggled between coercion, compromise, and collaboration (Pearson 1987; Kamat 2001). Did parts of the subaltern population thus engage in a type of agentive self-subjugation, which has been misinterpreted as "voluntary . . . conversion" (Robinson 1993: 67)? And is syncretism in general the enduring expression of a "culture of resistance" against Portuguese rule and Catholic hegemony in Goa (Axelrod and Fuerch 1996: 390; see also Newman 2001)?

The historical scholarship relevant to Goa becomes more complex when one contextualizes it within the critical historicization of Hinduism in recent years. Scholars largely agree today that the formation of Hinduism as a distinct religion is due to the incorporation and integration of a wide range of devotional, philosophical, and ritual traditions, both native and imported to the South Asian subcontinent. The term "Hindu," it has been shown, has its origins in the eleventh-century Persian term *al-Hind* indicating the land beyond the Indus River and, around the thirteenth century, gradually transformed into an ethnic marker of South Asian people distinguishing themselves from "Turks" (Talbot 1995: 700; Stietencron 1989). Only in the nineteenth century did the term "Hindu" gain its explicitly religious connotation and begin to designate the supra-local "imagined religious communities" of Hindus (Thapar 1989) that it marks today. The formation of Hinduism and Hindu identity thus was a gradual and protracted process marked by two major facilitating factors. One may be called external, insofar as it refers to the interrelated impact of European Orientalism and British colonialism. This external impact influenced the formation of Hinduism and the Hindu community by two means: (a) scholarly activities such as determining and tracing "origins," identifying and translating "hegemonic texts," and analyzing "cultural essences" of what was gradually consolidated as Hinduism (Inden 1986, 1990; King 1999); and (b) colonial technologies such as the mapping, census-taking, and legal codification distinguishing and thereby identifying the various religious and, by implication, caste communities of India (Cohn and Dirks 1988; Cohn 1996). A second factor may be called internal, as it refers to inherent qualities or mechanisms effective in consolidating the numerous Hindu traditions and practices into one religion. These qualities or mechanisms have been variously described with reference to notions and theories of polytheism (Daniélou 1964), hierarchy (Dumont 1970), inclusivism (Oberhammer 1983), orthopraxis (Fuller 1992), or encompassing habitus (Michaels 1998), all of which emphasize processes of assimilation, incorporation, and integration. While further identifying impulses for the "syndication" (Thapar 1997) of Hindu concepts and practices, and looking at interactions between "great and little traditions" (Redfield and Singer 1954), as well as cultural tendencies of "universalization and parochialization" (Marriott 1955; Sontheimer and Kulke 1989), all of these modern theories agree that the formation of Hinduism is marked by cultural features and historical dynamics that cannot be easily compared to the formation of Judaism, Christianity, Islam, or any of the Semitic religions that emerged from the Middle East. Lacking the impetus of a monotheistic claim for exclusivity (Assmann 2010), as well as the focus of a single charismatic founder, unitary text-based orthodoxy, and centralized ecclesiastical organization, Hinduism is characterized instead by its capacity for theological pluralism (Madan 2005), historical plasticity (Thapar 1997), semantic translatability (Burghart 1989), pragmatic diversity (Fuller 1992), and idiosyncratic variation (Doniger 2009), which make some scholars argue today—much to the dismay of radical Hindu nationalists claiming *Hindutva* or "Hinduness" to be the cultural essence of India—that it rather marks the cultural cohabitation of many than the theological orthodoxy of one religion (Stietencron 1989). When looking at Goa against the backdrop of these theoretical perspectives, the questions arising include, to what extent is Goa's hybrid culture related to the historical and cultural dynamics of Hinduism? Is there indeed something like a "Hindu polytheistic structural mold" that incorporates Christianity and other religions (Wilfred 1998)? Or even a genuine South Asian form of religious tolerance (Nandy 1990)? Which role does the system of castes play in the mediation of religious differences (Bayly 1989; Mosse 1994, 1997)?

The postcolonial critique of the "Orientalist Constructions of India" (Inden 1986), finally, renders reflections on the hybrid nature of Goa even more complex by referring to constructivist philosophy. The Orientalist discourse, Ronald Inden argues with reference to a longstanding scholarly legacy culminating in Louis Dumont's classic *Homo Hierarchicus* (1970), reduces Indian civilization to a cultural essence that marks the opposite of the culture of the West. The core of this essence is arguably the institution of caste, which, based on an ideology of purity and pollution and enacted through rigid ritual and social practices, is said to prevent all liberties and enfetter all agency in India. There are other, local reasons to look into the possibility that Goa's cultural hybridity and religious syncretism are influenced by caste allegiances and politics, which I discuss later. Here, the issue has to do with Inden's argument that to break free from such essentializing of India calls for a far-reaching epistemological revision of the scholarly perspective. This revision entails more than a critical reflection that overcomes asymmetrical power relations and allows Indians to take control of the representation of Indian culture. It calls for the radical rejection of the idea that cultures can be reduced to "essences" that preexist the epistemic conditioning of human cognition and the politics of representation. One question emerging from such criticism is whether Goa's hybridity is a genuine "Location of Culture" (Bhabha 1992) against which both Indian and Portuguese, Hindu and Catholic "essences" simply evanesce as historical and political casuistics. In fact, can one go so far as to argue that Goa, reduced to the site of an essentialist encounter between such forces, constitutes an "invention" as Ángela Barreto Xavier (2008) recently insinuated? If Goa's syncretism and hybridity, on the other hand, is merely an instance of the generic "Predicament of Culture" (Clifford 1988) and thus rejects reduction to cultural "essences," how do Goans relate to the religious identities and cultural differences that have become not only common currency of discourse and praxis but, above all, political reality? And, last but not least, how does the reassertion of identity and orthodoxy coexist with hybridization and syncretism?

While all these historical and theoretical perspectives contribute to understanding Goa's syncretic history and culture, the major intellectual challenge inspired by the term "syncretism" emerges from its ethnography. The critical point is that the syncretism I saw in Goa is not sufficiently described by saying that people are transgressing the boundaries dividing the traditions of Hindus and Catholics, let alone by indicating that this has any effect on their respective religious identities. Instead, all the people that I saw appreciating syncretistic expressions and engaging in syncretistic practices very self-consciously expressed and, at times, even anxiously asserted their respective identities as either Hindu or Catholic. This was not only done through the many explicit or implicit everyday ways of articulating one's religious identity, such as acting as a member of a distinct religious community, cultivating corresponding social contacts, observing specific holidays and lifecycle rituals, keeping typical dietary customs, talking distinct dialects of Konkani, wearing distinctive dresses or decorative accessories, and displaying religious symbols (even including wearing a Hindu *om* or Catholic cross tattooed onto the body). Notably, people engaging in syncretistic practices may express and assert their religious identities even in the very moments in which they are honoring a divine or saintly force belonging to another religious community or jointly performing a ritual with people from the other religious community. Hindus worshipping a Catholic saint at a church feast often express their distinct Hindu identity, for instance, by offering oil rather than candles to the saint, as Catholics would. And Hindus and Catholics participating in a common Jagar ceremony as a rule consciously keep apart from each other and act in separate groups or perform different rituals. If, for heuristic purposes, one were to define syncretism on the basis of ethnographic observations in Goa, one would thus have to say that it describes people who, on the one hand, self-consciously vow themselves to the sacred forces and principles of one religious community and tradition while, on the other hand, likewise self-consciously honor and trust the sacred forces or principles of another religious community or tradition.

In trying to understand this seemingly paradoxical syncretistic situation, one ethnographic moment gained particular significance for me. This was the utterance of a Catholic woman who commented on her devotional gesture toward a wayside shrine that contained icons of both a Hindu village goddess and the Catholic Mary with the phrase *devu ekuch re*, something that may be translated either as "there is only one god" or "God is One." Resonating with the summation of the Three Persons of the Holy Trinity in the Catholic prayer and the Hindu concept of Brahma transcending all differences, this phrase stayed with me not only because I heard the same or similar from other people, but also because it seemed to articulate a tolerant attitude at a time when religious pluralism came under serious attack in India. This was in the decade between 1990 and 2000 in which communal violence between Hindus and Muslims or Hindus and Sikhs recurrently broke out in parts of India, especially in urban metropolises. The violence was instigated, among other things, by the rise of militant Hindu nationalism that was propagating *Hindutva* as the essence of Indian culture and had its apex in the Babri Majid versus Ram Janmabhoomi controversy in the city of Ayodhya. This dispute occurred over a Muslim mosque built by the Mughal ruler Babur, which allegedly had replaced a Hindu temple dedicated to the god Rama in Ayodhya in the sixteenth century. Feelings ran high for many years over this controversy, and in 1992 led to the dramatic destruction of the mosque by a Hindu mob, triggering a wave of Hindu-Muslim violence all over India. Various indications showed that, in the heated debates dealing with this communal violence and the rise of the *Hindutva* movement egging it on, the longstanding peaceful coexistence of Hindus and Catholics in Goa gained a particular public appeal. Hence, newspapers in Goa praised the region as a paradise of communal harmony by publishing articles with headlines such as "Zagor: Rising above Religion" (Gomes and Shirodkar 1991), "A Common Faith" (D'Souza 1993), or "Sisters of Harmony" (De Souza and D'Souza 1987), which appreciatively highlighted the syncretistic practices in the local Jagar festivals and celebrated the cross-religious worship dedicated to the Virgin Mary and the Hindu Devi. In the aftermath of the violence, Hindu-Catholic syncretism found a widely positive echo in Goa's public discourse and regularly showed up in the rhetoric of local politicians, intellectual discussions, and events organized by cultural institutions such as Kala Academy, presenting Goa as a prime example of India's secularism, that is, the harmonious coexistence of diverse religious doctrines and communities. Even in Goa, however, the coexistence of Hindus and Catholics was not untouched by the spreading Hindu nationalism and strife over *Hindutva*. The effect of efforts to intensify and "sanskritize" the expression of Hinduism in public life showed up in many ways, ranging from the increasing display of Hindu images in public folklore to a change from bloody to vegetarian offerings in local religious ceremonies. In fact, in a number of places, people even started to "purify" their syncretistic ceremonies by removing age-old Catholic legacies in order to restore their allegedly proper Hindu origins and characteristics. For example, the date of a syncretistic ceremony might be shifted from a Catholic holiday to a Hindu one, or its location changed from a church to a temple site. In some villages, this even led to modifications of liturgical texts such as replacing the invocation of the Christian Trinity with the invocation of the Hindu *trimūrti*.

One question that I began asking myself was therefore whether syncretism and antisyncretism were indeed just a matter of political values, ideologies, and power relations. Were the syncretistic practices instances of liberal political trends and tolerant attitudes favoring religious pluralism, as public discourse suggested? And was it accurate to characterize the antisyncretistic trends as expressions of a political conservatism favoring religious orthodoxy? The relevance of these questions was underlined by the fact that while I was doing my fieldwork in Goa, a groundbreaking volume on the subject came out, edited by Charles Stewart and Rosalind Shaw (1994b). Entitled *Syncretism/Anti-Syncretism*, its subtitle, *The Politics of Religious Synthesis*, left no doubt that the editors saw the subject as an essentially political one, relegating its religious content, in modernist fashion, to a separate domain that was interpreted as being merely instrumental to political interests, ideologies, and agencies. In fact, as Peter Van der Veer (1994), one of the contributors to the volume, elaborates, syncretism is closely associated here with the modern division of religious and secular spheres that arguably initiated new interactions between religious differences mediated by the philosophical no-

tion of "natural religion" and the political agent of the nation state. This politicization of the subject, it was implied, freed the contested theological concept of
syncretism from the various ideological and theoretical problems inherent to its
earlier, often pejorative and essentialist meaning, thereby "relocating syncretism
in social science discourse" (Stewart 1995). The political approach also resonated
well with the politicization of religion at large in the context of the globally diag-
nosed "religious resurgence" and the rise of religious nationalism and religious
violence, all characterized as reactions to globalization and modernity (Sahliyeh
1990; Madan 1998; Juergensmeyer 2000).

Notwithstanding this contemporary currency of religious liberalism and the
scholarly trend of politicizing religion, my fieldwork indicates that these perspectives and approaches do not suffice to account for what I saw in Goa. That is,
the syncretism mediating between Hindus and Catholics could not, at least not
entirely, be interpreted by reference to liberal attitudes and political rationales.
To make it very clear, this is not to say that Goa's syncretism is apolitical or that
the people engaging in it are not tolerant. Syncretism is of course part of political interests, strategic action, and power relations. It marks a rhetorical value in
the political discourse, it is attacked by conservative forces, and it can even be a
strategy of subaltern resistance, as we will see. Similarly, tolerant attitudes cannot be categorically discarded from syncretistic expressions and practices, and
I am inclined to say that people appreciating them and engaging in them are as
tolerant and intolerant as anybody else who is not involved in syncretism. For
the vast majority of the syncretistic expressions and practices that I analyze here,
however, values and politics that in any explicit way addressed issues of religious
identity or difference clearly were not their primary, let alone exclusive, rationale,
and liberalism or tolerance certainly was not a dominant motive to appreciate or
engage in them.

This observation is buttressed in particular by ethnographic insights that indicate that the syncretism at stake is even more intricate than the seemingly paradoxical scenario of people who, all at once, self-consciously assert and transgress
the principles and boundaries of their respective religious traditions. Clearly, the
situation is more complex since those who participated in syncretistic behavior
did so with gestures indicating that their asserting their own religious tradition
and their engaging with the other tradition had nothing to do with each other.
Ethnographic evidence for this observation comes from the fact that people not
only never mentioned their own religious identities in discussion of their syncretistic practices but were even irritated and unsure how to respond when I,
mostly indirectly, asked questions about religious identities and differences in
the context of syncretistic practices. One such moment deserves mention because
it indirectly and over time indicated to me what actually was of importance to
people engaging in a syncretistic ritual. It occurred in the context of the Jagar
ritual of the village of Siolim (Bardez), that is, a ludic ceremony jointly performed

by Hindus and Catholics that brings Hindu and Catholic dramatic characters to the ritual stage. With the help of local people and friends, I had recorded, transcribed, and translated the lyrics and prayers of the ceremony, but the texts produced still had many gaps and open questions regarding their narratives and meanings. In fact, the text before me, apart from its hybrid Konkani-Portuguese linguistics and Hindu-Catholic semantics, was so thoroughly shot through with lexical incomprehensibilities, syntactical inconsistencies, and grammatical dubieties that I felt like I was looking at a genuine piece of what Clifford Geertz once described as the epitomic challenge of fieldwork, namely, "to read (in the sense of 'construct a reading of') a manuscript—foreign, faded, full of ellipses, incoherencies, suspicious emendations, and tendentious commentaries" (Geertz 1973: 10). I frequently had to rely on the performers' help with translating and understanding their songs and prayers. Once, sitting with them, I tried to find the meaning of a dramatic character called Teng Raja. We had discussed another dramatic character extensively, Firanghi Raja, or the "Foreign King," who obviously represented a Catholic. I hoped to find out what the religious allegiance of Teng Raja was and whether he perhaps was a Hindu antagonist of Firanghi Raja. So I asked. They did not immediately understand what I wanted to know, and I repeated my question a couple of times in varying formulations. Irritated by my persistent questioning, one of the old men eventually got up from his chair, performed a few characteristic dance steps, and, with a face signaling that he hoped that now everything was clear, said to me, "This is Teng Raja."

This incident became significant for me not only because it revealed a certain indifference by the performers to questions of religious identity and difference in the central narrative of their ritual play. More importantly, in time, this incident opened my eyes to the fact that questions not just about religious meanings but about meanings in general were for the performers of far less relevance than they were for me. I noticed that they had no problem with the fact that the religious hymns and stories presented during their ceremonies had linguistic flaws and semantic inconsistencies. At the same time, they took care that their prayers reproduced the phonetics and their dances followed the steps prescribed in the *kaido* or performative traditions of the Jagar, and that, in general, the drummers, singers, and dancers performed with great physical agility and bodily commitment. It still took me a long time to fully comprehend that Geertz's concern for symbolic consistency and textual semantics needs to be complemented by a similarly complex concern for the material embodiment and practical enactment of the signs and practices that I was observing. This theoretical insight was only gradually emerging from observations and understandings of what was of concern and significance for the people. Had all divine forces, gods, saints, ancestors, and tutelary beings relevant to the village been named in the *nomana* or invocation that opens the Jagar ceremonies? Was it certain that nobody was left out or forgotten? Did the icons and locations of all gods and saints receive the appropriate honors, offerings, and visits? Was there no ritual negligence, omission, or change that might have negative consequences for the protection of the village and the health of its inhabitants, animals, and crops? What proxy rituals would be done if the Jagar could not be performed because an important village dignitary had recently died? How much time needed to lapse after his death before the sacred drums could again be touched? Could a prominent local musician perform in the Jagar, even though his home was actually not quite within the village boundaries? Would the capacity to receive the *bhār*, that is, to be possessed by a local god who speaks in the ritual, indeed transfer from father to son? Was it possible to perform a fragment of the Jagar during a secular cultural performance at Kala Academy? Questions like these made me gradually understand that, for the participants, the materiality and activity of the ritual, expressed in concerns regarding its icons, locations, and performances, are of great importance and at times can even eclipse questions regarding its religious meanings and belongings.

Thus, if we cannot assume the syncretism between Hinduism and Catholicism in Goa to be the result of liberalism or tolerance, has little to do with politics regarding religious identities and differences, and to some extent even escapes the significance of meanings and the consistency of semantics, what then is its rationale? My work took an important turn when I began to realize that this question, which was crystallizing in my ethnographic research, was actually related to the main question that came out of my historical research, that is, what role religion played in the transformation of old and the emergence of new cultural differences at the historical beginning of colonialism and modernity. Hence, I began to understand that scrutinizing the circumstances that conditioned the cognition and re-cognition of a plurality of religions in the early-modern period would help me to appreciate what made Goan Hindus and Catholics engage in syncretistic practices today. Conversely, ethnographic insights into the principles and practices of today's Hindu-Catholic syncretism helped me to recognize the perspectives and processes that were involved in the protracted and reluctant recognition of religious pluralism in the early-modern period.

The heart of this book is therefore based on hypotheses that build on insights and critical questionings across its ethnographic and historical material. To be sure, this intersecting methodology has its limitations. In particular, I do not claim to present an exhaustive historical account of the early-modern encounter of Portuguese-Indian and Hindu-Catholic forces in India, nor to comprehensively illuminate the ethnography of Hindu and Catholic culture in modern-day Goa. Nevertheless, the methodological impact that the anthropological focus on alterity has on the historical perspective and, conversely, the effect that the historical perspective has on the ethnographic present lead to two hypotheses that deserve elaboration in the following pages. One is the proposal that the complexity of the mechanisms and rationales of Hindu-Catholic syncretism today supports the argument developed in the first chapter, that Vasco da Gama's error, that is, the confusion and, conversely, distinction of Hindus and Catholics in the early-modern period, was neither a quickly resolved affair nor can it be reduced to liberal values and attitudes. Instead, the historical distinction between Hindus and Catholics, and the related recognition of religious plurality, turn out to be an enormously protracted and contested process in which complex theological, epistemological, political, and practical conditions and transitions played a role. Moreover, the ethnographic insight that the rationale of modern syncretism is primarily not based on the negotiation of religious meanings but depends above all on the semiotic status, bodily enactment, and physical materiality of the religious signs, images, and objects at stake buttresses the hypothesis that the historical encounter between gentiles and Christians was not just about religious doctrines but was essentially about the emergence of a new, modern "semiotic ideology" (Keane 2007). "Similarity" and symbolism, it turns out, did not only constitute an intelligible "third ground" for translation and mediation in this process but also marked an iconic materiality that was prone to iconoclastic attacks and proselytic appropriation.

An important historical hypothesis guiding the book is that the principles of Goa's syncretism today do not emerge primarily from the modern doctrinal distinction between Hindus and Catholics but precede this distinction and, in a distinctly anachronistic way, undermine it. It is this hypothesis that challenges the idea, widely held in anthropology, that syncretism is in various ways an achievement or result of modernity. The historical and ethnographic material from Goa does not support the assumption that syncretism relies on the philosophical recognition of a "natural religion" or, for that matter, any other modern mediation of cultural differences based on the division of religious and secular domains and the organizing power of the nation-state, nor does it support the idea that syncretism can be reduced to semantic intelligibilities negotiated in the symbolic communication of functional necessities (Mosse 1994, 1997). Instead, the material suggests that syncretism marks a rupture and transition between premodern and modern modes of knowledge and signification, in which it is precisely the premodern embeddedness and embodiment of religion in social practices and material articulations that resists, to a notable extent, the hubris of the modern division of sign and signified, knower and known, the religious and the secular. This implicates in particular the hypothesis that Goan syncretism evades modernity's ubiquitous claim of universality and relies instead on rather parochial yet existential human concerns.

1 Vasco da Gama's Error
Conquest and Plurality

The true Religion can be but one, and that which God himselfe teacheth[,] . . .
all other religions being but strayings from him, whereby men wander in the
dark, and in labyrinthine error.

—Samuel Purchas, 1613 (Smith 1998: 272)

ON SUNDAY, 20 May 1498, after eleven months of adventurous navigation, the
small fleet of Vasco da Gama reached Malabar, the southwestern coast of India.
The Portuguese captain cautiously waited a few days on board to ascertain that
the local population had no hostile intentions against them and then went ashore
with some of his men to pay his respects to the local king. When he arrived in Calicut, the capitol of the little Indian kingdom, he had a curious adventure, which
was handed down by one of his crew members, most likely the soldier Álvaro
Velho,[1] to whom we owe the oldest manuscript of the *Journal of the First Voyage
of Vasco da Gama*.

> They took us to a large church and this is what we saw: The body of the church
> is as large as a monastery, all built of hewn stone and covered with tile. At the
> main entrance rises a pillar as high as a mast, on the top of which was perched
> a bird, apparently a cock. In addition to this there was another pillar as high
> as a man, and very stout. In the center of the body of the church rose a chapel,
> all built of hewn stone, with a bronze door sufficiently wide for a man to pass,
> and stone steps leading up to it. Within this sanctuary stood a small image
> which they said represented Our Lady. Along the walls, by the main entrance,
> hung seven small bells. In this church the captain-major said his prayers, and
> we with him. We did not go within the chapel, for it is the custom that only
> certain servants of the church, called *quafees*,[2] should enter. The quafees wore
> some threads passing over the left shoulder and under the right arm, in the
> same manner as our deacons wear the stole. They threw holy water over us,
> and gave us some white earth, which the Christians of this country are in
> the habit of putting on their foreheads, breast, around the neck, and on the
> forearms. They threw holy water upon the captain-major and gave him some

earth, which he gave in change to someone, giving them to understand that he would put it on later. Many other saints were painted on the walls of the church, wearing crowns. They were painted variously, with teeth protruding an inch from the mouth, and four or five arms. Below the church there was a large masonry tank, similar to many others which we had seen along the road. (Ravenstein 1998: 52–54)[3]

The episode in the Calicut "church" caused great sensation at its time. Even though this was not fully unexpected, the assumption of finding Christians in this faraway region of India was news of greatest significance for the king and the people of Portugal and was immediately communicated to other European nobles and the pope in Rome. To be sure, the iconography in the "Indian church" showed some bizarre details, and the appearance of "Indian Christians" who were said to "go naked down to their waist" was certainly peculiar to contemporary Europeans. These circumstances notwithstanding, the Portuguese seafarers had no doubts that "the city of Calicut [was] inhabited by Christians," some of whom, they felt, were wearing a special hair dress "as a sign that they are Christians" (ibid.: 49). In fact, they claimed to even have seen "another church" on their way to the king's palace showing "things like those described above" (ibid.: 55). To modern scholars it is of course obvious that Da Gama and his men had succumbed to a bold mistake. The details of their description clearly indicate that they had not been visiting a Christian church, but a Hindu temple in Calicut, most likely a Vishnu temple, as Sanjay Subrahmanyam argues (1997a: 132), adorned with an image of Garuda, the eagle-shaped vehicle of the Hindu god. The most intriguing question, which I address in this chapter, therefore is, how could Vasco da Gama fall prey to such a gross error?

Interestingly, the answers presented by leading historians in the field vary largely. Charles Boxer prosaically observes that "Da Gama on his arrival at Calicut was unable to distinguish between Hindu temples and Christian churches" ([1969] 1991: 34), and relates the explanation to the search for "Prester John," the legendary Christian priest who allegedly ruled a large kingdom somewhere in the East. More precisely, Boxer argues that it was the myth of a lost Eastern Christianity, the rediscovery of which had become a messianic vocation of the Portuguese royalty, that made Da Gama mistakenly find "friendly (though not rigidly Roman Catholic) Indian 'Christians'" (ibid.: 37).

Michael Pearson's analysis hints in a very different direction and relates the Calicut episode to what he perceives to be a "tolerant attitude" by some of the early-modern European explorers toward the foreign Indian world. The Portuguese, he notes, developed a curious "desire to find familiar things in Asia" (1987: 116). Beginning with Da Gama's error, Pearson shows, famed Portuguese chroniclers visiting India or writing about it in the sixteenth century such as Tomé Pires (1465–1520?), Duarte Barbosa (d. 1545), and Fernão Lopes de Castanheda (1480–1559) were fascinated by what they perceived as "similarities" between certain religious concepts and rituals of the gentiles and their own Christian beliefs and practices. In particular, the Holy Trinity, the Virgin Mary, and certain baptismal rites, as Pearson and Donald Lach (1994: 387, 401) point out, were seen as theologically comparable, if not genealogically related, notions and practices of gentiles and Christians. Pearson, however, also notes something utterly enigmatic about this curious "search for the similar." While understandable as an initial hermeneutic attempt to invest the alien with familiar traits, why did this attitude prevail for so long? Why, in particular, did Pires, Barbosa, Castanheda, and others continue to refer to Hindu-Christian affinities long after it seems to have been clarified that Hindus were not Christians, not even very lapsed ones. "How could they get it so wrong?" he asks ([1992] 2005b: 156). Even more puzzling, why did assumptions about Hindu-Christian affinities live on after the impact of the Counter-Reformation had turned the initially "peaceful" encounters between Portuguese and Indians, Christians and Hindus, into a hostile iconoclastic onslaught against Hindu culture? Pearson does not pretend to have plausible answers to these questions and, *faute de mieux,* explains them by philanthropic leanings. "It is possible," he writes, "that those who continued, despite the evidence, to find the Same were simply more humane, less intolerant than most of their fellows who launched vicious attacks on Hinduism" (ibid.).

Sanjay Subrahmanyam pays the closest attention to the Calicut episode of all modern scholars of Indo-Portuguese history, yet he conspicuously abstains from addressing the intricacies mentioned by Pearson. For Subrahmanyam, Da Gama's error simply was a short-lived "gaffe" triggered by "the fact that the Portuguese were momentarily convinced that large Christian kingdoms awaited them in Asia, and could be used as allies against the Mamluks and other Middle Eastern Muslim rivals" (2001: 26). He buttresses his thesis in another book by relating it to the curious information regarding the Christians living in the East that was delivered to the Portuguese captain by a man known as Gaspar da Gama or Gaspar of India. This Gaspar, a Jewish merchant with profound experience in the Indian trade who Da Gama had captured off the Kanara Coast and baptized a Christian in his name, certainly must have impressed his new Christian master when he presented Vasco Da Gama with a fantastic list showing no less than "ten Christian kingdoms" spread over India and the Far East, all allegedly waiting to support the Portuguese with mighty armies in their war against the "Moors" (1997a: 152–153).

Subrahmanyam also points out that the situation in South India must have been confusing for Da Gama as a group of Christians did in fact—and do to this day—live in southern India. These Christians are known as St. Thomas Christians because they trace their mythological origin back to proselytizing activities of the Apostle Thomas. Scattered rumors about these Thomas Christians were spread in Europe since the medieval age and gradually solidified in the Renaissance and early-modern period, when first Marco Polo (1254–1324), then Nicolò de Conti (ca. 1385–1469) reported to have seen the grave of the Apostle Thomas in a city called Mylapur (Chennai, Tamil Nadu) in southern India. At the time of Da Gama's visit, the numbers of these Thomas Christians are uncertain and are estimated at anywhere between thirty and seventy thousand (Bayly 1989: 247; Frykenberg 2003: 41). Although there is no certified evidence for Subrahmanyam's assumption that Da Gama or anyone of his crew may in fact have met with St. Thomas Christians in Malabar during their first voyage (Subrahmanyam 1997a: 119), it is easy to imagine that news about their existence had influenced Da Gama's perception of the situation in this faraway country. Most importantly though, Subrahmanyam argues that Da Gama's error was rectified almost instantaneously, something he attributes to the fact that, arguably, proper knowledge about the religious identity of the "gentiles" had long been available in Europe. "By the return to Lisbon of the second Portuguese voyage of Pedro Álvares Cabral (1500–1)," Subrahmanyam notes, "matters had been clarified to a large extent and the knowledge already possessed from the fifteenth century descriptions like that of Nicòlo de Conti had been reconsolidated: the term 'Gentile' (*gentio*) was now used to designate Hindus and Buddhists alike, and to distinguish them from Christians and Moors" (2001: 26).

In summary, historians are largely at variance regarding the interpretation of the Calicut episode and raise more questions than answers. What motivated the curious error of the Portuguese captain: expectations to find the mythical Christianity of the East, philanthropic leanings toward the familiar in the alien, or wishful thinking regarding allies in the conflict with the Muslims? Was Da Gama's error thus an anachronistic short-lived gaffe or even a harbinger of an Enlightenment perspective of cultural relativism, or were other epistemic conditions of cognition and perception involved? What does the episode in Calicut tell us about the dynamics of the attitudes of the Christian Self toward the Indian Other in the early-modern colonial encounter?

Prester John and the Search for Eastern Christianity

The assumption that Da Gama's confusion in Calicut was the result of longstanding rumors about certain Christians living in the East is supported by the celebrated disclosure, "We came in search of Christians and spices," reportedly made by one of his sailors on their arrival at Malabar (Ravenstein [1898] 1998: 48). In accordance with this information, Velho's travelogue shows that the Portuguese, once they had reached the coastline of East Africa, were constantly searching for hints and signs indicating the presence of Christians on their route. In Mozambique, they rejoiced for the first time when some of the natives, whom they repeatedly interrogated on this issue, allegedly spoke about "many cities" in the region that were populated by Christians. Moreover, they understood their native informants saying, that Prester John resided not far from this place; that he held many cities along the coast, and that the inhabitants of those cities were great merchants and owned big ships. The residence of Prester John was said to be far in the interior and could be reached only on the back of camels. These Moors had also brought hither two Christian captives from India. This information and many other things that we heard rendered us so happy that we cried with joy, and prayed God to grant us health so that we might behold what we so much desired. (Ibid.: 24)

Unfortunately though, Da Gama's hopes to go on land the following day in the city of Mombasa and "hear jointly mass with the Christians reported to live there" were disappointed, as well as the hope of finding "many large cities of Christians and Moors, including one called Quambay (Gujarat)" on their way across the Arabian Sea (ibid.: 35, 47). Nevertheless, the Portuguese captain and his men refused to give up their efforts to find Christians and continued to undertake tests and seek signs revealing the suspected Christian identity of local people, even where these signs seemed rather far-fetched. For instance, Da Gama's men claimed to have recognized two "Indian Christians" in Mozambique, describing them as "tawny men" who wore little clothing, had long beards, ate no beef, and spoke a language different from Arabic. Two rather curious forms of behavior convinced the Portuguese that these Indians, who were said to be owners of big vessels and who had visited one of the Portuguese ships, were in fact Christians. First, it was reported that, when the visitors were shown an altar-piece representing Our Lady, they immediately prostrated themselves, murmured prayers, and, most curiously, made "offerings of cloves, pepper and other things" to the image. Second, when Da Gama and his fleet left the harbor, the "Indian Christians" were said to have "fired many bombards from their vessels and when they saw him pass they raised their hands and shouted lustily 'Christ,' 'Christ'" (ibid.: 44–45).

On another occasion in Mombasa, Da Gama was invited into the house of "two men, almost white, who said to be Christians," something that the Portuguese captain found confirmed by a "paper" shown to him, which he interpreted as an "object of their adoration" depicting the "Holy Ghost" (ibid.: 36). These and similar incidents suggest that Da Gama was ready to stretch evidence, if only to keep the hope alive that he was going to find Christians in India. The details of the audience he had with the king of Malabar further confirm this. To begin with, Da Gama took the doorman of the palace to be a sort of "bishop . . . whose advice the king acts upon in all affairs of the church" and saluted him "in the manner of the country by putting the hands together, then raising them towards the Heaven, as it is done by Christians when addressing God" (ibid.: 56, 57). When meeting with the Zamorin, or king of Malabar, Da Gama told him that the Portuguese king, Dom Manuel, and his ancestors had undertaken "discoveries in the direction of India" for many years because they knew "that there [in India] were Christian kings like them." Therefore, he continued, "Dom Manuel . . . had ordered him not to return to Portugal until he should have discovered this King of the Christians [in the East], on pain of having his head cut off" (ibid.: 58).

These circumstances show that Vasco da Gama's search for Christians had little to do with modern notions of discovery. When the Portuguese captain spoke about discovery, he did not have in mind finding novelties or seeking new experiences, let alone changing his ideas or worldview. Instead, he sought to reconfirm what he already thought and, thus, was certain, against all evidence and facts, to find Christians and also, incidentally, immense riches and resources in India:

> We understood them to say—is therefore another information which he repeatedly believes to hear from the words exchanged with the natives in Africa—that all these things [silver, gloves, pepper, ginger, rings, pearls, jewels, and rubies] with the exception of gold were bought by these Moors; that further on, where we were to go, they abounded, and that precious stones, pearls and spices were so plentiful that there was no need to purchase them as they could be collected in baskets. (Ravenstein [1898] 1998: 23)

Like Christopher Columbus, Vasco da Gama pursued what Tzvetan Todorov called a "finalistic strategy of interpretation," that is, an interpretation whose operations were grounded not on experience but authority (1985: 26). The two early-modern explorers, in other words, took to be known in advance the meanings of the signs and gestures encountered on their journeys and, to a considerable extent, the messages conveyed to them in foreign languages. There are striking parallels therefore in how Columbus and Da Gama reasserted assumed knowledge against factual evidence. Convinced of finding a great and civilized continent, Columbus, in a celebrated episode of his journey, made his entire crew go on land in Cuba and swear a solemn oath that this was the great mainland of India for which they were searching, though a number of his men were doubtful (ibid.: 32). Da Gama was sure to find Christians in India and thus made his men, in a no less spectacular confusion, pray to images of saints in a Hindu temple in Calicut, though again some of them were not convinced that these were representations of saints. In fact, Hernan Lopes de Castanheda mentions in his version of the Calicut episode that a certain João de Sá, one of the men accompanying Da Gama to the "church," was doubtful and anxious that the "saints" he was ordered to worship may not be authentic. As a precaution, he therefore murmured, "If these are devils, I worship God" (Castanheda 1582: 44–45).

What made the two explorers so self-asserted about their assumed knowledge were not only certain authoritative texts, such as Pierre d'Ailly's *Imago mundi* for Columbus and the mysterious *Acts of Thomas* for Da Gama, which supposedly prefigured and predicted what they were hoping to find.[4] More specifically, the two explorers joined Luís de Camões (1524–1580) in trusting in what might be called a Christian epistemology that assumed the truth about the world in its entirety had been prefigured by Christian doctrine, if perhaps in an encapsulated form or cryptic signs waiting to be deciphered. History of literature scholar Shankar Raman, analyzing the great epic *Os Lusíadas* (Camões [1571] 1973), which Camões had composed on the occasion of Vasco da Gama's first voyage to India, comes to a similar conclusion when summarizing the great poet's view about the foreign land of India: "It is illogical to believe that God could have created parts of the world that were not from the very beginning available in some way to [Christian] man and thus part, even dimly, of man's knowledge, since proper contemplation of the created world requires such knowledge. Ergo, these lands must already have been known, our failure to acknowledge them a mere consequence of not having read the ancient texts with the requisite care" (Raman 2001: 69).

Among the "ancient texts" that arguably inspired Vasco da Gama's search for Christians in India were, as already mentioned, the *Acts of Thomas*. Dated to the second century, these documents are of unknown origin and provenance and have survived in Syriac (Aramaic) versions believed to have been produced in fourth-century Edessa (Greece). They are regarded as the oldest documents reflecting Christian traditions in southern India. The *Acts of Thomas* are interpreted as evidence of missionary activities undertaken by the apostle Thomas and, together with written and oral Malayali and Tamil literature, are claimed today as proof of the ancient and independent Christian origins of the Thomas or Syrian Christian communities of Kerala and Tamil Nadu (Frykenberg 2003: 34ff.). Although considered apocryphal by the Western church, the *Acts of Thomas* were a major source of myths and rumors circulating in medieval Europe about a Christianity of considerable proportion and power that allegedly was lost or hidden in the vast territories of the Indies somewhere between Ethiopia in the west and Cathay (China) in the east. Two sites became especially important for the dissemination of myths and news regarding these lost Eastern Christians. One was the Near East and, in particular, Jerusalem, where Western pilgrims not only learned about the idiosyncrasies of the Christian churches of Jerusalem, Constantinople, Alexandria, and Antioch, but also their various Armenian, Jakobite, Maronite, Chaldean, and Syrian subdivisions, some of which were said to have relations with the lost Christians of the East (Rogers 1962; Aubin 1976). The other site was the Western church in Rome whose leaders and theologians entertained ambiguous attitudes toward the lost Eastern Christianity. On the one hand, the Western church had a longstanding record of efforts at trying to unify the theological principles and political actions of the Christian churches of East and West, something that included repeated attempts to contact and communicate with the enigmatic Eastern Christians associated with St. Thomas and Prester John. On the other hand, it was a continuous concern of the Western church to counteract heretic deviations from Christian doctrine, something that led to an interest in monitoring segments of the Eastern Christians that were suspected of adhering to the Nestorian doctrines that had led to various secessions from the Greek or Orthodox churches during the Middle Ages.

Historically significant thus in contexts of Christian diversity and diversification, the discourse on the lost Eastern Christians gained new and critical significance in early modernity when Western Christianity not only was facing another dramatic episode of internal diversification by the emerging Protestant Reformation but also was increasingly entangled in encounters at the colonial frontier with until then largely unknown religious traditions in Asia and America. Not surprisingly, it was in the fifteenth and sixteenth centuries that another set of apocryphal texts relating the story of a mysterious Eastern Christianity gained public attention in Western Europe. These were the *Letters of Prester John*, which were taken to provide evidence of the existence of a formidable exotic Christianity located somewhere beyond the Islamic world. This imaginary Eastern Christianity was commonly depicted as an ideal kingdom in which a wise priest, Prester John, ruled in perfect Christian morality and splendid material prosperity over a powerful army and a happy nation (Aubin 1976; Rogers 1962; Slessarev 1959). Surfacing first in a Latin version in the twelfth century, the full impact of this literary imagination was reached in the fifteenth and sixteenth centuries, when Italian, Dutch, French, German, and English versions of the *Letters* made the subject into a bestselling literary genre. The enormous popularity and commercial success of the Prester John literature was owed to a combination of utopian ideas and exotic images that provided both edification and diversion to people in Western Europe afflicted by episodes of Black Death, religious wars, and a serious crisis of the feudal order and economy of their societies. Most successful chapbook versions of the genre, such as Andrea da Barberino's *Guerino da Meschino,* a fictitious travelogue into Prester John's kingdom, published in 1473 in Padua, and Giuliano Dati's *Treatise of the Supreme Prester John, Pope and Emperor of India and of Ethiopia,* a rhymed version of the *Letter of Prester John,* published in 1493 in Rome, combined the longstanding mythology of the St. Thomas Christians surmised in India with the alleged news of Prester John's kingdom said to be located somewhere in Ethiopia or India (Rogers 1962: 94, 97, passim). The popular genre also brought together classical and modern sources, that is Augustine, Pliny the Elder, and Strabo on the one hand, and Marco Polo, Nicolò de Conti, and Poggio Bracciolini on the other, to buttress and illustrate publications such as *De ritu et moribus indorum* (On the Rites and Customs of the Indians) or *Treatise on the Ten Nations and Sects of Christians,* which were frequently published in one and the same collection. Notably, the exoticism of the religious Other and the diversity of the religious Self thus intermingled in popular perception and fantasy. Another noteworthy leitmotiv of the time was the arrival of high-ranking Oriental dignitaries in the West, a subject that found a most intriguing artistic interpretation in a painting by Benozzo Gozzoli, completed around 1461, depicting—as Francis Rogers cogently notes—the celebrated

Magi, whose story had but recently been popularized by John of Hildesheim, not as the distant Melchior, Balthazar, and Jasper but as the contemporary Patriarch Joseph II and Emperor John III Palaeolugus of Constantinople, who indeed had visited Florence in the 1440s together with little Lorenzo de Medici (ibid.: 51).

Notably, though, St. Thomas Christians and Prester John's legendary Christian kingdom were not only the subject of popular literature and art but also of most real and serious politics. Of course, Pope Eugene IV's (1383–1447) letter to his "dearly beloved son in Christ, Prester John, illustrious King and Emperor of Ethiopia" could not induce its addressee to participate in the Council of Florence (1438–1442) at which the long-awaited decree of union between the Roman and Greek churches was proclaimed, for the simple reason that this addressee existed only in his imagination (ibid.: 37). Nevertheless, by the mid-fifteenth century, papal authorities and their royal supporters took serious efforts to make the Christians believed to live in India or Ethiopia part of a grand plan that had been determined at the Council of Basel (1431–1438). The goal of this plan was nothing less than

> to recover the Holy Land of Jerusalem and other lands which formerly belonged to Christians, and to bring back and restore to the one Christian fold, under one shepherd, the Roman Pontiff of the Universal Church, the schismatic Greeks and Armenians and, as far as possible, even those very Indians who hold to the faith of St. Thomas the apostle, so that there may be one fold and one shepherd in the world, subject to the name and obedience of one true God, who is Jesus. (Ibid.: 57)

Alberto da Sartena, the newly appointed "[papal] commissary for India proper, Ethiopia, Egypt and Jerusalem," was commissioned the task of communicating with the mysterious Eastern Christians and undertook various travels to Palestine and Cairo between 1435 and 1440, though he never reached Ethiopia or India (ibid.: 41). It was a natural development, therefore, that the King of Portugal, whom Pope Nicholas V (1397–1455) in the celebrated bull *Romanus Pontifex* had granted the exclusive right of conquest and possession in Africa and beyond, also took on the grand project of the unification of all known and unknown parts of Christianity: "He [the Portuguese King] would best perform his duty to God in this matter [of exploration], if by his effort and industry that sea [to the south and east] might become navigable as far as to the Indians who are said to worship the name of Christ, and thus he might be able to enter into relation with them, and to incite them to aid the Christians against the Saracens and other such enemies of the faith" (ibid.: 64).

Gentiles and Religious Plurality

It is against this background that I return to Subrahmanyam's remark that Da Gama's error in Calicut was a short-lived, anachronistic "gaffe" and that proper knowledge about the religious identity of the Indian gentiles was current in Europe long before the first sea passage to India. In particular we may recall Subrahmanyam's reference to news about India, which the Italian traveler Nicolò de Conti had brought to Europe in the fifteenth century and which, according to him, made a clear distinction between Hindus and Buddhists, collectively called gentiles, and Muslims and Christians (2001: 26).

Subrahmanyam's view seems to be supported by the fact that objections against Da Gama's assumption that Calicut was populated by Christians were reported almost instantaneously. Important to note in particular are documents from Girolamo Sernici, a Florentine merchant living in Lisbon when Da Gama returned from his voyage in July 1499. Writing letters about the event to a gentleman in Italy, Sernici first reported the exciting news about a city in India named "Chalichut" that was "peopled by Christian Indians" (Ravenstein [1898] 1998: 125). In a second letter written a couple of weeks later, he revised his report referring to new information received from "the pilot whom they took by force," that is, Gaspar da Gama: "He says that in those countries there are many gentiles, that is idolaters, and only a few Christians; that the supposed church and belfries are in reality temples of idolaters, and that the pictures within them are those of idols and not saints" (ibid.: 137ff.).

Subrahmanyam's argument that this quick rectification of Da Gama's error should be seen against the background that proper knowledge about the religious identity of the Indian gentiles had been current in Europe since the mid-fifteenth century is indirectly supported by Joan-Pau Rubiés. Rubiés analyzes the travelogue of the Venetian merchant Nicolò de Conti, who traveled for more than twenty years through Persia, India, and the Far East and, after his return, dictated his experiences to Poggio Bracciolini (1380–1459), the secretary of Pope Eugene IV (2000). Although a rather short and elliptical itinerary, the De Conti–Bracciolini account shows some interest in cultural issues and contains *inter alia* a description of religious ceremonies in Bisnaga (Vijyanagara) and news about the priestly classes of Cambay (Gujarat) and Zeilam (Ceylon). While being positively impressed by the city and kingdom of Vijayanagara as well as by the sophistication of the "race of Brahmins" of Ceylon, the Italian merchant and papal humanist obviously were rather disgusted by certain religious practices that De Conti had seen in India, which they classified as "idolatry." A lengthy description follows in the travelogue that reports not only on the alleged worship of idols of "false gods" and "demons" but also mentions a range of inhuman and cruel practices including stories of self-immolation, self-mutilation, and ritual murder. After having highlighted these details, Rubiés, surprisingly, qualifies the De Conti–Bracciolini report as an early "account of Eastern religion" (2000: 106). He gives two reasons for this assessment. The two Italians, Rubiés argues, took care to notice that the people sacrificing their lives were driven by powerful and socially esteemed religious motifs, something he interprets as an acknowledgment of their "free will" by the two Italian narrators. Moreover, Rubiés points out, the account uses a certain referential language to describe what De Conti saw in India, such as "they say" and "they consider," in which Rubiés sees traces of an "acceptance of diverse beliefs in diverse social contexts [that] raises (at least potentially) the possibility of relativism" (ibid.: 109).

Were Nicolò de Conti and Poggio Bracciolini thus indeed harbingers of modernity who anticipated concepts of religious plurality and cultural relativism? Doubts about this hypothesis seem justified given the emphasis the two Italians put on the observation that the Indian gentiles "are all idolaters" (Major [1857] 2005: 9). Although idolatry was already an old stigma, leading to discrimination of all those who were described as "infidels," "pagans," or "heathens" in European Christian discourse, the term gained new significance and acrimoniousness in the emerging modernity. This growing significance of "idolatry" stemmed from the fact that in the great cataclysm which eventually culminated in the Protestant Reformation and Catholic renewal in the sixteenth century, the alleged semiotic offence of mistaking the image for its prototype, that is, of worshipping the idol instead of what it stands for clearly asserted and aggravated the dividing line between Christians and so-called pagans. In this context, De Conti's and Bracciolini's highlighting of stories of how gentiles during religious ceremonies "cut off their own head, [thereby] yielding up their lives as a sacrifice to their idols," or had their "wives . . . burn themselves [with their dead husbands] in order to add to the pomp of the funeral" (Major [1857] 2005: 26, 6), are to be seen as an intensification of the allegation that the gentiles were engaging more with the material reification and performative dramatization of their religious beliefs than with their inner meanings.

To be sure, De Conti and Bracciolini did have some interest in religious diversity. Notably, however, this interest concentrated on Christian populations. Hence, the Italians found and distinguished three varieties of Christians in the countries of the East. First were the "Nestorian Christians" who were said to be "heretics" having their center in the city of Mylapur, where "the body of Saint Thomas lies buried in a very large and beautiful church" (ibid.: 7). Next mentioned were Christians said to live in a "kingdom twenty days journey from Cathay (China)" who were also "heretics" but have "churches . . . larger and more ornamented than ours" (ibid.: 33). Finally, Christians of Ethiopia and Egypt were mentioned, among whom "the period from Christmas to Lent is kept as a festival, being devoted to feasting and dancing." Obviously alluding here to the longstanding glorification of the alleged Eastern Christians associated with the legendary Prester John, De Conti and Bracciolini added that in the country of these Ethiopian and Egyptian Christians, no one ever suffered from "pestilence" but some people even lived to "more than a hundred and twenty years old" (ibid.:

36ff.). Contrary to these distinctions and qualifications of diverse Christians, all others—Hindus, Buddhists, and Muslims—were subsumed under the one notion of idolaters, though some of them triggered certain reminiscences for the Italians, who seemed to have retained ambiguities about the real nature of the gentiles and, in particular, the suspicion that they had some affinity with Christians: "All worship idols nevertheless when they rise in the morning from their beds they turn towards the east, and with their hands joined together say, 'God in Trinity and His law defend us'" (ibid.: 13).

Gentiles and the Search for the Similar

The question of to what extent the encounter of Portuguese and Indians, missionaries and gentiles, facilitated the emergence of a new, that is, modern perspective on religious diversity and cultural difference is critically connected with the question of why actual and imagined "similarities" between Christians and gentiles had such a fascinating attraction for the early-modern explorers, chroniclers, and missionaries. A prominent Portuguese chronicler who noticed such similarities was Tomé Pires (1465–1520?). Traveling in India, Malacca, and China between 1511 and 1516, he noted in his major work *Suma Oriental,* published around 1512 (Albuquerque 1994: 2:907ff.), "The whole of Malabar believes, as we do, in the Trinity of Father, Son, and Holy Ghost, three in one, the only true God. From Cambay to Bengal all the people hold this [faith]" (Pires [1944] 1967: 66). Regarding the people of Gujarat, Pires was even convinced that these similarities were remnants of a Christian heritage that had fallen into decay: "The heathens of Cambay are great idolaters and soft, weak people. Some of them are men who in their religion lead good lives, they are chaste, true men and very abstemious. They believe in Our Lady and in the Trinity, and there is no doubt that they were once Christians and that they gradually lost their faith because of the Mohammedans" (ibid.: 39).

Duarte Barbosa (d. 1545), who lived and worked in India from 1500 to 1506 and 1511 to 1545, and whose *Livro das Coisas da Índia* was written around 1515 in Calicut (Albuquerque 1994: 1:116ff.), produced the first detailed European description of Hindu society (Barbosa [1518] 1918–1921).[5] His elaborations are based on observations in Guzerate (Gujarat) and Malabar (Kerala). In Guzerate, he pointed out, the gentiles were divided into two sorts or classes. One were the "Baneanes" who are "great merchants" and whose description tells us today were Jains (ibid.: 1:110ff.). The other were the "Bramenes," described as "priests" who have a particular respect for Christian principles and saints:

> These Bramenes or Heathen have in their creed many resemblances to the Holy Trinity, and hold in great honor the relation of the Triune Three, and always make their prayers to the true God, Creator and maker of all things, who is three persons and one God, and they say that there are many other gods who

are rulers under him, in whom also they believe. These Bramenes and Heathen wheresoever they find our churches enter them and make prayers and adorations to our Images, always asking for Santa Maria, like men who have some knowledge and understanding of these matters; and they honor the Church as it is our manner, saying that between them and us there is little difference. (Ibid.: 1:115ff.)

For Malabar, Barbosa's account distinguishes no less than eighteen "castes" from Bramenes (Brahmins) through Nayres (Nayars) to Mainatos (Dalits), most of whom were said to have "their own sort of idolatry" and some their own "pagodes" or temples (ibid.: 2:33ff.). After describing in detail how the Bramenes worshiped their "idols" through elaborate ceremonies, processions, and regular offerings, the report points out that they also "honor the Trinity," to which they refer as "Berma [Brahma], Besma [Vishnu] and Maceru [Maheshvara] who are three persons and only one God, whom they confess to have since the beginning of the world." Barbosa added, however, that "they have no knowledge nor information concerning the life of our Lord Jesus Christ" so that they seem to live in a peculiar state of half-truth: "They believe and respect many truths, yet do not tell them truly" (ibid.: 2:37).

As pointed out by Pearson (1987: 116) and Lach (1994: 387, 401), the allusions to Christians living in Calicut and moreover to certain Christian roots among the gentiles at various places in western India survived in Portuguese travelogues and chronicles throughout the sixteenth and even the early seventeenth centuries. João de Barros's (1496–1570) *Décadas da Ásia* (written in the middle decades of the sixteenth century), Fernão Lopes de Castanheda's (1480–1559) *História do descobrimento et conquista da Índia pelos portugueses* (published between 1551 and 1554), and Damiao de Góis's (1502–1574) *Cronica do felicissimo rei Dom Manuel* (published 1566–1567) all reproduced the celebrated Calicut episode reconfirming, more or less directly, the Portuguese captain's assumption of having discovered a Christian church. The historically latest reproduction of the Calicut episode so-far unearthed can be found in Frei Paulo de Trindade's (1570–1651) *Conquista espiritual de Oriente,* a history of the Franciscan order in India, written between 1630 and 1636 in India (Trindade 1962–1967: 1:viiff.). This version again presents an almost word-by-word reproduction of Velho's original; Trindade enriches the story, though, by weaving together various genealogical and narrative threads of Christian mythology. According to "ancient annals," he reports, the historical king of Calicut was one of the Three Holy Magi who, after his celebrated visit to Bethlehem, had been baptized by the Apostle Thomas. The appeal of authenticity of this artful connecting of the Christians of Calicut and the Thomas Christians is further enhanced by the fact that Trindade takes the story to rectify earlier narrations, which had located the place of origin of the Magi in Persia, by claiming new evidence that at least one of them came from India (ibid.: 2:297). Moreover, Trindade presents the Calicut episode, more than 150 years after the fact, as evidence of the divine providence that had placed the Portuguese conquest of the Orient under the protection of the Christian Maria. He states, "The great captain D. Vasco da Gama, as we had reported, found a chapel dedicated to the Holy Virgin Mother of God and Our Lady when he reached India. He received no small consolation that heaven had ready for him in the midst of so much infidelity, the house and image of the Queen of Angels which assured him the prediction that the Portuguese would be Her protégés" (ibid.: 2:298).

Notably, however, there were also Portuguese chroniclers who rejected the assumption that Christians had been living in Calicut at the time of Da Gama's arrival and who denied that there existed similarities between the religious beliefs and practices of Christians and gentiles. One of them was Diogo do Couto (1542–1616), who spent about fifteen years in India as a soldier and writer and, in the late sixteenth century, took over from João de Barros responsibility as state chronicler for continuing the series *Décadas da Ásia* (Albuquerque 1994: 1:318ff.). Couto demystified allusions to Christianity in India most effectively in a passage of his *Década Quinta da Ásia* in which he dealt with the three supreme Hindu gods *Brahemâ* (Brahma), *Bisnû* (Vishnu), and *Rudrâ* (Shiva). After explaining the association of the gods with the three elements earth, water, and fire, and after elaborating their various functions, he explicitly refused the assumption that the beliefs and practices of the gentiles, based on this threefold nature of the divine, could have any relationship with the Christian Trinity:

> And from this [similarity] some scholars took reason to consider whether these gentiles have knowledge of the Holiest Trinity. João de Barros erred in this way because they [the gentiles] cannot know [the Holy Trinity], and also Damião de Gois makes the same mistake, because the gentile theologians did not have the same practice we do. And even today many do err as to what the Brahmans do in hearing them say that, like we worship three persons in one divinity, they also do to the three in the one *Mamurte* as we had said [before]. (Couto 1937: 391)

This insertion deserves closer inspection because Couto belonged to a group of Portuguese scholars writing in the sixteenth century who were obviously impressed by the social complexity, material richness, and cultural sophistication of Hindu society and culture, and who laid the cornerstones for its systematic exploration. Barbosa was one of them, providing the first elaborate description of the complex hierarchies and regulations constituting the system of castes in Gujarat and Malabar. Gaspar Correia (1492–1567) became known for his enthused account of the royal rituals, festivals, and temples in the kingdom of Vijayanagara (Karnataka) (Subrahmanyam 2001: 39ff.). Couto, finally, deserves the greatest attention for two chapters in his *Década Quinta da Ásia* in which he dealt extensively and in great detail with what at a later point in time became known as Hinduism. The two chapters evidence that the Portuguese chronicler had developed significant interest in this subject and had collected arguably the vastest knowledge in European writing about it both from his own observations and from other sources. In particular, Couto, who most probably did not read Sanskrit or any other Indian language, must have engaged in extensive conversations with learned Brahmans about Hindu beliefs and practices and, above all, their ancient books and writings. No doubt his remarkable interest generated for him a great and genuine respect for the foreign religious culture, something that is reflected in the fact that he was among the first Europeans to explicitly use the term *religião* or "religion" to describe what others contemptuously called *gentilismo*, "idolatry" or "paganism" (Couto 1937: 382).

In chapter three of the *Década Quinta da Ásia*, entitled *About the Views, Rites and Ceremonies of All the Gentiles of Industan, Living between the Indus and the Ganges. And about What Is Said about the Origins of Their Scriptures Which Their Theologians Teach in Their Schools*, he thus wrote,

> It should be known that among the gentiles of the Orient there is maintained and sustained but one view of God, the creation and corruption of creatures, which is a lesson to be read in their schools by their Bragmanes, who are teachers of their religion. Of this they have many books in their Latin, which they call Geredão [Sanskrit], which contain all that they are to believe, and all the ceremonies they are to do. These books are divided into bodies, members, and articles, whose originals are ones which they call Vedaos, which are divided in four parts, and these in another fifty-two in this way: six are called Xastra, which are the bodies; eighteen are called Purana, which are the members; twenty-eight are called Agamon, which are the articles. (Ibid.: 382)

Couto went on to speak of their *causa prima*, which, "they say," is "God, a pure spirit, embodied, infinite, almighty, omniscient, all benevolence, omnipresent, whom they call Xarues, Xivaru, which means creator of all" (ibid.: 383). He then talked about their notion of "angels whom they call Monixavaru, which means saints" and of "souls who must be immortal, but if one has sinned, when he dies, his soul passes through a living being, where it is purged before it deserves to ascend into heaven" (ibid.: 384). This is why, he concluded, the gentiles take great care of animals, and some do not even kill bedbugs because these all may be human souls purged for their sins. The souls of the worst sinners are said to transform into the most filthy animals and the worst of all into dogs. Many souls however are believed to pass through the bodies of cows which are therefore most venerated among them: "In the kingdom of Cambaia [Gujarat] we have seen it many times that, when a cow was urinating in the streets, the Baneas [Jains], men and women, came out and reached their hands and took the urine and spread it over their heads, saying some words, just like we do it with the Holy Water" (ibid.: 384). At this point, Couto inserted an interesting reference saying that this "brutish view" (*openião bruta*) can already be found among the "ancient Gentiles" (*antigos gentios*), since it was Êpedocles Agregentino (Empedocles of

Agrigentum; ca. 490–430 BCE), the Greek philosopher known for his theory of natural elements, who said that all "spirits of the air, the sea and the earth" who have "lived badly" have to be purged before "they deserve entering into glory" (ibid.: 384). Others in India who had managed to see more of the truth, he continued, tell that in their "second Heaven" there is one place called Xorvago where all those relax who had lived a good life and another place that is called Naraca that is full of fire and as many types of tortures as there are types of sins performed by angels of the third category, "who are depicted in all possible ugliness, as we do for the devil, and called by many names, the most common ones being: Diagal or Saitan, name of what is known everywhere and [even] till those savages could not be lost" (ibid.: 385). The chapter ends with a note on the four worst sins— "killing, stealing, drinking wine and taking some one else's wife"—and modes of atonement such as going on pilgrimages and making sacrifices in temples. The main and most common mode of worship, Couto wrote, are performed in temples including "Ramanacor near Manar," that is, Rameshvaram in Tamil Nadu; "Xilabarao, eight *legoas* from Negapatao," that is, a today-unknown temple in Nagapattinam, Tamil Nadu; "Canjavar," that is, Khajurao in Madhya Pradesh; "Triquinimale in the kingdom of Gigi," that is, Koneswaram in Trincomalee in Sri Lanka; "Tripiti and Tremel in the kingdom of Bisnaga," that is, Tirumale-Tirupati of Vijayanagara in Karnataka; "Jagarnatte," that is, Jagarnath in Orissa; and "Vixavat in Bengalla," that is, most likely Visvanathan in Benares. He added the temples of "Tanavare in Ceylon . . . Pico in Adao . . . Jaquette . . . and infinitely many others where the devil is well venerated" (ibid.: 387).

Chapter four is entitled *About the Other Three Parts of Their Sources and All Other Rites and Customs of the Gentiles and about Their Three Rulers and about the Mistake That Some Made in Assuming That They Have Knowledge about the Holiest Trinity. And about the Distinctions of Their Castes and about How They Preserve These.* It starts with a comment on the divine rulers (*regentes*) who govern the cosmos and the elements: "These blind gentiles say that this *primera causa* that they take for God is so mighty that, for not having to care about lowly things, he gives all celestial bodies to rulers so that they move and govern them" (ibid.: 390). The chapter then goes on to specify five divine rulers, all of whom are said to have wives or even appear as women, that is, goddesses, and their respective spheres: one who governs all the planets called Xadaxivão and his wife, Hûmanî; one who governs fire called Rudra and his wife, Parvadi; one who governs air called Measura and his wife, Maenomadi; one who governs water called Bisnu and his wife, Lacami; and one who governs earth called Brahemâ and his wife, Xarasuadi.

> These five, they say, govern all created matter, but [above all] there are three who are worshipped as gods, that is, Brahemâ, Bisnū and Rudra, who are the rulers of Earth, Water and Fire, because one creates, the other proliferates and the other consumes, and because they are the cause of creation, breeding and

decay of all. And these three, they call Máá Murte, which means the "three supreme ones" and they affirm that they had been generated by the same God. And like that they portray them together, one body and three faces, as we see them in the temple of Elefanta, where we even see that figure . . . with three faces as large as a big barrel, made in stone like marble with a miter on its head, round with three cone ends, like the ones of our Pontiffs, a piece that can count as one of the wonders of the world. And in memory of these three rulers all Gentiles wear a thread braided of three lines around their neck. (Ibid.: 391)

Two other passages and finally an episode from the remaining part of the chapter about how Indians perceived the Portuguese themselves are worth mentioning. In one passage that closely follows the description of the five cosmic rulers, Couto made reference again to classical knowledge of his time by stating that "this idolatry [of the Indian gentiles] seems to have spread in all the Orient from the ancient Egyptians" who likewise worshipped the stars and elements as deities (ibid.: 391). This statement relates to the observation that the gentiles are indeed making "speculations about natural causes," in particular the signs, courses, qualities, and conjunctions of the planets, and that they have "great experts" among them who predict floods, droughts, famines, wars, and other events. He concluded, however, when ignorant people saw that these predictions had come true, they took them for miracles and worshiped the experts. In order to increase their authority and influence, these experts therefore, by the help of "the Moors, the hypocrites of the world," engaged in magic art and sorcery and did tricks and deceptions that were "the signal of the devil" (ibid.: 394). In another section, Couto referred to a "most appreciated and erudite book called Valvuer," that was written in the city of Maliador (Mylapur, Chennai, Tamil Nadu) "at the time of the venerated St. Thomas": "This book contains 1330 verses dealing with the knowledge of a single Creator, with the respect one owed him, with the contempt for the idols, and the praise of penitence, humility and abstinence . . . [and] for these things and others written it is to be presumed that they had knowledge of the apostle St. Thomas and learned from him his doctrine" (ibid.: 392). Toward the end of the chapter, Couto reports an episode from a journey he and two companions undertook from Goa to Chaul (Maharashtra), which gives an interesting insight into how the Portuguese were perceived and treated by local Indians outside of the territory of Portuguese control. For lack of any other supply, the small Portuguese party once had to rely on "Bragmanes" for food. Although the food was served with "great care and ceremony," the Portuguese were puzzled by the great ritual precautions taken by the Brahmans in the interaction. It was winter and the Portuguese were asked to doff their outer wear on an outside veranda, then fed inside the house. The plates, though, were placed about "ten to twelve steps away" from Couto and his men, who had to get up to reach the food and return the plates themselves, avoiding any direct contact with their hosts. After they had eaten, "they [the gentiles] brought vessels with water which they poured on the plates from which we had eaten and after making us execute many purifications they washed with great . . . ceremony the verandas on which we had dressed, as if we were ill from some disease contagion" (ibid.: 394).

In summary, then, Couto had an ambiguous attitude toward the religious culture of the gentiles. His interest in and even respect for their theology, literature, and cosmology is undeniable, yet he did not spare his contempt and uttered numerous derogatory remarks regarding their "blindness," "brutish views," "idolatry," and even "veneration of the devil." In fact, the great chronicler opened his celebrated essay *About the Views, Rites and Ceremonies of All the Gentiles of Industan* with a derogatory remark that deserves closer inspection because it triggered an interesting interpretation by Subrahmanyam. Couto began his essay by "giving thanks to the Almighty God for the mercy that he did us, in giving us knowledge of Himself [and] in making us see the ugly, nefarious, and crass rites of these blind gentiles" (ibid.: 382). Obviously irritated about this passage, Subrahmanyam reaches for a drastic interpretation, suggesting that the negative remark was a self-conscious act by which Couto pulled "the teeth of the Counter-Reformation and its censorship" (Subrahmanyam 2001: 36). Without much evidence, the historian thus turns the Portuguese chronicler here into a rebel against contemporary authorities and insinuates that Couto consciously inserted his negative remarks about the gentiles in order to deceive censors about his otherwise sympathetic description.

Notably, in presenting this interpretation, Subrahmanyam suppresses the second half of the critical sentence quoted, which further qualifies "the ugly, nefarious, and brute rites of these blind Gentiles" by adding, "that were mentioned in the diversity of earthly animals in the world which St. Peter saw in his vision of the vessel poring them out, as can be seen in our Acts of the Apostles, number one" (Couto 1937: 382).[6] In other words, Couto made reference here to a story from the Acts of the Apostles, that is the fifth book of the New Testament, which is ascribed to the Apostle Luke and which deals among other things with what in modern parlance might be called religious diversity. More precisely, the story describes a vision that the Apostle Peter had when he was falling into a trance while hungry:

> In this vision the apostle saw a vessel coming down from heaven. In this vessel were all sorts of wild animals, reptiles and birds. Then Peter heard the voice of God telling him: Get up, Peter, kill and eat. The apostle replied: No, Lord, I have never eaten any thing common or unclean. Upon this, the voice spoke to Peter again: What God has cleansed, do not you call common. This was done three times, and then the vessel was taken up again into heaven. (McGarvey 1872: 133; see also Acts of the Apostles 10:9–16)

Bible scholars agree that Peter's vision deals metaphorically with the problem of commensality, that is, the living and eating together of Jewish Christians and gentiles in late antiquity. Given that the principle Torah distinction between clean and unclean food marks the critical subject here, Clinton Wahlen points out that the story introduces a third category of "common" or "doubtfully pure food" (2005: 505). It is this third category of food, he argues, that widened the possibilities of social contact for Jewish Christians to include also "potentially defiled" yet "God-fearing Gentiles," who were distinguished from the "(intrinsic) uncleanness [of] pagans" who continued to be excluded from social contact (ibid.: 515). Returning to the interpretation of Couto's negative remarks regarding the Indian gentiles, the reference to the biblical story does not suggest that the chronicler was engaged in any kind of "double bookkeeping" but rather that he identified himself with the situation of St. Peter and felt a strong and genuine dilemma regarding how to assess and deal with the gentiles who, on the one hand, seemed to him ignorant, nefarious, and even unclean, and, on the other hand, were cultured, sophisticated, even God-fearing.

These uncertainties about the status of gentiles were not uncommon in late-medieval and early-modern times. The book of Genesis, after all, lists among the locations of the descendants of Noah "the isles of the gentiles divided in their lands; every one after his tongue, after their families, in their nations" (Genesis 10:5) and thus indicates that there existed or still exists a genealogical relationship among gentiles, Jews, and Christians. Are gentiles then genuine pagans or did some or all of them once have knowledge of Christian Truth? If the latter, what were the reasons for their apostasy from Christendom: geographical dispersal, as both the terms "pagan" and "heathen" seem to indicate, or moral decay, as the term "idolater" seems to specify with its reference to the notorious relapse of the Jews worshipping the Golden Calf (Exodus 32:4)? How were the various religious cultures of the gentiles related to the divisions and heresies of Christianity? Another, even more disquieting theological hypothesis questioned whether part or all of the religious culture of the gentiles had in fact been manipulated and fabricated by the devil in order to deceive people and take them off the right path. That Couto too saw diabolic influences in the religious culture of the Indian gentiles becomes evident in a remark he made right after the passage quoted earlier, in which he showed himself so obviously impressed by the erudite books of the gentiles, which evoked reminiscences of his own Christian culture and Latin scriptures. "All these books [that is the Vedaos, Xastras, Puranas, and Agamon] are written in heroic and pompous verses and words, an invention that the devil (*o demonio*) had fabricated so that their versatility and seductiveness obliged them to hear them and be affected by them. Like this he [the devil] made so much that whatever Brahman he wanted to make believe a lie in thought or verses did so with so much devotion and authority" (Couto 1937: 383). In other words, the devil is a malicious beguiler who—especially when helped by the "Moors," whom Couto had identified earlier as the "hypocrites of the world"—makes false gods, beliefs, and practices look true so that the "blind gentiles" are fooled and made to believe and do what is wrong.

This idea that alleged similarities between pagan concepts and practices and Christian culture are actually audacious acts of simulacrum or deception fabricated by the devil was common in the early-modern world. We find it clearly expressed in the travelogue of Manuel Godinho (b. 1633), the Portuguese Jesuit who traveled in 1663 along the western coast of India. Engaging in dialogues over theological questions with Hindu Brahmans of Gujarat, Godinho's description of their "errors" shows that not only the curious "search for similarities" but also the persistent suspicion that these similarities might be diabolic fraud occupied the minds of the early-modern explorers and missionaries:

> This is the fundamental error in which these Brahmins, who are more conversant with the matters of our holy Faith, get involved when they come to discuss it. . . . If you explain to them that it is incorrect to worship many deities, they reply the Christians also do the same, since they have the Father, the Son and the Holy Spirit as their deities and, if you tell them that they are not three deities but three persons in one God, they argue in a similar manner about their fictitious trinity. The common enemy has managed to ape the true God everywhere in blind paganism, simulating the mysteries of the Faith, so that, even when truth is later proclaimed, men cannot distinguish it from the false-hoods in which they were brought up, for, when one is shortsighted and things present some similarity, one thing is easily mistaken for another. And then, since the devil knew to counterfeit our things so well as to be able to disguise his own, he simulated for the Brahmins even the cloister, temples, habits, choir and other monastic practices. (Godinho [1665] 1990: 42)

In conclusion, the scholarly interpretations of Vasco Da Gama's error vary a great deal. Subrahmanyam classifies the misperception of the Portuguese captain as a temporary "gaffe," that is, an anachronistic relapse to a time before the knowledge had been established that Christians, Muslims, and those called gentiles had distinct religions. Pearson associates Da Gama's error and, by extension, the mindset of those who thought to recognize significant similarities between the religious cultures of Christians and gentiles with a distinctly "tolerant attitude." The interpretations by the two leading scholars in the field could not be more different, except for the fact that both judge the Portuguese captain against a modern notion of religious plurality.

To be sure, there are good reasons to justify the contextualization of the circumstances of the celebrated error with new perspectives and experiences brought by the revolutionary changes of emerging modernity. Da Gama's grand voyage indeed initiated the lasting and widening encounter of European Christianity with the religious diversity of India and Asia. There also can be no doubt that there were people who almost instantaneously recognized that the alleged Indian Christians were in fact gentiles. Among those were even scholars, such as Diogo do Couto, who laid the foundation for the systematic study of what centuries later was recognized as Hinduism. Intriguingly, the material under investigation, however, also provides substantial indications why it took so long for the recognition of the existence of a multiplicity of independent religions across the globe. Ironically, this recognition was delayed in the early-modern period not because the gentiles were, as was done later in classical modernity, conceived as the radical and racial Other, but because they were perceived as a hidden and distorted form of the religious Self. The longevity of this conceptual absorption of the Other arguably stemmed from its basis in multiple narrative, epistemological, political, and theological grounds. Ancient legends about a lost Eastern Christianity, we have seen, held their ground even against most obvious experiential evidence because they were old, because they offered political hope for a Christian reunion against the global superiority of Islam, and because their allegedly text-based authority still overruled the seemingly ephemeral knowledge gained by discovery and practical encounter. To imagine and eventually recognize that gentiles have genuine and autonomous religions proved problematic in early modernity because it was difficult to conceptualize history differently from the model of biblical genealogy and divine revelation. The term "gentile" thus retained its ambiguous, even dazzling meaning, which oscillated between genuine pagan, apostatized Christian, and someone misguided and deceived by the only imaginable Other to the Christian Truth, that is, the Antichrist or devil. The association of the gentiles with corrupted forms of Christianity, as Sushil Srivastava cogently argues, ended only as late as the early twentieth century, when the term "gentile" became consistently rendered as "heathen" in English translations of early-modern Portuguese travelogues and chronicles such as Mansel Longworth Dames's 1918 edition of *The Book of Duarte Barbosa* (2001: 589).

Rather than a quick or tolerant recognition of religious plurality, the circumstances of Vasco da Gama's error and the "search for the similar" thus indicate the long-lasting and fundamental problems originating from the fact that he found himself in a profound dilemma when facing a religious culture of previously unseen complexity, sophistication, and pomp without however being, epistemologically speaking, ready, and, theologically speaking, willing to acknowledge it as a religion. In simpler terms, the problem was how to acknowledge a religion other than Christianity if, by scholastic definition and orthodox belief, Christianity was the only religion or "Truth" possible. One solution to this problem, which arguably explains the paradoxes inherent in Da Gama's error and the mystery of its persistence over time, is a kind of "assimilationism" (Todorov 1985) that can be described by this formula: if the temples, iconographies, and ceremonies of the gentiles were a religion, then they had to be Christian or at least had to have some genealogical relation or theological affinity with Christianity; if they had no Christian origins or affinities, then they could not be a religion but had to be paganism or, what in many ways was the same, a work of the devil.

2   Image Wars

Iconoclasm, Idolatry, and Survival

> Goa will be taken from the infidel, and will come in time to be the queen of all
> the East, raised to a pinnacle by the triumphs of the conquerors; from which
> proud eminence they will keep severely in check, the idolatrous heathen, and
> all such as may be tempted to wage war against your beloved people.
>
> —Camões [1571] 1973: 65ff.

By the second half of the sixteenth century, Portuguese-Catholic forces
launched a ferocious iconoclastic campaign against Hindu culture in India that
seemed to bring an end to all ambiguities and confusions regarding the identities
of gentiles and Christians. The campaign was directed primarily against Hindu
temples and images, and affected above all India's western coast. The severest
damage was done to Goa, the core colony of the Estado da Índia, as well as Baçaim, Bombai, Damão, and Chaul, its so-called *Provincias do Norte* or Northern
Provinces.[1] From the outset, the campaign looked like a war against images driv-
en by the old Judeo-Christian hostility against "idolatry" and provided a perfect
theological justification for colonial conquest. In Goa, it was nothing less than
devastating, and in little more than two decades, between 1540 and 1560, led to
the destruction or removal of all Hindu temples, shrines, and images. The campaign also banned and suppressed the performance of public Hindu rituals, so
that by 1600, most Hindus who were not willing to convert to Christianity had
either been expelled or fled Goa.

This destruction and demoralization notwithstanding, a second look shows
unintended and ambiguous results for the campaign. The foreign intruders did
not just destroy Hindu images and monuments but, in an obviously strategic
manner, systematically replaced them with Catholic ones. The campaign thus
effected a war between images rather than a war against images. This practice
was of course not uncommon in the contemporary contexts of political conquest.
Ottoman Muslims had transformed the Christian Hagia Sophia in Constantinople into a mosque; Spanish *reconquistadores* planted a Christian cathedral in

the Moorish Mesquita of Cordoba; the Portuguese king made Lisbon's largest synagogue into a church. In Goa, though, the attack on the images arguably had special effects because it did not just target singular and outstanding religious landmarks. Instead, it systematically destroyed all Hindu temples, shrines, and images and replaced them with Christian equivalents. This procedure triggered paradoxical consequences that counteracted the iconoclastic thrust and, ironically, allowed the Catholic images to contribute to the memory, survival, and, in the long run, even recuperation of the Hindu monuments they replaced. The campaign also reveals ambiguities and inconsistencies in the longstanding Christian theological debate regarding the use of images in religious praxis, and brings together, in intriguing synchronicity, the religious encounter of Christians and gentiles at the colonial frontier with the division of Protestants and Catholics in Europe.

Iconoclasm

A first hint that the Portuguese-Catholic regime had plans for an attack against Hindu temples and images after Afonso de Albuquerque conquered the Islands of Goa in 1510 can be found in a letter written by Bishop Duarte Nunez, the leader of the first clerical *visita* to India in 1522, to the Portuguese King João III (r. 1521–1557; Biermann 1953). In this letter, Nunez not only suggests the destruction of Hindu temples and images but, interestingly, also proposes to replace the Hindu temples with Christian churches:

> Regarding the people of Goa they have in their island their temples decked out with figures of the enemy of the Cross and [?] statues, and they celebrate their feasts every year; these feasts are attended by many Christians, our own people as well as recent native Christians. It is a big mistake to continue to show favour to their idolatry. It would be to the service of God to destroy in this island alone these temples and to raise in their stead churches with saints. And whoever wants to live in this island let him become a Christian and he shall possess his lands and houses as he has till now done; if he does not want to do so, let him leave the island. (Silva Rego 1948–1958: 1:452)

Notably, Nunez's suggestion was not put into effect for another twenty years, and there is no evidence of a systematic destruction of Hindu temples until Martim Afonso de Sousa assumed the office of governor of the Estado da Índia from 1542 to 1545. De Sousa, who had arrived in Goa in 1541 on the same ship as Francis Xavier (1506–1552)—the charismatic founder of the Society of Jesus who was to become the celebrated "Apostle of Asia"—came to India with an obviously premeditated plan to attack and destroy major *pagodes* in India. The plan targeted in particular the famous Tirumale-Tirupati temple complex in Andhra Pradesh, which in the sixteenth century was an important religious and economic asset of the rulers of the kingdom of Vijayanagara (Subrahmanyam 2001). Although he eventually gave up this audacious plan due to the military superiority of Vijay-anagara, there was nothing to prevent the new governor from directing violence against other Hindu temples within the Portuguese-controlled territories.

The area first affected was the Islands of Goa, that is, the islands of Chorão, Divar, Jua, and Tiswadi in the estuary of the Mandovi River, where the Portuguese-Catholic regime had built its capitol and headquarters. The destruction of the temples there was only the beginning. Viceroy and Governor of India João de Castro (in office 1545–1548), acting on behalf of João III, continued the campaign and extended its reach to Bardez, Salcete, and Baçaim. The sources also indicate that high clericals of the newly established Diocese of Goa, in particular João de Albuquerque, the first bishop (in office 1538–1553), and Miguel Vaz, the vicar general (in office 1532–1547), were actively involved (D'Costa 1962: 163). Moreover, there is evidence that the campaign intensified. A 1550 order entitled "Provision of Dom João de Castro to Tear Down the Temples on Order of the King" shows that the campaign against the *pagodes* now targeted not only Hindu temples but—playing on the dual meaning of the term *pagode,* which can stand for "temple" as well as "idol" in early-modern Portuguese—was also extended to the destruction of Hindu idols and images. The provision further banned the celebration of all Hindu festivals, ceremonies, and rites, and prohibited the Hindus remaining in the Islands of Goa from using the services of Brahmanical priests from the *terra firma,* that is the adjacent mainland not under Portuguese control. Based on a letter from the king to the governor, the order reads as follows:

> Dom João de Castro, friend. I, the King, send you many greetings. As you know, idolatry is such a big offense against God that I will not tolerate it to exist in these countries [India] that are under my Lordship and, because I have been informed that there exist in the Ilhas de Goa some idols, in public and in hiding, which have done such great harm to Our Lord, . . . I strongly recommend to You and order that from now on, . . . You assert that there will not be any of the said idols, neither in public nor hidden, in the said Island of Goa and that no craftsmen shall make them from stone, or wood, or copper, or any other metal. And likewise that in the entire Island there should be no Gentile festivals in public, nor should its inhabitants bring Brahman priests from the mainland; and [I] order that the houses of all Brahmins and Gentiles, which are suspected to have the said images, are searched, and the proper enactment of all these issues should be asserted by severe penalties. (Wicki 1969: 162ff.)

The provision was confirmed by Bishop João d'Albuquerque, who acknowledged his duty to "destroy this very bad idolatry . . . in the countries of Your Lordship, the Islands [of Goa] and in Baçaim." He went on to address Padre Belchior Gonçalvez and the Jesuits proselytizing in Salcete; Simão Travaços, the vicar general of Baçaim; and the friars of the Franciscan order who were active in Bardez, empowering them to "destroy and tear down existing temples and temples under construction or repair, wherever they are found." All this, he added, is part of the obligation to "extinguish the sect of Maphamede [Islam] and Gentilica [Hindu] and all that is opposing the faith of Our Lord Jesus Christ in my diocese" (ibid.: 164). The reconfirmation and repetition of these and similar orders and prohibitions during the rule of King Sebastião (r. 1557–1578) and Governor Constantino de Braganca (in office 1558–1561) made the sixteenth century the period during which the Hindus of Goa and the Northern Provinces lost most of their temples, shrines, and idols to this ruthless iconoclastic violence. The nature and intention of this violence becomes clear, once again, from an order issued by Queen Doma Catarina of Austria in 1559, acting as regent during the minority of her grandson King Sebastião. In this order, she condemns

> the many offences and harms done to Our Lord by the infidels and gentiles adoring and celebrating in public their idols and images and performing diabolic rites within my Lordship and in presence of Christians . . . [and orders] . . . that, in the said island of Goa and its other annexed territories, there should be no more idols, nor images within nor outside of any house and all those found should be burned and disfigured [*desfação*], nor should it be possible to make them from wood, nor stone, nor any metal, nor any other material, nor should it be allowed to have any public gentile festival indoor or outside, nor should Brahmanical Gentile priests be allowed, . . . nor [temple] pools for the Gentiles, nor should they be allowed to burn [their dead]. (Ibid.: 63ff.)

Dimensions of Destruction

The iconoclastic policies articulated in the legislation issued by the various Portuguese kings in Lisbon in the middle decades of the sixteenth century undoubtedly were of the utmost ruthlessness and aimed at the complete destruction of the religious culture of Hindus in the extended Goa. The *Livro do Pai dos Cristãos*, a compendium of royal laws and decrees issued *a favor da Cristandade*, "to promote Christianity" in Goa (Wicki 1969: xii), lists six laws between 1549 and 1566 that explicitly order the destruction of temples and prohibit the repair of existing or construction of new ones (ibid.). An early indication that the campaign had devastating effects in the Islands of Goa comes from Nicollo Lancilotto, a visiting Italian Jesuit, who on his arrival in 1545 reported, "There are no more temples in this island, but there remains an infinite number of Moors, Gentiles and bad Christians" (D'Costa 1962: 163). This assessment notwithstanding, it is not easy to determine the damage of the iconoclastic campaign. Uncertainty results from a number of circumstances. First, we have only insufficient and indirect information about the number and the quality of temples that existed in Goa before the arrival of the Portuguese. There is some indication that a number of large temples were in Islands of Goa, which was the heartland of the Chalukya (600–700 CE), Silahara (800–1000 CE), and Kadamba (1000–1400 CE) dynasties and also the site of major historical cities such as Gopakapattana (modern Velha Goa, Tiswadi; Mitragotri 1999). Archaeologist Gritli von Mitterwallner writes that "there must have once existed many temples" there (1983a: 24).[2] We have little information, however, about the situation in the villages and hinterland of Bardez and Salcete. Indirect evidence comes from old property names and records indicating that in most villages, special plots of land were dedicated to the respective *ganvdevāta* or village deities. That means either temples or shrines had been built on this land or its products were used for the maintenance of temples and shrines and the payment of temple priests and servants, as well as the organization of religious rituals and festivals. Other evidence includes property names and records as well as archaeological findings indicating that many old churches in the area were built at or nearby locations at which there had been temples before the coming of the Portuguese. In fact, some archaeological findings even indicate that some of the old churches were built by using the very rubble of the temples they replaced (Mitterwallner 1983b; Doshi and Shirodkar 1983). Historians commonly estimate the temples destroyed in the hundreds. D'Costa refers to unspecified "native sources," when speaking of 160 temples that were destroyed in the Islands of Goa (1962: 163); Pearson estimates that 300 temples were destroyed in each one of the three provinces of the Old Conquests, the Islands of Goa, Bardez, and Salcete in the 1540s ([1984] 2005a: 41). It has to be stressed though that none of these numbers are buttressed by concrete evidence, and that estimations based on early-modern Portuguese sources are especially uncertain because the term *pagode* stood for both "temple" and "idol."

Uncertainty about how much damage the iconoclastic campaign actually effected also results from the fact that the content of the legislation cannot be taken to exactly reflect social reality in sixteenth-century Goa. Michael Pearson in particular highlights how much the "normative decrees" issued by the king and archbishop were in contrast with the multireligious and cosmopolitan life in the city of Goa, something that found best contemporary expression in a celebrated passage published by the Dutch nobleman John Huyghen van Linschoten who visited Goa in 1598 and described it as such:

> (The Portuguese) dwell in the towne among all sorts of nations, as Indians, Heathens, Moores, Jewes, Armenians, Gusarates, Benians, Bramenes, and of all Indian nations and people, which doe all dwell and traficke therein, everie man holding his owne religion, without constraining any man to do against his conscience, only touching their ceremonies of burning the dead, and the living, of marrying and other superstitions and devilish inventions, they are forbidden by the Archbishop to use them openly, or in the Island, but they may freelie use them upon the firme land, and secretly in their houses. (Pearson [1984] 2005a: 42)

A common explanation for such seeming inconsistency is that early-modern Portuguese rule and Catholic hegemony in India was notoriously inefficient. Structures of command and control were imperfect, means of communication were long and uncertain, and there was ample room for local interpretation and corruption of Lisbon's orders and policies, something that Pearson describes as the "pre-modern casualness" of Portuguese rule and administration in India (1987: 19).[3] Subrahmanyam further demystifies the contemporary imperial aspiration of the Estado da Índia and the glorification of *Goa Dourada* by arguing that it is even questionable "whether the Portuguese truly had an empire in any meaningful sense in that period," given the fact that early-modern Hindu polities were far more dynamic and powerful than contemporary Portuguese sources commonly make us believe (1993: 1, 28, passim).

The documents collected in the *Livro do Pai dos Cristãos* (Wicki 1969) provide other indirect evidences indicating that the execution of temple destruction and the oppression of Hindu practices may not have been as effective as its harsh legislation suggests; it may, in fact, have met with considerable local resistance. Noteworthy here in particular is a letter written by King Dom João V to his viceroy in Goa, Dom Vasco Fernandez Sezar de Menezes, in March 1714 in which the king bitterly complained about the "great omission and abuse" that his legislation was experiencing in the Indian colony. He went on to admonish the local authorities that they had not succeeded in preventing the *gentios vassalos,* that is, Hindus living in Portuguese-controlled territories and collaborating with the colonial rulers as doctors, merchants, and political middle men, from continuing to pursue their religious traditions. In particular, it becomes clear that the Hindus on the Islands of Goa not only regularly traveled to the mainland to pray to their deities and celebrate their festivals but also used the money they made in Portuguese Goa to build new temples there (ibid.: 326ff.). Another form of local resistance undermining the suppression of Hindu influence in the Portuguese-controlled territories was that certain Hindus maintained considerable social status and political influence, something that allowed them to perform highly symbolic practices, such as walking the streets with showy parasols or being carried in sedan chairs, privileges that actually were reserved by law to Portuguese noblemen (ibid.: 190ff., 218ff.; Chandeigne 1996). The Brahmans of Goa were especially able to embark on this level of disobedience because they had preserved such economic power that, in complete contravention of the legislation listed in the *Livro do Pai dos Cristãos* favoring local Christians in the distribution of the *rendas* or tax-farming contracts, they had been able to acquire more than 80 percent of the tax-farming contracts for themselves (Pearson 1973b: 37).

To assess and appreciate the damage done by the iconoclastic campaign, however, one cannot look only at the destruction of individual temples or the status of elite sections of Hindu society. One also needs to consider the meaning and significance that religious monuments and images had and have to this day for Hindu society and culture in the region. The marking of villages and landscape with temples, shrines, and icons of deities, ancestors, and tutelary beings is pivotal for Hindu society and culture in Goa and elsewhere in India. It plays an important role in structuring geography and landscape, articulates social distinctions and hierarchies, constitutes cultural memory, and is crucial for people's orientation in space, society, and time. Moreover, religious monuments, images, and sites are indispensable for their evocation of the divine and other sacred forces. Icons are closely associated with ideas and practices related to security and danger, peace and conflict, illness and healing; they play important roles for the identities of families and castes by specifying their places of home and belonging and tracing their origins and descent. It cannot be surprising therefore that, to this day, religious images and icons are omnipresent in Goans' life. They can be seen by the hundreds in every village and town, and mark countless spots in the fields and forests; they are displayed in temples and homes, public buildings and private shops, and adorn thousands of cars, busses, motorcycles, and boats. Religious monuments, images, and icons receive wide and regular attention: temples and shrines are carefully maintained and decorated, and images and icons of gods and goddesses are treated like kings or queens, fed daily, bathed, dressed, entertained, and worshipped (Eck 1981). Hindus approach them for help and protection, and to divine the future; they are carried through settlements and fields during the seasonal festivals. Images, icons, and paraphernalia of deities, ancestors, and tutelary beings also play an important role in rituals and festivals in which the stratification of castes and the principles of seniority are displayed and negotiated, and they are essential in religious ceremonies that mark the yearly seasons and coordinate ritual and reproductive cycles. It is against this background that the magnitude of the iconoclastic onslaught against Hindu monuments and images becomes comprehensible. Obviously, the attack targeted a life vein of Hindu culture and society, depriving it of its symbolically articulated and ritually enacted social order and threatening its economic and reproductive survival.

Not surprisingly, the iconoclastic campaign therefore resulted in the almost complete surrender of the Hindu population, driving a majority into Christian conversion and forcing those who were not willing to convert to abandon their homes and property and flee from their villages and lands in large numbers. By 1700, the demographic effect of the onslaught had reached its peak, with 90 percent of the population of the Islands of Goa, Bardez, and Salcete becoming Catholic (Srivastava 1990; De Souza 1975: 30). Moreover, reports document that, at the height of the iconoclastic violence, entire Hindu communities in Goa approached Catholic missionaries and asked to be converted to Catholicism. In at least one case, Hindus seem to have even destroyed their own temple asking for the construction of a church (Robinson 1993: 75). Rowena Robinson's research challenges, however, the assertions made by Jesuit historians like Henry Heras (1933) and Anthony D'Costa (1962) that these dramatic events contained "voluntary elements of conversion" even amid the violent encounters of the sixteenth century. Highlighting the symbolic significance of the divine for the local society and culture, Robinson cogently argues that conversion to Catholicism for the local people was practically "the only way of preventing their world from falling completely into pieces" (1993: 76).

Idolatry

When addressing the question of what triggered the early-modern iconoclastic campaign in India and what were its rationales, scholars usually make reference to the particular nature of the Portuguese colonial expansion. Combining mercantile interests with religious motives, the political institution of the *Padroado,* that is, the privilege of the Portuguese royalty to patronize and supervise all missionary activities in Asia, formally organized the cooperation of Church and Crown, Cross and Sword. As Carmen Bernand and Serge Gruzinski note in the early-modern Spanish-American context, "Idolatry was a splendid politico-military alibi because it legitimized the [colonial] conquest" (1988: 14). That the colonial expansion responded to two major European crises developing in roughly the same period—the late-medieval crisis of feudalism and the early-modern conflict between the Protestant Reformation and the Catholic Church—further supports scholarly conventions that treat religion and politics as functionally and ideologically interrelated in the colonial project (Boxer [1969] 1991; Pearson 1987; De Souza 1990; Subrahmanyam 2001).

More specifically, the violence against Hindu culture is related to the celebrated Council of Trent, which, spread out over three papal pontificates and no less than twenty-five sessions held between 1545 and 1563 in Trento and Bologna, Italy, formulated the Catholic response to the Protestant Reformation. Commonly considered as propagating a kind of Counter-Reformation, the council both mitigated and countered the Protestant challenge by reforming certain grievances of contemporary Catholicism and boosting its renewal, especially by enforcing its overseas missions. In Goa, the Council directly effected three major events: the introduction of the *Casa do Santo Officio,* that is, the Portuguese Inquisition in 1560, which targeted "Protestant heretics" and newly converted Christians suspected of relapsing into non-Christian practices (Lima 1996); a series of four *Concílios Provinciales* held between 1567 and 1606 that worked out detailed policies intensifying the Christian conversion in Asia (Cunha Rivara [1862] 1992); and the notorious campaign against Hindu culture including the destruction of Hindu temples and images in the extended Goa and the repression of Hindu rites. Francis Xavier is commonly identified as a major agent of Counter-Reformation ideology and said to have initiated its execution in Asia. Additional evidence buttressing the argument that the events in India were closely related to religious politics in Europe is the striking contemporaneity of the iconoclastic violence in both places. Notably, the agents of the Portuguese-Catholic colonial regime attacked and destroyed the Hindu monuments and images in Goa more or less exactly in the same period in which the activists of the Protestant movement went out to destroy and deface Catholic images in the churches and chapels of Germany, France, the Netherlands, and Bohemia.

While this is the major political background of the campaign, it is the first of the Ten Commandments in the Hebrew Bible that reminds us of its theological rationale: "I am the Lord your God, who brought you out of the land of Egypt, out of the house of bondage. You shall have no other gods before me. You shall not make for yourself a graven image, or any likeness of anything that is in heaven above, or that is in the earth beneath, or that is in the water under the earth; you shall not bow down to them or serve them" (Exodus 20:2–5). The prohibition against images in religious practice is thus an old Judeo-Christian axiom. Arguably, it originated in the biblical moment of the "Mosaic distinction" (Assmann 2010), that is, the moment when Moses revealed to his people the divine declaration of the exclusive Truth of the Jewish doctrine and the disavowal of all other religions. Interestingly, though, the new norm was immediately challenged and violated. Hence, while Moses climbed Mount Sinai to receive the Decalogue, the biblical story reports that his followers relapsed into old practices, creating and worshipping the idol of a Golden Calf representing the God of Israel (Exodus 32:1–34:2).

Thereafter, the quarrel about the status and use of images became one of the most protracted and dramatic controversies in the Christian tradition. It was debated at numerous church meetings and councils, engaged countless theological scholars, confronted and separated various Christian denominations and sects, and triggered a series of violent encounters and wars. Notwithstanding its repeated banning and persecution, the use of images was never fully given up by the people and, at various times, also gained theological justification and support from the highest order. Pope Gregory the Great (540–604) defended the display and liturgical use of images because he acknowledged them as "the books of the illiterate" and suggested allowing converted gentiles to continue using their "churches" on the ground that this was a powerful and legitimate incentive for others to convert (Jedin 1935: 423; Turner and Turner 1978: 51ff.). Gregory's iconophilic attitude was confirmed by the Second Council of Nicaea in 787 at which it was argued that the ban of images in the Old Testament was superseded by the coming of Christ, whose incarnation justified the material representation of the divine and holy. At other times, images became the object of disagreement and conflict, triggering the notorious Byzantine iconoclasm between 730 and 787. Initiated by Emperor Leo III, this conflict turned into a full-fledged war with widespread bloodshed and destruction between the opposing parties of *iconodules,* or image worshippers, and *iconoclasts,* or image breakers. Focusing on theories regarding the nature of Christ, the argument of the adversaries of the images was that Christ combined in himself, in inseparable union, a human and divine nature of which only his human nature could be depicted. Concluding from here that the depiction of Christ in images and icons unavoidably violated his inseparable dual nature, *iconodules* were accused and persecuted for committing a deadly sin when making and worshipping images of Christ, the Trinity, and the saints.

During the Middle Ages and well into modernity, the debates over the use and status of religious images kept clerics and scholars busily discussing the issue in the light of numerous theological laws and moral principles. The dogma of the singularity of divine creation, morals of decency regarding the body, the authenticity of natural forms, and the ways demons and the devil were suspected to act became major arguments for the rejection of images. The assumption that everything in the universe was created by the One God alone became a reason to suspect images—human artifice imitating nature—of constituting blasphemy (Camille 1989: 33). Pictorial art was also despised for its capacity to "make what is not," as Saint Paul put it (ibid.: 37), and to show what was prohibited to look at. The depiction of forms and shapes not found in nature, such as Janus, the two-faced Roman god, and the representation of nude bodies, such as Artemis, the Greek goddess, made the figures of the classical pantheon into epitomes of forbidden idols. Another serious reservation against pictorial representation was its alleged tendency toward deception. Images were despised for faking nature not only "in the way we look down upon artificial flowers today" (ibid.: 36). Three-dimensional sculptures were moreover considered dangerous simulacra and potential hidden sites of demons, fallen angels, or the devil, forces that might allow the sculptures to come alive and speak or act like living beings, thereby bewitching or possessing people.

Humanist and Protestant reformers made the image question a central issue of philosophical and theological debates in the sixteenth century. Although Martin Luther (1483–1546) pursued only a moderate critique of the use of images in Christian practice, Erasmus of Rotterdam (1466–1536), John Calvin (1509–1564), and Ulrich Zwingli (1484–1531) attacked religious images harshly and triggered a widespread *Bildersturm* or wave of iconoclastic destruction in Catholic churches and chapels in Germany, France, the Netherlands, Bohemia, and other European countries in the middle of the sixteenth century (Jedin 1935; Freedberg 1982). Underlying the controversies were questions about the status and value of liturgical images, objects, and practices. Is the *Gnadenwirkung,* that is, the emanation of grace, restricted to certain sacraments, as Protestant theologians argued, or are images, icons, and relics also instrumental in the mediation and transfer of grace, as most Catholic theologians argued? Does one need to read and understand the Christian scriptures in order to partake in the redemptive power of the Christian doctrine, or does mere phonetic recitation of sacred formulas and prayers, the performance of rituals, and the handling of sacred substances and objects have the same effect? While discussing these and other questions in Humanist and Reformation circles, delegations of Catholic theologians from the highest-ranking universities in Europe tried to establish what appears today a hairsplitting distinction between *latria,* that is, illegitimate worship of images, and *veneratio,* that is, legitimate veneration of images. The distinction, it was insinuated, marked the difference between pagans and Christians (Jedin 1935: 177). "Is it likely," David Freedberg asks, "that the countless men [in early-modern Europe] who went on pilgrimages to particular images, who sought aid from a favourite painting or sculpture, or who went to be healed by the miracle-working powers of a specific shrine made this kind of distinction? All the evidence suggests not" (1982: 139).

Scholarly controversies and practical inconsistencies notwithstanding, the use of religious images became the central criterion for the qualification of the cultural differences that European Christians encountered at the colonial frontier. Hence, the notion of the "idolater" became a general synonym for pagan and heathen marking the common Other of the *Christenmenschen,* that is, the "Christian human being" in whose German linguistic designation still resonates the assumption that only Christians are fully human. "Idolatry" became a descriptive shorthand used in contemporary travelogues, chronicles, and missionary reports for all sorts of qualities, practices, and objects found among the gentiles in the colonies. Still adhering to the unspecified connection made in the biblical law between the worship of "other gods" and the making of "graven images," this philosophy indiscriminately defamed and stigmatized all that was considered non-Christian. In Goa and India, the violent iconoclastic attack was thus not only directed at the destruction of Hindu monuments and images but also attempted to stop and eradicate all Hindu practices, rituals, festivals, and customs. The contemporary literature amplified the defamation of idolatry in India by ascribing to it all sorts of horrifying practices such as the burning of women at the funeral pyres of their husbands, the self-mutilation of devotees in front of their idols, and even the alleged ritual suicide of people who let themselves be crushed by the chariots of deities carried through the streets at religious festivals (Rubiés 2000; Major [1857] 2005). Interestingly, the stigmatization and discrimination against idolatry became also a favored subject of contemporary artwork that accompanied written reports from the colonial world. A case in point is an early depiction of a Hindu god illustrating the travelogue of Ludovico di Varthema who visited India around 1505. Portraying the Hindu god not only, as Partha Mitter (1977) aptly put it, as one of the "much maligned monsters" of the East, the illustration also pays conscious effort to graphically depict the "sinful worship" that was dedicated to the idol (see figure 2.1).

Figure 2.1. Calicut Idol from "The Travels of Ludovico di Varthema in Egypt, Syria, Arabia Deserta and Arabia Felix, in Persia, India, and Ethiopia, A.D. 1503 to 1508." From Mitter 1977: 20.

Iconoclasm thus became a widespread corollary to colonial conquest and missionary activity. Notably, the violent onslaught in India not only attacked Hindu monuments and images but also banned and prohibited a wide range of objects and substances used in Hindu religious practice. What deserves attention here is the fact that the royal and clerical orders for the attacks made painstaking efforts to name and identify each and every material of which the condemned idols were made, such as stone, wood, copper, and any other material. This peculiar concern for the material quality of the idols corresponds with the catalogue of objects that the agents of the Portuguese Inquisition had prohibited from the local Christian liturgy including certain local plants and flowers, rice, coconut, turmeric, betel leaves, and areca nuts, among other things. In fact, researching the suppression of "gentile practices" among converted Christians in early seventeenth-century Goa, Rowena Robinson notes that "it is . . . not so much the rituals that are being opposed, but more significantly, the substances used therein" (2000: 2425). Trying to unmake all "Hindu habitus" among local Catholics, she continues, the Inquisition banned all sorts of customary social practices such as the keeping of Indian names, the wearing of Indian dresses, and the singing of the Konkani verses known as *vovio* (ibid.: 2427). Goan historians extend the list and report that even local customs such as cooking rice without salt, removing one's footwear in the home, and, for men, squatting down when urinating was banned by inquisitorial law (Angle 1994; Cunha n.d.: 18). How much the Catholic encounter with Hindu culture was thus a confrontation in which substances and bodily practices played a critical role comes finally to the fore in the fact that, in a reversal of the prohibition for Catholic converts to use Hindu pollution-removing substances such as cow dung, the agents of the iconoclastic attack themselves consciously used cow meat to either desecrate Hindu religious sites or reassert people's conversion by forcefully making them consume beef.

This critical attention paid to the material and performative expression of Hindu culture indicates that not only theological and cognitive principles but also the practice and materiality of signification were at stake in the Portuguese-Catholic attack. In order to appreciate this larger perspective, it is important to notice that the scholastic attempts to distinguish between pagan idolatry and Christian veneration of images at the Council of Trent was conceptualized on the one hand in the backdrop of the Platonic distinction of body and soul, image and prototype, and, on the other, responded to the Protestant claim that the redemptive effect of the Christian Truth was a matter of inner belief and intellectual comprehension rather than externalized representation through images and rituals. The position taken by Count Alberto Pio of Pardi, one of the clerics attending the Council of Trent, defended the use of images against the critique of Erasmus of Rotterdam by distinguishing between "internal veneration of God [*innerer Gottesverehrung*], *cultus latriae*, which is not appropriate for images, and external veneration of God [*äusserer Gottesverehrung*], the unfolding of which needs the stimulation of images" (Jedin 1935: 153). Pardi continued his argument by defending "the spiritual pagan image service" (*vergeistigter heidnischer Bilderdienst*) of classical antiquity vis-à-vis the "external veneration of God" by arguing that it was rejected by the Christian doctrine "not because it was fundamentally wrong, but because it depicted creatures and demons" (ibid.). How critical and difficult it was to distinguish between the two forms of veneration comes to the fore in the documents of another high-ranking clerical meeting that preceded and anticipated the image debate at the Council of Trent. This was the bishops' convention that gathered in 1561 in Poissy, France, which, interestingly, also included a discussion with Calvinist theologians on the issue of "the central dogma of the presence of Christ in the Eucharist" (ibid.: 170). A major result of the meeting was an instruction to parochial priests regarding the veneration of images, which Hubert Jedin summarizes as follows:

> The images are displayed in the churches above all so that the spectator is reminded of the redemption by Jesus Christ and to illustrate the faith and piety of the saints. . . . They are to be venerated, but not with that internal devotion [*inneren Kult*] that belongs to God alone and that consists of the tri-

une Faith, Hope and Love, but by those lower external modes of expression [*niederen äusseren Ausdrucksformen*] . . . genuflection, prostration, raising of hands which are the same as in the *latreutic* [cult] that belongs to God alone. . . . The priests are ordered to illuminate the people that nothing divine and no genuine power inheres in the images. They shall reject superstitious ideas and practices, that have become common, take care that obscene, ridiculous and inappropriate paintings and sculptures are removed and in general, by instructing their parishioners, prevent the creeping in of idolatry. Permission of the bishop is needed for the display of new images. (Ibid.: 171–172)

While the bishops in Poissy and the clerics at the Council of Trent thus permitted the use and veneration of religious images under certain conditions, the council emphasized that visual depictions were most critical where abstract aspects of the divine that had no mundane or natural equivalent were at stake. In particular, depictions of the Holy Trinity and the Holy Spirit became subjects of critique and debate, and the council rejected representations of the Trinity by a male figure with three faces, as had become common practice in France, or portrayals of the Holy Spirit as an old man holding the globe in his hand, as was common in parts of Germany. This notwithstanding, Catholic clerics and scholars again found compromises and decided that the Trinity and the Holy Spirit could be depicted by models and symbols that were mentioned in biblical scriptures. Hence, a vision of the prophet Daniel was said to justify the depiction of God as Father (Daniel 7:13–14) and the biblical story of Pentecost was taken to legitimize the depiction of the Holy Spirit as a dove (Acts of Apostles 2:1–31). These details reveal the position of the Catholic congregation in another major contemporary debate, that is, the debate over the relation between image and text. Protestant reformers and all those who argued that God cannot be depicted acknowledged only two ways of partaking in the divine grace: the reading of biblical scriptures and the two sacraments that arguably had been initiated by Christ himself, baptism and the Eucharistic Supper. All other objects and practices commonly involved in contemporary Christian observances such as images, icons, relics, paraphernalia, sacred substances, bodily exercises, postures, and gestures were rejected by the reformers and, in the worst case, considered idolatry. While the Catholic congregation obviously did not follow the Protestant Reformers in this radical rejection of images, it did acknowledge their basic semiotic principles and tried to carefully, if also perhaps not convincingly, distinguish between legitimate and illegitimate uses of images and other modes of devotional expression. More importantly, the recommended practices regarding the depiction of the Trinity and the Holy Spirit show that the Catholic response to some extent also reenacted the Protestant appreciation of biblical scriptures and of text at large vis-à-vis images and rituals.

The sixteenth-century image debate can thus be summarized to reflect a major transformation of the Christian notion of religion, changing it from revealed, embodied, and enacted Truth to interiorized, acquired, expressive faith, something that included important changes in the concept of knowledge and the system of signification. These changes substituted premodern ideas of an iconic, that is, bodily articulated or materially reified similarity mediating between sign and signified, knowledge and knower, by modern notions of the autonomy of knower and knowledge and a symbolic, that is, neutral and arbitrary code communicating among knowledge, sign, and meaning. In the religious field this new "semiotic ideology" (Keane 2007) was reflected above all in theological principles and practical attitudes controlling and disciplining the use of images, rituals, and the body, and favoring the significance of text, education, and personal creed (Asad 1993, 2003; Freedberg 1982, 1989; Belting 2000; Camille 1989).

In the debate about images and idolatry, these modern transformations became important above all by rendering the theologically defined image ban a scientific issue. Idolatry, in other words, changed its status from a sin that combines the depiction of the nondepictable with the worship of the forbidden into a cognitive mistake, that is, the confusion of the image for the prototype, the sign for the signified. This transformation henceforth marked the distance between Christians and idolaters with unmistakable certainty and scientific coherence, defining Christians as those who know to distinguish between images and prototypes and, therefore, do not worship religious images, and despising idolaters as those who confuse the distinction between images and prototypes and, therefore, worship the images themselves, that is, wrongly paying ritual attention to material objects and substances, external appearances and bodily practices.

It is this condensation of the age-old Judeo-Christian debate about images in religious practice in a scientific or semiotic principle that explains the extraordinary vehemence of the early-modern condemnation of idolatry and iconoclastic attack. Intriguingly, though, the renewed image ban left many theological ambiguities open and generated unintended consequences in its practical execution. While Protestants for the most part felt that religious images were generally disposable, to Catholics the matter was about reinterpreting the details of their status and use in Christian liturgy. Moreover, the very nature of iconoclasm turned out to be ambiguous, since, at least partially, it reasserted the significance of what it attacked. It was these ambiguities and unintended consequences that, in Goa, encouraged Catholics to continue the use of images and, ironically, even made the images part of conceptual and practical interactions with Hindus.

Survival

A Christian image displayed in the church of the village of Siolim (Bardez) in Goa palpably demonstrates the ambiguities triggered by the iconoclastic attack on Hindu culture (see figure 2.2). The image represents a statue of St. Anthony of Padua (1195–1231), the Portuguese-born Franciscan monk, in his function as

Figure 2.2. St. Anthony and the Snake, Siolim, Goa. Photograph by Gasper D'Souza.

patron saint of Siolim. The image is peculiar because it shows the saint in an unusual posture. While conventionally presented in the habit of a Franciscan monk holding a book in his arm on which baby Jesus sits, the Siolim image shows the saint with a string in his right hand from which hangs a strangulated snake. A local legend explains this curious scene: In the year 1600, the legend reports, Franciscan missionaries carried with them a statue of St. Anthony on their passage to India. Already in sight of the Konkan coastline, the pious travelers got into a heavy storm that threatened to sink their ship. In great fear, they prayed to St. Anthony, vowing to build him a church wherever they reached land safely. Miraculously, the storm calmed down, and the missionaries landed near the village Siolim where they started to build the promised church in the saint's name. While doing so, they met with an unexpected obstacle, however. A big snake appeared, threatening them and persistently obstructing their work, tearing down overnight what the workers had built during the day. This went on and on, the legend continues, until one day the friars, not knowing what else to do, placed the statue of St. Anthony into the worksite. There the saint worked another miracle. The next morning, the malicious snake was found dead, strangled by the statue of St. Anthony itself, and the construction of the church could be completed (Ataide de Lobo 1907, 1931; D'Cruz 1994).

Today, the people of Siolim, Hindus as well as Catholics, have an interesting interpretation of the miraculous image. To them, the snake represents the Hindu god Vetal, a Konkan manifestation of the great Shiva, who quite regularly manifests himself as a snake and had a temple in Siolim in precolonial times that was located at or near the site where the church of St. Anthony today stands. People's recollection that St. Anthony's church had thus replaced an ancient temple of Vetal is confirmed by sixteenth-century documents vouching for the existence of a *Vetalache tolli ani xet,* that is, a "land and field of Vetal" set aside for the building and its economic subsidy right next to the location of toady's church (D'Cruz 1994: 6).

Two interesting syncretistic practices twine around St. Anthony of Siolim and the Hindu god Vetal whom Anthony superseded. The first is dedicated to Vetal whose icon at the time of the destruction of Siolim's Hindu temples was salvaged and clandestinely brought to Palle (Bicholim), a village then located outside the reach of the Portuguese-Catholic regime. The people of Siolim never forgot the whereabouts of their former village god and regularly visited Palle to make offerings to their ancient Vetal. In fact, a local church chronicle from 1931 reports that even some Catholics from Siolim followed what is contemptuously called the *incoerente costume,* that is, "the inappropriate custom" to accompany their Hindu village fellows to Palle to also pay their respects to the ancient village god (Ataide de Lobo 1931: 15).

Another syncretistic practice is dedicated to St. Anthony, the Catholic patron saint of Siolim who, to this day, is not only honored by Catholics but also many Hindus of Siolim. Hence, Hindu shopkeepers display St. Anthony's image next to Hindu iconography in their shops, and Hindu villagers routinely pay their respects and make offerings to the saint's shrine outside the church, saluting his statue with flowers and devotional gestures when it is carried through the village at festive occasions. Especially at his annual feast day on 19 June, some Siolim Hindus regularly take part in the holy masses read in the name of the patron saint inside the church and—since taking Holy Communion resonates for them with their own concept of *prasāda,* that is, the reception of food ritually offered to a god—some of them would also not be disinclined to receive the altar bread distributed at the occasion although the Catholic vicar regularly announces that this part of the ritual is reserved for Christians only. Devotional homage paid by Hindus to St. Anthony are also common during the Jagar ceremony that is jointly performed by Hindus and Catholic in Siolim every year. As I describe in more detail in chapter 5, one of St. Anthony's chapels is the site where the Catholics involved in the festival collect and pray before they proceed to the *mand,* that is, the place of ceremonies where they join their Hindu fellows for the nightlong ceremonies. During these ceremonies, St. Anthony is invoked and honored by Catholics and Hindus in prayers and songs identifying him, among other things, as *Bhaktā Firanghi kuḍīyecyā, tuje librar Menin Jesu kelta,* that is, the "Saint belonging to the European race, on whose book Baby Jesus plays."

Although particularly expressive, the curious image of Siolim's patron saint is not the only indication that Hindu images and icons survived their destruction and replacement by Catholic images and icons. The modalities of this survival vary, of course. In some cases, people remember and continue to venerate the "old identity" of a saint's image that replaced the icon of a Hindu god or tutelary being. Hindus also pray, present offerings, or otherwise express their respects to saints' images, sometimes using offerings that are typical for Hindu gods such as the burning of oil lamps or incense. In other cases, people travel to places where Hindu images had been displaced to pay homage to "erstwhile gods" of their village or region. A form of commemoration that is becoming more and more popular in recent times is the temporary or even permanent reinstallation of Hindu images in their former villages or towns.

In general, these forms of survival of Hindu images reinforce the truism that all iconoclastic violence, to some extent, acknowledges and reconfirms what it attacks and destroys (Freedberg 1989). Hence, when the missionaries destroyed and replaced the Hindu images, local people often perceived the violent act as confirming the "power" of the affected images.[4] A closer inspection suggests though that in Goa, the connection between replacement and survival of Hindu images was and is more complex. It is important to recall that the replacement of Hindu images and monuments was done in a systematic and area-wide manner. Hence, historical, archaeological, and ethnographic evidence indicates that the Portuguese-Catholic iconoclasm did not only attack a few large and conspicuous Hindu temples but indeed affected the whole range of Hindu temples, shrines, and images marking the Goan settlements and landscape. This systematic procedure thus added to the reconfirmation of the iconic agency of the Hindu monuments and images by exactly replicating the details of their territorial distribution and spatial association.

In order to appreciate the significance of this peculiar circumstance, it is important to recall what David Shulman called "the phenomenon of localization" in Hindu religiosity (Erndl 1993: 60), that is, the eminent manifestation in space of divinity and sainthood in Hindu mythology and praxis. Most Hindu gods are associated with mountains or rivers, embodied in landscapes and regions, and identified with settlements and wards. Kathleen Erndl points out that female divinity in particular is articulated in local manifestations that are known as *śakthī pīṭhās* or "places of power" (ibid.: 32). In Goa and elsewhere in India, this spatial manifestation of Hindu divinity takes a most complex form in the village realm. Every village is associated with one or several *ganvdevāta*, or village gods, who are commonly seen as founders, ancestors, protectors, and members of the village and village community. All ancient gods of Goa and the Konkan—Sateri, Bhumika, Vetal, and Ravalnath—are in this way associated with particular villages. This association becomes most expressive where village goddesses are addressed by local epithets identifying them with their village's name so that, for instance, the goddess from the village Fatorpa is addressed as "Fatorpekarin," the one from Morjim as "Morzai," the one from Valpoi "Valpoikarin," and so on. As Erndl notes, "The deity and the place are identified with each other. It is difficult to say which is named after the other" (ibid.: 60). The most palpable expression of the intimate connection between *ganvdevāta* and village is certainly the idea that the body of the goddess constitutes the soil of the village itself.

The association of *ganvdevāta* with towns, villages, and regions is complemented by minor gods or tutelary beings associated with subdivisions or distinct localities in the settlements and landscape. These minor gods are generically known either as *rakhne*, a term derived from the Konkani word for "guardian," or simply *jāgeveile*, which literally means "those from the place." Like *ganvdevāta*, *rakhne* are associated with particular territories or localities. In order to identify these, Goans draw a ritual distinction between the territories of the *rān*, that is, the forest and uncultivated land, and the *vāḍo*, the settlement including cultivated land.[5] There is evidence that many *rakhne* were originally associated with the territories of the *rān*, and their abodes and shrines are located either at sites in the uncultivated land or at places that mark the boundaries between cultivated and uncultivated land. Commonly imagined as superhuman and sometimes giant beings, *rakhne* are believed to assist *ganvdevāta* in shielding the cultivated and productive areas of the villages from natural dangers such as wild animals, storms, or the intrusion of seawater. Most of the *rakhne* sites are thus located at the boundaries of fields and forests, or at dams that separate *khazān,* or low-lands, used for rice cultivation or salt production from lagoons, rivers, and the sea. Likewise, *rakhne* shrines appear on bridges, hilltops, or at crossroads that mark boundaries between forests and fields or between different villages. Another generic name for them is therefore *śīmeveile,* which refers to the Konkani word *śīmo,* meaning "boundary" or "border." Today, of course, the rapid expansion of villages and cities means that some of the formerly peripheral *rakhne* sites have been incorporated into settlement areas, thus transforming *jāgeveile* or *śīmeveile* into proper village or even city gods. These modern developments notwithstanding, it continues to be a rule for pious Hindus that whenever the borders associated with *ganvdevāta* or *śīmeveile* are transgressed, such as when people marry, change residence, purchase property, or undertake ritual activities across them, particular border-crossing rituals have to be performed. A widely practiced ritual is *śīmeband,* literally "closing the borders," at which the icons of all relevant *śīmeveile* are ceremoniously visited and honored and during which the settlement borders cannot be transgressed for one full night. Another generic name for minor deities in Goa and the Konkan is *deunchār.* The exact meaning is not known, but local mythology usually describes *deunchār* as giant guardians walking through the territories with which they are associated, filling the air with the tinkling of the bells on their feet and lighting their paths with torches at night. In some temples in South Maharashtra, *deunchār* are offered huge leather sandals by their devotees, possibly suggesting that their name is a combination of the terms *dev* for "god" and *chāra* for "walking," thus designating a kind of "divine walker."

It is against the background of this complex manifestation and distribution in space of Hindu divinity that the effects of the replacement policy of the early-modern Portuguese-Catholic attack needs to be assessed. Not only can we reconstruct that each and every Hindu village goddess and god was replaced by a Catholic patron saint; the ubiquitous distribution of Catholic crosses, saints' images, and shrines also indicates that the replacement affected each and every minor deity and tutelary being in Goa. Hence, today Catholic crosses, shrines, and monuments appear on exactly the same central and liminal locations, marketplaces, borders, bridges, and crossroads that are also demarcated for Hindu *rakhne, śīmeveile,* and *deunchār.*

When trying to account for this parallelism in the spatial association and distribution of Hindu and Catholic monuments, it is important to consider that iconoclastic replacement may not be its only background or rationale. Similar to Shulman's notion of "the phenomenon of localization" in Hindu mythology and practice, William Christian Jr. speaks of the "localistic religiosity" in early-modern Catholicism in Spain (Christian 1989: 20). By this term, he refers to a multitude of religious objects and practices that were closely associated with locations or spaces generating a distinct religious marking and mapping of the Catholic settlements and landscape. These phenomena were no novelty in six-teenth-century Iberia. Peter Brown (1991) has shown that marking the landscape with religious sites and monuments has old roots in Christian Europe and can be traced back to late antiquity, when influential patrician families began to patron-ize the tombs of saints that later became popular pilgrim centers. These centers, Brown argues, were essential for the spread of Christianity in medieval Europe. Christian, then, speaks about an intensification of such kind of "Christianization of the landscape" in Iberia after the twelfth century, when the use of devotional images became especially popular. He points out two contexts in particular in which images emerged as geographical landmarks. One was the association of villages or towns with patron saints. These associations not only stood for the spiritual protection of the settlements by their saintly patrons but also became a major source of social prestige and political power for their inhabitants. Hence, local families, religious brotherhoods, and, in the case of cities, guilds of mer-chants and artisans were competing over the patronage and control of the local saints' cults, something that found expression not only in the attempts of mu-tually outplaying each other in the purchase of precious relics and sumptuous images of the saintly patrons, but also in the local rivalries of who could assert for himself the right to carry and display the saintly paraphernalia in public cer-emonies and processions.

Another major form of localistic religiosity in which images played a spe-cial role was the devotional practices centering around miracles. Two types of locations were especially known for their miracle-working aura and predestined to become popular pilgrim centers. One was churches, chapels, and monaster-ies housing famous relics patronized by aristocrats or rich citizens. The other was sites at which the Catholic Mary or other saints had made an apparition, something that typically happened in remote areas witnessed by common people such as shepherds, children, or women (Christian 1989: 76ff.).[6] A. H. de Oliveira Marques confirms the extraordinary attention paid to "miracle-working images that had become the objects of zealous devotion" in early-modern Portugal (1971: 212). In sum, the early-modern Iberian situation thus suggests that the system-atic marking of Goa with Catholic images and monuments may not only have been the effect of the iconoclastic replacement of Hindu images and monuments but also the result of a genuine similarity of Hindu and Catholic concepts and practices regarding the manifestation and distribution of the divine and holy in space. Most likely, it was a combination of both.

Whatever its background, the systematic replacement and spatial duplica-tion of Hindu monuments and images by Catholic ones prepared the ground for a distinct subversion of the iconoclastic campaign against Hindu culture. Before this could take effect, however, a number of critical developments and changes had to happen. At first, in the sixteenth century, thousands of Hindus who were not willing to give up their religious beliefs were expelled or fled the areas that became the Old Conquests of Goa. As Paul Axelrod and Michelle Fuerch (1996) have recently elaborated, many of the exiled and fleeing Hindus took with them the images and icons of their major village gods and reinstalled them either in already existing or newly built temples in the areas that were to become the New Conquests. This led to the emergence of a large Hindu "diaspora culture" in the seven provinces of the New Conquests, which, eventually, were integrated into Portuguese-controlled Goa in the second half of the eighteenth century (ibid.: 388). Literally encircling the predominantly Catholic areas of the Old Conquests, this Hindu diaspora became especially self-conscious about its religious identity as well as its origins and traditions in the core lands of Goa. Hence, many temples in the New Conquests became the new home for images and icons of "displaced deities" from the Old Conquests and developed into well-bestowed religious centers entertaining a festive and ceremonial culture of commemoration. Noteworthy, for instance, is the village community of Chimbel (Tiswadi), which keeps alive in a special way the memory of its former village goddess, Bhagavati. For that purpose, Bhagavati's icon—which in the sixteenth century had been secretly brought to the village of Marcel (Bicholim)—pays regular ceremonial visits to its former home. Every year in the Hindu month of Chaitra (March-April), the icon goes by truck and palanquin on a ten-kilometer trip from Marcel to Chimbel where it is displayed for fifteen days in a temporary shrine. On these occasions, the goddess receives great honors not only from the people of both villages but also from Hindus and Catholics asking her for protection and boons (ibid.: 393ff.).[7]

Robert Newman, the doyen of modern Goa ethnography (2001: chs. 5, 6), describes another case of how a Hindu goddess whose temple was destroyed in the sixteenth century "survived" with the help of her image. This is Shanta Durga, the village goddess of Cuncolim in Salcete, whose devotees resisted the Portuguese-Catholic subjugation with courage and determination. Maintaining a state of "intermittent rebellion" by not paying taxes and defying missionary attempts at conversion, the villagers' confrontation with Portuguese-Catholic forces reached a climax in 1583, when the foreign rulers burned down the temple of Shanta Durga and polluted its tank with cow intestines. The villagers retaliated by killing five Jesuits who had been involved in the atrocities, at which point the Portuguese regime dispossessed all land-owing families and gave the land to Portuguese noblemen and Jesuits. What the violent subjugation could not prevent, though, was the salvaging of the icon of Shanta Durga by Hindus from Cuncolim, who brought it to the village of Fatorpa (Quepem), at the time part of the territory of Idal Khan, the Muslim ruler of the neighboring Bahmani state. There the goddess became the focus of great devotion that continued even after

Fatorpa was incorporated into Portuguese Goa in the eighteenth century. To this day, her annual temple feast in the Hindu month of Margashirsh (December-January) attracts thousands of devotees and pilgrims from both villages. At this occasion, Cuncolkarin, the Hindu goddess of Cuncolim, also receives veneration from Hindus and Catholics seeking healing, boons, or futures foretold. Newman writes that during the ceremony,

> inside the temple, before the image of Shantadurga, Catholic women in black saris kneel and cross themselves, then pray devoutly, palms together, to "Mamãe Saibin," the Holy Mother. Such behavior naturally is not condoned by the Catholic Church, nor is it common in most other parts of India. In Goa, though, Catholic participation is long established. The priests of this temple know many Catholic families by name because they come to the festival every year and donate money for goods. The Catholics take receipts for their offerings, signifying that this is neither a surreptitious or sporadic relationship. (Ibid.: 119)

Another development that stimulated syncretistic practices was the erection of Hindu and Catholic images, shrines, and monuments in close proximity in the Goan settlements and landscape. This development was fostered by the political and economic circumstances that, over time, allowed Hindus to return to the territories of the Old Conquests and to take up there the practice of their religion. Politically, this was first facilitated by Marquis de Pombal (1699–1782), the enlightened Portuguese governor who, in the mid-eighteenth century, began to gradually liberalize religious politics in Portugal. Pombal's secularizing and anticlerical impulses brought for Goa and the Estado da Índia the termination of the Inquisition, the expulsion of the Jesuits, and religious freedom for Hindus in the New Conquests. A major consequence was that the territories of the New Conquests that were integrated into Goa in the second half of the eighteenth century were never exposed to the kind of iconoclastic violence and religious suppression that had so radically transformed society and culture in the Old Conquests. Although Pombal's policies were partly revised again in later periods, the political liberalization of Portugal and its reverberation in the Asian colonies further progressed when Portugal in 1843 became a constitutional monarchy and, in 1910, a republic. The revival of Hindu culture in Goa was further enhanced by the fact that, after the short heyday of the Cidade de Goa in the seventeenth century, the economy of the Estado da Índia experienced a steady decline and, in response, a massive labor emigration of Goan Catholics. Together, the political and economic developments effected a drastic shift of the religious demography of Goa. The population shifted from 35.5 percent Hindus and 64.5 percent Christians in 1851 to 50 percent Hindus and 50 percent Christians in 1900, with a steady increase of the Hindu majority thereafter (Angle 1994: 17). Today, Goa has 65 percent Hindus and 27 percent Christians.

Figure 2.3. Hindu-Catholic Twin Shrine, Mapusa, Goa. Photograph by Gabriele Henn.

One major implication of the revival of Hinduism in the territories of the Old Conquests was, of course, the building and rebuilding of Hindu temples and shrines. As a consequence, every village and town over time got not only one or several Catholic churches and one or several Hindu temples but also myriad wayside shrines and other tokens of Catholic saints and Hindu deities. Notably, this revival of Hinduism affected the religious monuments of the two communities as they became more or less numerically balanced. The peculiar replacement and spatial replication of Hindu monuments by Catholic monuments in the sixteenth century also meant that, after the recent revival of Hindu culture, many Hindu and Catholic shrines are located in close contiguity. Most explicit forms of this religious double-occupancy are Hindu-Catholic twin shrines that can be found in two variations. One shows Hindu and Christian shrines in close spatial proximity, side by side or back to back (see figure 2.3). A notable example appears in the central market of the city of Mapusa (Bardez) where, divided by an old tree, a shrine of Our Lady of Vailankanni, a popular Indian incorporation of the Catholic Maria, is located back to back with a shrine of Shri Dev Bodgeshvar, a popular local god of the city. Another variation of twin shrines consists of shrines that shelter icons or images of both religious traditions under one roof. An outstanding example is again a shrine of Our Lady of Vailankanni located at the central plaza of the city of Margao (Salcete), which also displays an image of Damodar, the Hindu *grāmadev* of the city. Cases of adjacent, contiguous, or twin Hindu-

Catholic shrines like these abound in Goa and obviously attract devotional attention and practices from members of both religious communities.

Like the ritual honors dedicated to the displaced or homecoming Hindu deities, the practices dedicated to adjacent or twin shrines are connected to the acknowledgment of common Hindu-Catholic concepts of spatial belonging, protective territorial forces, and ritual control of precarious localities. Notably, however, in the contexts of close commonality and syncretistic worship, differences remain and are reasserted. Hence, distinct religious identities may be marked not only by differing offerings brought by Hindus and Catholics to one and the same shrine, when Catholics for instance offer candles and fruits and Hindus bring oil lamps and flowers. Distinctions can also be found with regard to the identities of honored sacred beings where Catholic saints are given cigarettes and candles and Hindu *rakhne* are given *viḍo* (chewing tobacco) and flowers. It is important to note thus that seemingly syncretistic practices may not implicate any transgression of doctrinal boundaries, let alone blur religious identities; what at first glance looks like syncretism may at closer inspection turn out to be an iconic expression of two traditions competing for the same place.

3 Christian *Purāṇas*

Hermeneutic, Similarity, and Violence

> [Cambay] . . . is inhabited by a people called Guzarates . . . among whom there
> are some men, like philosophers and religious men, who are called Bramenes,
> who believe in the Holy Trinity, Father, Son, Holy Ghost, and many other
> things of our very sacred law.
>
> —Dom João de Castro (Pearson [1992] 2005b: 154)

INCONSISTENCIES AND CONTROVERSIES lived on in other areas of the Catholic mission field in India. Instigated by Francis Xavier, an important goal of the missionaries was to render the Christian message comprehensible to the local population. Apart from the use of images, music, theater, and rituals, all of which played a significant role in contemporary proselytizing strategies, great attention was paid to the ability to communicate with Indian people in their own languages. Thus, the Jesuits made great efforts not only to learn but to systematically study Indian languages and teach them to newly arriving missionaries and seminarians trained in India. For this purpose, a considerable number of vocabularies and grammars of Indian languages—Tamil, Malayalam, Marathi, Konkani, and Gujarati—were produced, which today are considered to represent the start of European scholarship in Indian linguistics. Moreover, missionary scholars began to compose educational Christian texts in the Indian vernaculars, in particular biblical stories, hagiographies, catechisms, and confession manuals, which were widely disseminated with the help of newly imported printing presses. Recognizing that these translations required more than merely linguistic skills, the missionary scholars also took a distinct interest in Hindu literature, especially the popular epics of the Mahabharata and Ramayana, the ancient collections of myths known as *purāṇas,* and the devotional literature of Hindu *bhakti* religiosity, which they used as literary models for the composition of Christian texts. Most famous was the *Kristapurana,* the adaptation of the Christian Bible in Marathi composed by the English Jesuit Thomas Stephens, which adopted the style of Hindu religious literature so perfectly that Stephens to this day is, along-side famous Hindu poet-saints such as Jnaneshvara (1271?–1296) and Ekanatha (1533–1609), one of the most-lauded *bhakti* poets of Western India. In sum, the Jesuits developed an impressive hermeneutic effort and linguistic skill in their compositions of Indian-language Christian texts, since they did not just translate Christian meanings to Indian idioms but also consciously borrowed from poetic models, aesthetic styles, and the lexical expressivity of local Hindu literature that was familiar to actual or potential converts.

Efforts to assimilate Hindu expressions and customs in the life of Catholic converts took place in other forms and at other locations. In Goa, missionar-ies adopted the popular Jagar ceremonies that were regularly performed during local temple festivals into the Catholic liturgy of church feasts, and made the ceremony called *fama,* which was originally performed during the Hindu spring festival of *Holi,* part of Catholic ritual. Notably, these assimilations happened only after "cleansing" the local customs of their original Hindu meanings, that is, replacing their references to Hindu village gods with references to Catholic patron saints. In Tamil Nadu, the Italian Jesuit Roberto Nobili became known for an assimilative method of conversion that, around the same time, also created a furor in the Jesuit mission in China. This method was called *accommodatio* and implicated, above all, that Christian converts were allowed to continue with certain ritual customs—including, in China, practices related to the memoriza-tion of ancestors and, in India, practices related to caste ranking—that the Jesuits considered merely social in nature.

Although praised today for their supposed cultural empathy and herme-neutic interests, at their time the assimilative efforts and literary activities of the Jesuits, however, triggered serious clerical controversy and were eventually banned. At least in Goa, they also were accompanied by awkward political cir-cumstances. Hence, Thomas Stephens prepared his *Kristapurana* just after the period in which Hindu temples and images were destroyed all over Goa and all Hindu expressions and ritual practices were banned under threat of serious pen-alty. In fact, modern Goan historians claim that part of the violent campaign against Hindu culture was also the systematic destruction of precisely those Hindu books and manuscripts whose literary styles Stephens and other Jesuits diligently emulated in their production of Indian-language Christian literature. The problem I address in this chapter, therefore, refers to the seemingly paradoxi-cal attitude of the Christian missionary approach in early-modern Goa. How is it possible that the extraordinary literary efforts and adaptive exertions of the Jesuits went hand in hand with the systematic destruction of Hindu monuments and the suppression of Hindu expression? Did the producers of the Christian *purāṇas* comply with the destruction of Hindu temples and possibly even Hindu books? Or was the synchronicity of the literary and stylistic adaptations and the suppression and destruction of Hindu expressivity merely coincidental? Why are modern philologists translating and interpreting Stephens's *Kristapurana* today so conspicuously silent about its violent concomitants? How were hermeneutics and violence, translation and conversion, related in the early-modern proselytizing policies?

Kristapurana: Adaptation

The efforts undertaken by Jesuit missionaries to learn, study, and teach Indian languages were truly remarkable. There is some indication that the earliest initiatives in this direction were taken by Francis Xavier, who is known for pointing out in his letters to Rome that the slow conversion rate achieved by the Franciscans on the Malabar Coast could be speeded up if missionaries were able to speak to the fishing communities there in their own languages. In Goa, Xavier's suggestions bore results in a series of local *Concílios* held in 1567, 1575, 1585, 1592, and 1606, all of which strongly recommended that parish priests learn the local languages. In fact, in 1609, it was ordered that no priest could be appointed vicar of a parish unless he was conversant with the local language, and vicars already appointed who were ignorant of local languages were to lose their positions unless they learned a language within six months (Cunha Rivara [1862] 1992: 226ff.). In the middle of the sixteenth century, the linguistic project of Christian proselytization in India was fostered by the import of the latest technical novelty of the time, the printing press with movable letters (Priolkar 1958). Around 1550, four printing presses had reached India and were installed in Old Goa and Kerala (Ambalakadu, Cochin, and Panikkayal; Priolkar 1967; Pereira n.d.). What followed was a period of little more than a century of industrious printing on the Malabar Coast and in Goa, dedicated overwhelmingly to the publication of texts of a religious nature: catechisms, Bible adaptations, hagiographies, manuals for confession, and religious treatises of various sorts.[1] In Goa, the first Indian-language book was the adaptation of the Bible that became famous under the title *Kristapurana*[2] and was composed by the English Jesuit Thomas Stephens in what he variously refers to as *lingua Bramana* or *Bramana Marastta,* and which scholars today identify as "Old Marathi" (Van Skyhawk 1999: 363). Printed for the first time in 1619, Stephens's masterwork, which itself was re-edited twice in in 1649 and 1654,[3] initiated a brief but prolific era of Marathi- and Konkani-language productions of Christian texts in Goa, to which Stephens added another theological work printed in 1622,[4] *Doutrina Christá em Lingua Bramana-Canarim ordenada á manera de dialogo, para ensinar os meninos* (Christian doctrine in Brahman-Konkani language, organized in the form of dialogue for the education of children). For the whole period from 1616 to 1674, when the last printing in early-modern Goa is documented, Priolkar (1967: 17ff.) counts eleven major Indian-language Christian texts.

Two features of the seventeenth-century Marathi- and Konkani-language Christian texts are especially noteworthy. First, they were all printed in roman script only, though some of their authors, notably Stephens, tried to have their compositions printed in Devanagari. The reasons why the Jesuit authorities, in particular Alessandro Valignano, the *visitor* of Jesuit activities in Asia, refused to have texts printed in Devanagari are unclear and seem to have ranged from technical difficulties in casting the characters to the changed attitude of Valignano after his visit to Japan, since he now considered Indians racially and intellectually inferior and thus unworthy of having Christian literature in their own script (Dias 1995). Second, many of the early-modern Marathi- and Konkani-language Christian texts, unlike those in Tamil, were written not in prose but in verse, that is, in the quatrain verses locally known as *ovī*. It was Stephens who, by introducing this new practice, considerably embellished the literary style of Indian-language Christian texts and rendered them closer to styles familiar to their Indian readership. The *ovī* meter and poetic composition and style adapted by the Christian *purāṇa* literature were, and to this day still are, the classical characteristics of the devotional lyrics (*abharats, kīrtanas, āratīs*) of the Hindu *bhakti* literature of Maharashtra and the Konkan. Literally translated as "participation" or "devotion," *bhakti* characterizes a piety that favors an intimate relationship with a personalized god and, to some extent, constitutes a demotic counter-current to certain aspects of Brahmanical theology and temple religiosity. In linguistic and literary terms, *bhakti* religiosity helped to boost the regional languages (Prakrit) against the claimed exclusivity of Sanskrit in religious writings by stimulating the production of a rich body of devotional literature in the various regional vernaculars. In Maharashtra, the *bhakti* literature has especially deep historical roots going back to the famous poet-saint Jnaneshvara and, in Stephens's times, it experienced a second heyday in the work of another poet-saint, Ekanatha.

It is therefore highly likely that Stephens's *Kristapurana* was inspired by and modeled after Ekanatha's work. According to Hugh Van Skyhawk,

> In keeping with the devotional nature of Bhakti, Stephens rendered the contents of the Old Testament in brief . . . and expanded upon the life of Christ in the New Testament. . . . Instead of using the religious terminology of Latin or Portuguese, he chose or coined corresponding terms from Sanskrit and the regional language Marathi. Similarly, the metre and the rhetorical devices used in the *Kristapurāṇa* derive from Bhakti literature in Old Marathi. Only with regard to its specifically Christian contents and intention does the *Purāṇa* from the quill of the first Englishman in Goa differ from the works of Ekanātha or Śrī Sant Jñāneśvar, . . . not, however, in its literary form and composition. (1999: 366)

Stephens's way of telling the story of Christ was well received by the local population, as documented in a Jesuit letter sent to Italy in 1621 and quoted by Shanta-ram P. Bandelu, the editor of a modern version of the *Kristapurana*, published in Pune in 1956: "This work is so delightful that not only do the Christians derive much profit from it, but even the non-Christians speak of it with pride. On Sundays and feast-days this book, or Puranna, as it is called, is being read in the churches with as much profit as it gets applause" (Van Skyhawk 1999: 363). It is therefore little wonder that Stephens's masterwork not only attracted imitators but also generated a Christian *purāṇa* style that developed widely into various genres of Christian devotional and folk literature in Goa and among Goan diaspora groups in Karnataka, South Kanara, and Maharashtra. Among his imitators, two deserve special mention. Étienne de la Croix (1579–1643), the French Jesuit who preceded Stephens as the rector of the Jesuit college in Rachol, Goa, composed a *Discourso sobre a vida do Apostolo Sam Pedro,* also written in the *ovī* verse form, which was printed in 1643 and became known as the "Peter Puranna" (Tulpule 1979: 382; Priolkar 1967: 18). The other imitator is Antonio de Saldanha (d. 1663), a Portuguese Jesuit who published a hagiography of his namesake St. Antonio of Padua, a first version of which was printed in Goa in 1655. This version was composed in prose *na lingua da terra corrente,* "in the common local language," that is, Konkani (Cunha Rivara 1858: 127) and was re-edited in 1963 under the title *Sancto Antonichi Acharya,* "The Miracles of St. Antony" (Saldanha [1655] 1963). A second version, whose first publication is also dated to sometime in the seventeenth century, was composed in the Marathi *ovī* verse form and re-edited in 1956 under the title *Sancto Antonichi Jivitvakatha,* "The Life of St. Antonio." According to Saldanha (ibid.: xvi), the style of the "Anthony Puranna," shows great similarities with the work of the Marathi poet Mahipati (1637–1712). Finally, Joachim Heliodoro da Cunha Rivara (1858: 131–172) reprinted and translated into Portuguese extensive abridgments of a *Christian Puranna,* a copy of which was found in the Biblioteca Publica of Nova Goa, albeit without a title page, so that its author is unknown. Cunha Rivara classifies this work as having been printed in the "Jesuit office" in Goa around the middle of the seventeenth century and, for convenience, called it the Library Purana (ibid.: 132).

Of all the works written in the Christian *purāṇa* style, modern scholars without exception agree that Stephens's *Kristapurana* shows the greatest literary skill and poetic art and the greatest sophistication in mediating between Hindu and Christian thought. Van Skyhawk praises Stephen's "ability to express Christian beliefs and teachings in the images of folk Hinduism" (1999: 365), even, as he comments elsewhere, at the cost of "contribut[ing] unwillingly to a syncretism of Hinduism and Christianity, that was to continue in Goa up to the present day" (ibid.: 368). Van Skyhawk is joined by Shankar G. Tulpule for whom "Fr. Stephens has succeeded in the difficult task of presenting Christ in such an oriental garb as appeals in the Hindu mind without abandoning the principles of the Christian religion. The Purāṇa is like a sanctuary in the centre of which is the image of

Christ while the structure and decoration that surrounds it are in genuine Hindu style" (Falcao 2003: vii).

The most thorough appraisal of Stephens's work has recently been presented by the Salesian scholar Nelson Falcao (2003). As Falcao describes the *Kristapurana*, the material has a clear Christian outline that is structured in two parts. The first, or *Pailo Purāṇa*, tells of the major events described in the Old Testament: the creation of the world, the nature of the angels and the fall of Lucifer, the creation of Adam and Eve, their original sin and banishment from paradise, the unfaithful life of people and the great flood, the preservation of Noah, and the call of Abraham. The second part, or *Dusoro Purāṇa*, tells of the coming of Christ the Redeemer; his mother, Mary, and his birth; John the Baptist; and the life and teaching of Christ; his passion, death, resurrection, and ascension to heaven. By presenting these biblical themes in the poetic meter and style of the *bhakti* literature and putting the Old Testament themes into about four thousand and the New Testament themes into about seven thousand *ovī* or quatrains, respectively, Stephens interpreted the Christian story to his Indian readers and listeners. More than that, he used and generated Marathi and Sanskrit terms to name the persons and describe the course of the Christian epic: *Deva Bapā* (God Father), *Vaikuṇṭharāyā* (Lord of Heaven), *Parameśvara* (Lord God), *Sarvācyā Racaṇārā* (Maker of All). He has sent *Devasuta* (His son), *Jeju Kristarājā* (Jesus the King),[5] *Visvatāraku* (Savior of the World), *Jñānadipu Paripurṇā* (Lamp of Perfect Knowledge), and *Dharmaiticā Denakarū* (Sun of Righteousness), to earth in order to defeat *Mārūvā* (Satan), *Devacāra* (the evil ghost), *Ajāgara* (serpent), and *papa* (sin), in order to cut off *doṣa banda* (the bonds of guilt), eradicate *āvidyā* (ignorance), and bring *diptī* (light), *jñāna* (knowledge), and *muktī* (liberation) to the people of the world, thus reconciling *svarga* and *saṃsāra* (heaven and earth; ibid.: 25–34).

In a similarly creative and poetic way, Stephens also told the story of *Bhāgyevaṇta Mari* (the Blessed Mary), for whose description and praise he used more than eighty different names and titles, such as *Devamātā* (Mother of God), *Vaikuṇṭhapatice Māte Aṅkuvāri* (Virgin Mother of the Lord of Heaven), *Pavitra Mātā* (Holy Mother), *Sadevi Aṅkuvāri* (Blessed Virgin), *Devadutāṅci Rāṇī* (Queen of the Angels), *Candrabimba Suṇdari* (Beautiful as the Moon), *Surya Nirmaḷa* (Spotless as the Sun), *Sadaivi Bhāgeveti Striyāmajī* (Most Blessed among Women), *Svargīci Rāṇī* (Queen of Heaven), and *Kṛpe Karūṇeci* (Fountain of Grace and Compassion; ibid.: 36). More important still, Stephens succeeded in creating a kind of Hindu equivalent for every step and principle in Christian doctrine. He thus made it entirely clear to his Indian readers that *Krista Tāraka* (Christ the Savior) had come to redeem the people of the world from their *ādipurūsace karma* (Original Sin) and *papa karma* (Karma of Evil) by *aganape samapila* (sacrificing himself) so that everybody who underwent *jñāna-snāna* (baptism, literally "bathing in knowledge") followed *śāstra-rītu pāḷavyā* (the "laws and rites of the scripture") and participated in *Kiristace bhakti-pujā* (Christian worship, that is, the Eucharist) and *bhakti-satva* ("devotion of goodness") could indeed acquire *muktī* (redemption) and reach *mokṣa* (salvation; ibid.: 197ff.).[6]

Malabar Rites: Disputation

Who, then, would not agree with Falcao that "Stephens succeeds in building bridges between Christian and Hindu worlds of consciousness" (ibid.: 170)? Except that the irritating hostility against Hindu culture continued to surround the early-modern Jesuit literary activities in India. As discussed in the previous chapter, the combined forces of the Portuguese Crown and the Catholic Church had initiated a violent campaign against Hindu culture in Goa and other parts of the Estado da Índia around the middle of the sixteenth century aimed at the complete destruction of all Hindu temples, shrines, and images and the radical suppression of all forms of Hindu religious practice and expression. Moreover, the Portuguese scholar of Konkani linguistics Cunha Rivara and, following him, the Goan historian Anand Kakba Priolkar argue that the campaign also targeted for destruction the "books of the gentiles." More precisely, they reference a letter written by João de Albuquerque, the bishop of Goa, to the king of Portugal on 28 November 1548 that indicates that Albuquerque was "going to collect the books of the gentiles in order to stop their idolatry" (Cunha Rivara 1858: 14; see also Priolkar 1967: 76). "In the first heat of conquest," Cunha Rivara further contextualizes the letter, "all temples were destroyed, all emblems of gentile cults shattered, all books written in the vernacular languages burned, like convicts or suspects telling the principles and doctrines of idolatry" (1858: 13). Although the historical letter of the bishop of Goa unfortunately cannot be located today, the circumstantial evidence, at least, does not rule out that in the large-scale destruction of monuments, images, and objects associated with the condemned "idolatry of the gentiles," their books and manuscripts were also destroyed.[7] That the possession and use of religious books with non-Christian content was strictly forbidden for Muslims, Hindus, and, above all, Catholic converts in the Portuguese-controlled territories of India is certain. Some further evidence for this appears in the fifth decree of the first *Concílio* in Goa in 1567, which prohibited Muslims from having "false relics, invocations (*nomina*), and books of their perfidious sect," as well as regarding *gentios* "that anyone preaches in public or in private about the things of their false religion, and anyone listens to such sermons, or anyone has books dealing with it" (Cunha Rivara [1862] 1992: 13, 14). That the missionaries were dealing with Hindu texts and manuscripts is amply evidenced, among other things, in a list of references taken from the work of Étienne de la Croix which shows that this French Jesuit used at least twenty-six different Hindu sources in the composition of his Peter Purana. The number of Hindu texts available to Stephens, Falcao estimates, was even larger and included, next to Marathi and Sanskrit, also Old Tamil texts (Falcao 2003: 12). Recent discoveries in the public library of Braga in Portugal testify moreover that the Jesuit scholars had copied Hindu texts and transliterated them into roman script (Rodrigues 1990; Patil 1999).

Important in this context, the clerical attitude toward the Jesuit efforts at adapting Hindu literary styles, ritual genres, and social customs in Catholic liturgy and practice were never uncontested and, from the very beginning, met with serious clerical criticism. An example here is the famous controversy triggered by the method of conversion for which Roberto Nobili coined the name *accommodatio*. Unlike other missionaries, Nobili did not enforce with this method a radical social and cultural transformation of the converts' lives. Instead, he allowed converts to continue a number of practices that were of crucial social significance, especially to Brahmans, such as wearing *yajnopavita,* the sacred thread, and *kudumi,* the Brahman hair tuft, and applying *tilakam,* sandal-paste signs on the forehead, all of which were considered emblems indicating the high-caste status of their bearers. He also permitted converts to maintain their vegetarian diets, and to continue to perform prescribed baths and other Hindu cultural routines. Moreover, Nobili replicated among Catholic converts the Hindu caste principles and, in particular, strictly separated high-caste and low-caste Catholics in churches and religious services. He himself learned Sanskrit and Tamil and studied Hindu theology so that he could regularly engage in scholarly debates with local Hindu priests, and, more extraordinary still, adopted the lifestyle of a Tamil Brahmin himself by wearing the Brahmanical habit, following a vegetarian diet, and in many ways leading the life of a Hindu Brahman. He also adopted the Hindu title of *sannyāsin,* which he considered the local equivalent of "scholarly monk."

As Ines Županov (2001) has amply documented recently, however, Nobili's extraordinary methods triggered a century-long dispute over what was called the "Malabar rites." This dispute was fought out in myriad letters circulating among Madurai, Goa, and Rome, as well as a series of meetings and investigations that took place in these cities. Its basic lines were drawn up between Nobili and his supporters who, as Županov illustrates (2001: 35, 109), basically claimed that the practices at issue were merely social in nature and had nothing to do with religious values and beliefs, while opponents held that they were indeed of a religious nature and therefore could not be separated from the "superstitions" and "false beliefs" of the Gentiles. Brought up *inter alia* at a meeting of the Archbishop of Goa, the Bishop of Cranganore, and "the best theologians" present in Goa in 1619, the dispute was first officially decided in favor of Nobili. Following this vote, Pope Gregory XV (r. 1621–1623) declared in his Apostolic Letter of 1623 that, "until the Holy See provides otherwise," Christian converts would be allowed to wear the Brahman thread, hair tuft, and sandal-paste marks, and to perform regular baths, provided these were not part of any "pagan ritual" (Nazareth [1873] 1894: 131).

Gregory's decree, however, was immediately rescinded. The Archbishop of Goa, notes church chronicler Casimiro Christovão de Nazareth, had already argued in the meeting of 1619 "that in no way should one allow them [the Christian converts] to wear that [Brahman] thread, no matter whether it is or is not a sign of nobility." He also made it quite clear that, in opposition to the pope, "[he] favors the adversaries of the Jesuits" (ibid.: 120, 133). The issue remained contested throughout the seventeenth century until, in 1704 and repeatedly in later years, high-ranking clerics dismissed or seriously curtailed the *accommodatio* policies and practices in India, China, and other overseas missions. In the meantime, Stephens's efforts on behalf of the production of Indian-language Christian texts were officially ended in 1684 by the notorious decree of Viceroy Francisco de Tavora (1646–1710). This decree ordered that, henceforth, all official church communication was to be in Portuguese, and that Goans were to abandon their mother tongue and learn Portuguese instead (Cunha Rivara 1858: 35; Priolkar 1967: 64). The second part of this order was obviously not enforceable, and Konkani remained the mother tongue of the majority of Goans, despite its lasting neglect in the colonial politics of education, while Portuguese only gradually became the language of high-caste Catholics. Nevertheless, the Tavora decree clearly indicated the antiadaptionist attitude in the educative and Church policies and marked the end of the production of Christian *purāṇas* and their prohibition for Christian instruction. Similarly, locally derived ceremonies and rituals such the Jagar and the *fama,* which had become a common part of Catholic popular religion and folklore, were now defamed and prohibited as "pagan reminiscenses" and persecuted by heavy punishment such as excommunication (see chapter 5). Moreover, there are indications that the turn against the use of local languages in Christian instruction and communication was more than just an issue of cultural re-education and, indeed, had a clear religious component. Hence, the ban of Konkani was used in particular for the prohibition of folkloric practices such as the singing of songs at weddings and other domestic ceremonies in the quatrain meter *ovī,* which was the literary mark of the traditional local Hindu *bhakti* literature and which had found its way into Catholic folklore through the popular Christian *purāṇas* (Cunha Rivara 1858: 67; Nazareth [1873] 1894: 243). An especially radical injunction against the contested *accommodatio* was eventually set by the apostolic legate Charles Thomas Maillard de Tournon (1668–1710), who visited the Christian missions in India and China in the early part of the eighteenth century and issued a decree in 1704 that ended all adaptionist experiments, denouncing in particular the toleration of *a leitura dos livros fabulosos dos gentios,* "the reading of the fictitious books of the Gentiles" (Nazareth [1873] 1894: 200; Catholic Encyclopedia n.d.: s.v. Malabar Rites).

"Library Purana": Refutation

The seemingly paradoxical parallelism of hermeneutics and violence, and the protracted controversy over the adaptionist Jesuit methods, hint that the early-modern composers of the Christian *purāṇas* had an ambiguous relationship with the Hindu literature. This ambiguous attitude comes to the fore most clearly in the textual fragment of another Christian *purāṇa* that Cunha Rivara discovered in the mid-nineteenth century in the Biblioteca Publica de Nova-Goa. Although unfortunately not traceable anymore today, Cunha Rivara's discovery is still valuable because he extensively copied passages from its original roman-script Konkani version, to which he added a Portuguese translation. He dates the document, which he notes existed at his time both in a printed and handwritten manuscript, to the mid-seventeenth century and, because it was missing pages at its beginning and end, simply calls it the *Puranna da Bibliotheca*, that is, the "Library Purana" (Cunha Rivara 1858: 131–132).

Comparison of this rare document with Stephens's celebrated *Kristapurana* reveals both concordances and deviations. Hence, the Library Purana reproduces all major stylistic characteristics of the *Kristapurana*: subdivided into three *purāṇas*, it copies the style of the Hindu *bhakti* literature, in particular its quatrain meter and rich devotional vocabulary in presenting a biblical theme, the story of the Apostle Peter. The Library Purana, however, clearly diverges from Stephens's *Kristapurana* in its major literary and theological thrusts. The main goal of the *Kristapurana*, it has been argued, is to generate an adaptation of the Christian theme in the local Indian and, by default, Hindu idiom and expressivity. The stated major goal of the Library Purana, by contrast, is to refute and disempower the principles and forces of what it calls the *Conconni Ponni*, that is, the beliefs and practices of the Konkan people.[8]

The book begins with the first *purāṇa*, which tells the story of St. Peter: how he attended the last supper with Christ; how, after Jesus's capture, he denied him; how Peter nevertheless was selected to disseminate the Christian law first among the Jews, then among the *Concanis*, that is, the "people of the Konkan." The second *purāṇa* continues with a reference to the tenth book of the Acts of the Apostles, which describes how St. Peter acted among the *gentios* and how God, by the help of an angel, calls a certain Cornelio, "captain of the army," to act as a helper to St. Peter (ibid.: 140). Although only alluded to in the Library Purana, this background story, interestingly, calls upon the same biblical context to which Diogo do Couto also referred in his section *About the Views, Rites and Ceremonies of All the Gentiles of Industan* in the *Década Quinta da Ásia* (see chapter 1) and illustrates the deep ambiguities in which the early-modern explorers and missionaries saw themselves acting in the foreign land of the gentiles. The story describes Cornelio as a "pious man who worshipped the true God like all his household, gave alms freely to the people, and prayed to God continually," even though he was a gentile and had not been circumcised (Catholic Encyclopedia n.d.; Acts of the Apostles 10:1, 2). Therefore, the Jewish people accompanying Peter were concerned that Peter be "contaminated if he consorts with one of another race," upon which Peter tells them, "God has been showing me that we ought not to speak of any man as profane or unclean" (ibid.: 28–29). The story finally describes a scene in which Peter, talking to Jews and gentiles, gets surprising spiritual help from the Holy Ghost, coming upon all those who listened to him and enabling them to proclaim the greatness of God in different languages. Seeing this, the "faithful of the circumcision" showed surprise that the grace of the Holy Ghost was poured out upon the Gentiles also, upon which Peter says, "Who will grudge us the water for baptizing these men, that have received the Holy Spirit just as we did?" (ibid.: 45–48).

While recognizing thus that the gentiles, at least potentially, are capable of being clean and converted, the title of the second *purāṇa* indicates how unforgiving the program and reality of such conversion was. It reads, *Geantŏ cuddham Conconeacheam Devanche bhŏgenaché chedŏnŏ pŏri lihunŏ ahe,* which translates approximately as, "Here it is written about the refutation of the worship of the false or blind Konkan gods."[9] Different classes of "false or blind gods" are then distinguished and addressed in the various books of the second *purāṇa* beginning with the refutation of the worship of "men, plants, and snakes." Before the text turns to the defamation of these gods, it however first lists the refutation of *Gonesso,* or Ganesha. This circumstance is interesting because it shows how close the Christian *purāṇa* indeed is to its *bhakti* literary model, even where it completely perverts its purpose, since devotional *bhakti* hymns invariably begin with the invocation of Ganesha, the spiritual "overcomer of obstacles." Thereafter, the catalogue of *qhonddono,* that is, *khāḍan* or "refutations," list a series of gods said to be mentioned in *gentivo gronthí,* the "scriptures of the gentiles." *Nagues,* also called *Nagŏ Nagues,* the god Nageshi, who is often worshipped as a snake, is named, as is *Tulossi,* the goddess Tulsi, who is embodied in the sacred Tulsi plant, and *Vŏttam pimpollanssŏ,* that is, the sacred "peepal tree" (*ficus religiosa*). Variously mentioned and condemned is the worship of the cow, as well as the fact that "the gentiles refuse to eat beef." Finally, the condemnation of the worship of *Santeri Devo,* the goddess Sateri, demonstrates the significance that this ancient and popular goddess has in Goa and the Konkan, since the work dedicates to her not one but two quatrains in which she is described as having "no divinity" but only "falsehood" and "nullity," and that her worship by the gentiles is "of no avail" (Cunha Rivara 1858: 139ff.).

The third book is dedicated to the refutation of *Purosso,* that is, "ancestors"; *Addisto,* another type of deified human; and *Soitana,* Satan or the devil. The individual verses condemn the worship of people who died from suicide, warn that the devil may disguise himself as an ancestor and by the help of his *bottos,* or priests, may offer *prossados,* that is, "oracles" and other deceptive advice to people (ibid.: 144ff.). The fourth book deals with the refutation of the worship of *Betalle,* that is, the ancient Konkan god Vetal, and *Bhuto* or *bhūta,* a well-known Konkani designation for ghosts, all of whom are classified as forms of the devil. Obviously aware of the fact that Goan Hindus often venerate both Vetal and certain forms of *bhūta* as *raqhonai,* that is, guardians of villages, fields, and borders, the book explicitly notes that none of these local tutelary beings can be seen as a "friend of God" nor can the services of their *gaddis,* that is, "local priests," who are all defamed as magicians, be trusted. Instead, the work emphasizes that only "angels" can be seen as "guardians" and "servants of God," and only the "prayers of the apostles," "relics" of Catholic saints, and "the sign of the cross" can prevent misfortune and protect people against the devil (ibid.: 148ff.).

The list of the refutation of "false or blind gods" continues with mentions of Brahma, Vistnum (Vishnu), and Mahessu (Mahadev), and eventually condemns *tetisso cotteche cuddeponno,* the "33 million [forms of] falseness" or "blindness" that are said to be mentioned in the scriptures of the *Vedo* and *Puranna.* All of these forces, it is variously emphasized, are "neither gods," "nor representing the origin of the universe," but are "weak," "ignorant," and "do not offer any path of salvation" (ibid.: 153ff.). The short fragment of the third and final *purāṇa* asserts that, in their stead, only *Poromesvoro,* the "Omnipotent [Christian] God" is "true," "unique," "without beginning and end," "without differences," "the Father of the universe," and "powerful," and has given *Fé,* the "Faith" that is the Truth (ibid.: 168ff.).

In summary, it is noteworthy how well-informed the unknown author of the Library Purana was about gods and religious practices in Goa and the Konkan, as well as major gods and theological principles of Hinduism at large. In fact, it shows that the author not only was well acquainted, as all known authors of Christian *purāṇas* had been, with the variously mentioned *gentivo gronthí* or "gentile scriptures," in particular, the *conconneancheá granthā puranna; chearí vedo;* and *Devaché xastrŏ,* that is, the "Konkan *purāṇa*"; the "four Vedas"; and the "godly *śāstras*" (ibid.: 165ff.). Obviously, he also had quite a bit of knowledge about local gods and religious practices that must have come from genuine ethnographic interest and experience. Likewise, most of the text is educative and explains, for instance, that neither the elements—Wind, Earth, Sea, and Fire— are gods, nor the planets—Sun and Moon—possess any divinity, thereby using language in a distinctly descriptive and rationalizing way. It is, however, also important to point out that, in large parts, the text has the character of a prayer or, more precisely, a *nomana,* that is, "invocation," or *khāḍana,* that is, "refutation" or "exorcism." Here, language is not used in a descriptive or symbolic way but in a ritualistic, that is, iconic, way that aims to variously invoke or ban the spiritual forces it is dealing with. Presenting itself as a Christian *purāṇa* in this fashion, therefore, does more than adopt models from Hindu *bhakti* literature to Christian messages. Arguably, the Christian *purāṇa* literature also strives to imitate or more precisely mimetically appropriate the spiritual forces embodied in the *bhakti* literature in order to disempower and control all the "false gods" it painstakingly identifies in the Hindu texts and practices. An exemplary illustration of this iconic quality inherent in the Library Purana is the evocation of the Christian God in typical *bhakti* forms of name calling and prostration in order to disempower and destroy the devil and the demons of the *Conconni Ponni:*

> I invoke [*nomo*] the Lord, the Savior of the universe;
> You, of Whom the universe if filled, . . .
> Creator, Light of the Universe,
> And its Preserver;
>
> Your incomparable name,
> Has been given to the devil [*Soitaná*]
> Whom they praise on the throne,
> That is your symbol;
>
> Like this they shut their eyes,
> To the light of the truth,
> Not knowing since when,
> God and the anti-God [*Atheo*] are divided;
>
> In this way they are surrounded,
> By the darkness of the Conconni ponni,
> Not knowing the light and in obscurity,
> That is how they are!
>
> In order to destroy here,
> The worship of these demons,
> Give me grace, I beg You,
> Prostrating me at Your feet;
>
> When the gold and the alloy,
> Blend together in the mixture,
> From the appreciable name of the gold,
> Benefits also the alloy;
>
> But when the power of the fire,
> Pulls the gold and the alloy apart,
> The alloy does not benefit freely anymore,
> From the name of the gold;
>
> The gold stands for Your existence,
> And the alloy for the Devil and the demons,
> Such is the mixture of Conconni ponni,
> Which denies You. (Ibid.: 148–150)

Given the Library Purana's depreciation and defamation of the *Conconni Ponni,* the most striking feature of the text is how conceptually similar and theoretically inherent to the Self it presents this Other. Nothing of the *Conconni Ponni,* it seems, is really different or altogether new to the Christian author; all is just in reversed order like the devil and the "false gods" that hold the place of the True God, or its use of opposite equivalents like the "gentile scriptures" of the Vedas, *purāṇas* and *śāstras* that occupy the site of the Law and "divine revelation." In the same way, Vetal, the ghosts, and deified men pretend to do what their Christian equivalents—the angels, apostles, and other "friends of god"—do, and the many "useless" and "powerless" practices and objects of the gentiles prevent the people from recognizing the effective power that emanates from Christian practices and objects such as the prayers of the apostles, saints' relics, and the sign of the cross. In fact, the *Conconni Ponni,* we eventually learn, is to the Christian *Fé* not just what is "darkness" to "light" but rather marks an "alloy" of worthless metals, the gentile gods and beliefs, melted together with precious gold, the Christian God and Truth. Hence, the cleansing fire of proselytization is actually not converting the gentiles to something that is entirely new to them. Instead, conversion only extracts the Truth that was always there from the falseness that had smothered it, and opens the eyes of the "blind gentiles" for something that they were unable to see: the Truth of the Christian God and the falseness of their demons.

Hermeneutics—Similarity—Violence

How, then, can we account for the paradoxical circumstances and inconsistent attitudes in the proselytizing practices and policies of the Jesuits in early-modern Goa? How is it possible that their extraordinary literary skills and assimilative efforts went hand in hand with the systematic destruction of Hindu material culture and the suppression of Hindu expression? How were hermeneutics and violence, translation and conversion, related to each other? Did the Jesuit methods indeed foster modern ideas of cultural relativism and religious pluralism, as current-day scholarship insinuates?

When readdressing these questions, the modern philologists who are translating and commenting on Stephens's *Kristapurana* frustratingly seem to totally ignore the violent circumstances of which its production was a part. This striking silence is especially bewildering because the scholars, as we have seen, emphatically praise the hermeneutic empathy and aesthetic appreciation that the Jesuits supposedly had for the Indian languages and literature from which they drew their inspirations and for the Indian people whose cultural modes of expression they arguably attempted to emulate. How is it possible to speak of hermeneutic dialogue when the envisioned Other is muted or even eradicated? And how can one possibly conceive of intercultural bridge-building when the other side of the river has been destroyed, so to speak? After ruling out mere ignorance about the violent historical circumstances, the theoretical position of the scholars can only be explained by the fact that they did not see the literary activities of the Jesuits and the political violence against Hindu culture as intrinsically related. This implies in particular that they appreciate these activities as part of a modern concept of translation that mediates linguistic differences by reference to a neutral or middle ground. As Richard Burghart (1989) elaborated, this mediating "third ground" between source text and target text is in modern understanding constituted as that intelligibility that brings different linguistic expressions together in common and, at best, universal meanings related to each other on the ground of common and, ideally, universal meanings. Županov makes this common scholarly understanding of the early-modern Jesuit "translations" in India (Tulpule 1979; Van Skyhawk 1999; Falcao 2003) explicit by arguing that Nobili's *accommodatio* came close to "positions of cultural relativism, semiotic arbitrariness and theological nominalism" (Županov 2001: 98). Investing the activities of the Jesuits with such modern assumptions, philologists and historians thus exempt their scholarly presuppositions from any intrinsic impulse to destroy or suppress the Hindu originals and expressions from which they drew their insights and inspiration. The violence, they assume, may have had political and theological reasons and, in general, may have been considered necessary for the intended eradication of paganism, but it was not part of the epistemic and semiotic operations enacted in the production of the Indian-language Christian literature.

It is at this point, however, that another perspective becomes important for which, once again, the concept of "similarity" is critical. As we had seen, similarities played a crucial role from the very beginning of the colonial encounter. Not only did Vasco da Gama, on the basis of alleged similarities, mistake Hindus for Christians upon his first arrival in India, generations of Portuguese chroniclers and Christian missionaries also discovered similarities between gentiles and Christians and discussed a wide range of theories about genealogical relations, historical intersections, or diabolic deceptions to account for the affinities. Similarities were moreover critically involved in the contemporary theories of idolatry triggering debates on how images relate to their prototypes, whether and how visual representations have an impact on their onlookers, and whether and under what premises one might venerate religious images. It is against this background that we are justified in assuming that the significance of the concept of similarity in the early-modern colonial encounter constituted a profound semiotic and epistemic axiom regarding the connectedness of signs and things, which Michel Foucault illustrates in his classic *Les mots et les choses* with reference to language:

> Language resides halfway between the visible characters of nature and the clandestine consonance of the esoteric discourses. . . . In its pristine form, as it was given to Man by God, language was a certain and true sign of the things, because it resembled them. The names were deposited on what they

signified . . . by means of similarity. This transparency was destroyed in Babel as a form of punishment. The languages had been separated from each other and became incommensurable only after their resemblance with the things, which was the first *raison d'être* of language, was annihilated. (Foucault [1966] 1980: 67)

Distinguished by manifold scholarly classifications, Foucault further elaborates, similarity was part of a complex premodern epistemology that referred to contiguities in space as well as agreement of bodily forms, and implicated many sorts of conceptual analogies and sympathetic affinities. That the healing capacities of medicinal plants were most efficacious where the plants resembled either the organ or the illness to be healed, so that walnuts were used to treat brain tumors and lanceolate leaves were thought to cure knife injuries is only one conspicuous illustration of this vast premodern "episteme of similitude." Modern semiotics by and large condense this mode of thinking into the paradigm of iconicity, in which the icon works on the assumption that the sign and the signified are related by a substantial similarity or affinity (Burks 1949; Jakobson 1965). In other words, unlike the arbitrary cultural code of the symbol, which modern scholarship sees at work in translation and other linguistic transactions, the similarity of the icon is tangibly embodied in realistic images, onomatopoetic sounds, and mimetic reifications, and played and to this day plays a role in particular in religious belief and practice.

By returning then to the question of how hermeneutics and violence so seamlessly coexisted in the early-modern proselytizing process in India, the hypothesis is that the Jesuit literary activities and the policy of *accommodatio* were still not based in the full sense of the term on a modern concept of translation. Instead of facilitating a convergence of linguistic and cultural differences on a neutral or secular ground, Jesuit "translation" and *accommodatio*, to a considerable degree, still worked on premodern semiotic presuppositions and religious assumptions regarding the existence or nonexistence of substantial similarities between the different linguistic and cultural modes of expression. Translation, we recognize, still marked an operation that was deeply embedded in cultural models and religious beliefs. Richard Burghart gives an example from a different cultural context of how this combination of technical and religious paradigms in the constitution of translation or cultural mediation works. Hinduism's capacity to interrelate and mediate the vast plurality of Indic religious traditions, he argues, is based on a notion of the "ontic identity" of things that finds expression in Brahma, the essence of Hindu divinity. Because Brahma in principle has no form and no quality in mundane manifestation, he may take any form and any quality (Burghart 1989: 214 *passim*). It is this paradigm that, at best, allows Hindus to integrate a multitude of religious traditions into their lives, including sometimes Jesus Christ perceived as a manifestation of Krishna and, at worst, makes them claim that all religions have their ground in Hinduism, implicating in particular that Buddhism, Jainism, and Sikhism are all merely variations (ibid.: 221; Tambiah 1996: 245).

The early-modern Christian concept of "similarity" arguably constituted a likewise complex combination of semiotic and doctrinal perspectives in dealing with religious differences. Unfortunately, we do not know in any detail what Thomas Stephens thought about the "similarities" of Christian and gentile beliefs and practices that were allegedly so frequently discovered and certainly so seriously discussed in his time and scholarly environment. For Nobili it is documented that he, like many others around him, interpreted the "similarities" to the effect that "some fragments of the 'true faith,' the monotheistic god, the Trinity, etc., had been revealed to Tamils [and gentiles at large, for that matter] in a distant past" (Županov 2001: 3). He was therefore fascinated to find a large and old body of sophisticated theological literature in India, in particular the ancient Vedas, whose language, Sanskrit, he did not hesitate to compare to Latin, and was convinced that the name of the erudite Brahmans with whom he conversed about these texts was associated with the biblical Abraham. In fact, he was, as Županov puts it, "enthralled" by the idea that an alleged "lost part" of the Vedas might have been the Christian Gospel, such that he felt his task in India was not so much to introduce a new faith but to find and reconstruct a defective and corrupted form of the Christian Truth (ibid.: 74, 115).

At the same time, however, arguments about alleged "similarities" between Christian and gentile culture also played an important role in the despised practice of "idolatry" that had justified the Portuguese-Catholic regime to completely destroy the Hindu material culture in Goa. As demonstrated by the anonymous author of the Library Purana, "similarities" were interpreted here as perfidious deceptions fabricated by the "false gods" of the gentiles, as well as indications that underneath the surface of their "false beliefs" there were, if distorted and perverted, rudiments of the "Christian Truth." Studying the beliefs of the gentiles and translating the Christian message into their languages, in this perspective, therefore, implicated at least two corrective strategies. One was to "refute the false gods" of the gentiles and replace them by the one "True Christian God." Another was to extract "the Gold of the Christian Truth," as the unknown author of the Library Purana metaphorically put it, from "the worthless alloy with the gentile falsehood" in which it was allegedly smothered. Both these procedures certainly did not constitute any form of modern translation in the Jesuit production of Indian-language Christian texts. Instead, they manifest what the Goan linguist Anand Patil called a "battle of puranas" (Patil 1999) in which the Christian *purāṇas* defeated and replaced rather than translated the Hindu *purāṇas*.

To be sure, the question of how hermeneutics and violence were exactly related in the work of the composers of the Christian *purāṇas* and in Nobili's *accommodatio* cannot be definitively decided due to the lack of more detailed sources. Thomas Stephens and Roberto Nobili may indeed have held different and more liberal positions than the anonymous author of the Library Purana. What is striking, though, is that, unlike the assumption that the Jesuits were engaging in a modern practice of translation, the logic of the premodern paradigm of "similarities" to which they obviously were committed does not render hermeneutic and violence as mutually exclusive, but rather presents them as the two sides of the proverbial same coin.

4 Ganv

Place, Genealogy, and Bodies

"We're Christians . . . but first of all we're Hindus."

—A Goan priest quoted by Somerset Maugham, 1949 (Pearson 1987: 130)

Each Goan GANV or village constitutes a world of its own. It is regulated by an ancient organization that orders economy and redistribution, social life and hierarchies, ritual ceremonies and traditions, all of which are closely interrelated. It has a clear-cut territory that is structured in wards (*vade*), fields (*shet*), and wilderness (*ran*), all of which are marked by recognized boundaries guarded by tutelary beings and affirmed by rituals and processions. Myths and genealogies tell about origins, migrations, and important historical events that are also reflected in the iconographies and legends of ancestors, gods, and saints. Hindu village gods and Catholic patron saints are considered founders, members, and guardians of the village community, believed to attend its social gatherings and religious feasts and trusted to protect its territory and people. Closely identified with *their* respective village—carrying its name, inheriting its mythological past, marking its localities and spaces, and protecting its people's health and safety—these local gods and saints embody rather than simply represent the village. What Valentine Daniel says about the Tamil *ur*, or village (1987), is also true therefore for the Goan *ganv*, that is, that the divine or holy marks for its *ganvkār* or villagers both "the sign and the substance" of the village that provides for them home, that is, spatial belonging; memory, that is, genealogical rootedness; and bodily welfare, that is, protection and healing from all sorts of natural, spiritual, and bodily dangers and illnesses.

In this chapter I explore how Hindus and Catholics coexist and live together in Goa and what, at times, makes them trust and honor holy or saintly beings that belong to the respective other religious communities. While still using historical sources, this chapter starts the second section of the book, which will primarily rely on ethnographic research that I conducted in Goa between 1990 and 2010. The foci of this research, which for reason of comparison also included fieldtrips to Sindhudurg in Maharashtra, were (a) the popular religion that entwines Hindu *ganvdevāta* and Catholic patron saints, and (b) religious rituals and festivals that are known to include and attract both Hindus and Catholics. The underlying hypothesis of the chapter is that coexistence and syncretism between Hindus and Catholics in Goa are, to a large extent, conditioned and facilitated by the ways that Goans conceptualize and organize their village communities. In pursuing this argument, historical and ethnographic research from Goa and South India that suggests that the interrelations and intersections between Hindu and Christian communities may be effected by the interplay of caste organization, economic redistribution, and a system of stratified ritual honors proved especially interesting (Appadurai and Appadurai Breckenridge 1976; Axelrod and Fuerch 1998; Fuller 1976; Bayly 1989; Mosse 1994, 1997; Kaufmann 1982). In a first section, I take a close look therefore at the social, economic, and ritual organization of the Goan *ganv*. More specifically, I subdivide this section in order to reconstruct and compare the ancient village organization *ganvkārī* that predates the arrival of the Portuguese and to this day marks the ideal-typical living world of Goan Hindus (Kosambi [1962] 1992; De Souza 1979, 1990; Pereira 1978, 1981) with the colonial village organization *comunidade* that was established under Portuguese rule and to this day marks the ideal-typical living world of Goan Catholics (Xavier 1903–1907; Rubinoff 1988; Gomes 1987; Axelrod and Fuerch 1998). Needless to say, neither one of these village organizations ever formed a pristine state or static polity, which is why I also look at processes of political and religious transformation and discuss the much-debated question of to what extent the *comunidade* continues or discontinues the *ganvkārī*.

A closer look reveals that the constitution of the *ganv* does not rely on social structures and economic modes of production and redistribution alone. Quite obviously, the *ganv* is also effectively constituted through rituals, ideas, and practices related to the divine and saintly, that is, religion. The question then arises, how exactly is religion related to the social and economic? Does it provide legitimacy for social hierarchies and economic disparities? Is religion the symbolic expression and public articulation of socioeconomic reality? What role does religion play in the coexistence and syncretism between Hindus and Catholics? Does it express challenged theological principles such as the doctrine of an exclusive Catholic Truth whose missionizing zeal nonetheless enforces cultural compromises, or the concept of an all-embracing Hindu Brahma whose universality borders on cultural hegemony? In the second section of this chapter I pursue these questions by looking at the concepts and practices that connect people, villages, and patron gods and saints. This connection, it turns out, is not so much a matter of domains, that is, functional interactions between the social, the economic, and the religious, nor of religious doctrines, that is, Hindu and Christian theologies or ideologies, but of epistemological perspective and practical action. People see their village as an embodiment of gods and saints, thereby enacting an iconic relationship between metaphysics and praxis. As a practical effect of this iconic equation, popular religion constitutes the village as a triad of neighborhood, genealogy, and well-being, and it is the ritual concern for these practical values and objectives that, at times, overrules doctrinal differences and divisions.

The third section of the chapter looks at village festivals that emphatically articulate and consolidate the epistemic and practical foundation of popular religion and its interreligious capacities. The festival of Our Lady of Miracles, the patron saint of the town of Mapusa, and the ceremonies for Jagoryo, the tutelary god of the village Siolim, exemplify both the apex of popular religiosity and high points of the syncretistic intersection of Hindus and Catholics in Goa. They show that not religious differences—which paradoxically are reasserted rather than challenged in the syncretistic happenings—but ideas of local proximity, family relationship, and bodily healing are at stake when Hindus and Catholics join in common rituals.

Ganvkārī

The economic, social, and ritual community constituted by the *ganv* is encompassed in an ancient village organization known as *ganvkārī* (Baden Powell 1900; Pereira 1978, 1981; De Souza 1990). This organization was and to some extent still is based on the communal ownership of agricultural land by the *ganvkār,* that is, the family clans that claim to descend from the original settlers and hence hold the status of genuine villagers. Ideally and simplified, the productive village land was divided into three categories: The largest and usually best part of the farm land, called *ganvkār* land, was annually or biannually auctioned among the *ganvkār* households and thereafter used for their livelihood and private interest. A second part that is commonly known as *devāche bhāt* or "god's land" was used to cover all costs of the religious domain, including the maintenance of temples and shrines; the livelihood of priests, temple servants, and *devadāsi*[1] or performing artists; and the organization and performance of rituals, ceremonies, and festivals. The final part may be called communal land, which was often reserved for special productions such as *khazān,* the highly productive saline floodplains used for specialized agriculture and pisciculture, or coconut orchards, areca groves, and other tree or horticultural lands.[2] The use of the communal land was itself manifold. It was leased out to *mundkar* or *render,* that is, tenants, or its earnings were used for specialized service groups or castes such as village clerks and artisans, and the labor force working the village land. Communal land was also used to finance public works and to generate additional income for the village community. Apart from the exclusive right of bidding during the regular land auctions and membership in the various village councils, *ganvkār* enjoy two major privileges. One is to hold *jon,* annually redistributed shares in the profits made from the leasing of land and the earnings from the communal land. The other is that *ganvkār* usually have the village goddess or god as their *kuldevī* or *kuldev,* that is, family goddess or family god, something that also makes them *mahājān,* trustees of the central village temple.

Next to the division of *ganvkār* and service groups, two major hierarchies structure the village society. One divides the group of *ganvkār* into different *vangod* or patrilineal clans, so that there exists a first, second, third, and so on *vangod* in each village according to the number of *ganvkār* clans. The other hierarchy divides the village society into different castes, which are distinguished as the more strictly stratified *varnā* or ranks of Brahmins, Kshatriya, Vaishya, and Sudra, and the less clearly stratified *jāti,* that is, ethnic or occupational groups. Two groups do not belong, at least from the point of view of caste Hindus, to the caste system. These are the Mhar and Chamar, or Dalit, whom an obsolete terminology had classified as "Untouchables" because of their "impure status," and the tribal groups of Gaude, Kunbi, Velip, and Dhangar who used to live in and from marginal lands and forest areas. Although considered outside the caste system, it is notable that members of both of these groups traditionally hold or held "ritual honors" and performed functions in major religious ceremonies in many villages, something that reflects their seniority and functional importance in the ancient village system.

The stratification of the *vangod* distinguishes a number of social and ritual privileges that are commonly known as *mān,* or "honors," and their holders as *mānkari.* Hence, the households of the first rank and possibly other high-ranking *vangod* traditionally enjoyed priority and were served first during seasonal activities such as the thatching of house roofs before the monsoon or the sowing or harvesting of fields by the communal labor force. *Vangod* or *mānkari* privileges are most ostentatiously marked in the religious domain. At the various temple festivals, the male *mānkari* usually perform the role of *yajamān,* that is, primary donors of the offerings presented to the deities, and act as patrons and functionaries of the ceremonies. For that purpose, all *mānkari* must be present for the ceremonies and are entitled to wear special dresses, sit or walk next to the deities during the rituals, and carry their palanquins, umbrellas, ritual batons, or any other paraphernalia during processions. In response, *mānkari* are honored by receiving ceremonial gifts, such as betel nut, and are the first to receive the *prasāda,* the food or flowers ritually offered to a god. The hierarchies of the village community are most flamboyantly demonstrated and enacted during the *jātra,* or annual temple festival, when everybody has to wait for the *mānkari,* who are marked by conspicuous turbans or white shawls, to take their privileged positions in the temple. These are usually left and right of the deity's palanquin, which the *mānkari* then take turns in carrying through the village territories, visiting the temples and shrines of affiliated deities, tutelary beings, or village ancestors.

In the meantime, non-*ganvkār* villagers at each stop try to get near the deity to take the *darśana,* that is, exchange an auspicious glance with the *mūrti,* or deity's icon, or get one of the flowers decorating the palanquin as a kind of *prasāda.*

Due to the long-lasting impact of Portuguese colonialism in Goa, and particularly the large-scale destruction of its Hindu culture in the sixteenth century, only a few archival sources are available today that give detailed evidence about the pre-Portuguese history of the Goan people and their village and religious culture. One resource is the *Sahyadri Khanda of the Skanda Purana,* or "Book of the Western Mountains," an apparently recently organized and somewhat deficient edition of disparate texts (Levitt 1977; Figueiredo 1963)—the earliest ones of which date to the fifth and the latest to the thirteenth centuries (Levitt 1973: 82, 87)—that tell the mythological story of the people of the Konkan and Goa (Cunha 1877; Gaitonde 1972). An especially relevant example is the story of the migration of the Saraswat branch of the Panca Gauda Brahmans of North India to Goa. The mythical hero of this story is Parashurama, the sixth avatar of Vishnu, who, enraged by a misdeed of King Kartavirya, perpetrates a massacre among the Kshatriya. The hero then begs the sea-god Varuna for land or, according to another version, claims the land of Konkan and Malabar himself from the ocean by blows of his magical axe, in order to bestow it to Brahmans in expiation for his cruel deed (Walker 1983: 2:190; Doshi and Shirodkar 1983: 54). More precisely, the *Sahyadri Khanda* accounts for sixty-six Gaud Saraswat Brahman families who Parashurama had brought from Trihotra, the modern Tirhut in western Bengal, to settle in Goan villages.[3] The story of the historical migration of the Gaud Saraswat Brahmans is supported by passages of the *Sahyadri Khanda,* in particular the section *Mangish Mahatmya,* "Glory of Mangish," that are taken to refer to deities whom the Gaud Saraswat Brahmans have brought with them to Goa. These deities, Mangish, Mahalakshmi, Shanta Durga, Nagesh, and Saptakotishvara, are all worshipped in temples and shrines in Goa to this day (Mitragotri and Mathew 1991: 4; Wagle 1970: 9–10).

Facilitated by its enormous size and amorphous structure, the *Sahyadri Khanda,* however, has become the subject of contested interpretations. Modern scholars have questioned the "myth of the northern descent" of the Gaud Saraswat Brahman, arguing that their origins instead come from local priests who, at some point in history, gained Brahmanhood (Kosambi [1962] 1992: 166). Others see the region of the ancient river Saraswati in northwest India as the origins of the ancient Gaud Saraswat Brahman and claim Harappa as a "Saraswat Civilization" (Kamath 1992: 42). Historicizing the myth, it has been argued that the significance it gained in the late nineteenth and early twentieth centuries, and in particular its alleged reference to the northeastern origins of Gaud Saraswat Brahman, stems from the effects of Bengal-based Hindu reform movements in Bombay and the political formation of a Gaud Saraswat Brahman identity. In this context, interpretations of the *Sahyadri Khanda* also became part of debates between the Konkani-speaking Gaud Saraswat Brahman and the Marathi-speaking Kharhade and Deshastha Brahmans in Goa (Wagle 1970; Conlon 1974). The American scholar Stephan Hillyer Levitt translated stories from the *Sahyadri Khanda* that suggested the ancient existence of entire villages of Brahmans in the Konkan region who had been degraded in their caste status for various misfortunes and delinquencies, something that may explain why few Goan temples are exclusively patronized by Gaud Saraswat Brahmans today (Levitt 1973). Yet other scholars challenge the assumption drawn from the *Sahyadri Khanda* that major deities of modern Goa had been "imported" by immigrating Brahmans. Most of the Gaud Saraswat Brahman *kuladevatā* (family gods) mentioned in the *Sahyadri Khanda,* it is argued, are "sanskritized" local "folk deities" who had long been worshipped in Goa, in particular in the context of ancient Shakti, Linga, Nag, and Nath cults (Mitragotri and Mathew 1991; Shirodkar 1988, 1993). The argument that many deities presiding in Goan temples today are sanskritized local gods refers not only to the influence of Gaud Saraswat Brahmans but also to Kshatriya, in particular the *jāt* or subcaste named Maratha, whose members came from Maharashtra and gained prominence during the rule of the Hindu king Shivaji (1627–1680). A third *jāt* that arguably had sanskritizing effects on Goan Hinduism are Vaishya merchants, known as Vani in Goa. Today, most Goan Vani originate from Maharashtra, though historically Goa has been known for its longstanding contacts with Vaishya and Jain merchants from all along the western coast (Shirodkar and Mandal 1993; Shirodkar 1991).

Indications of historical transformations involving influences from diverse social strata and forces can also be found in the iconography and mythology of local deities. A case in point is a myth telling the origin and story of the goddess Morzai in the coastal village of Morjim (Pernem). Once upon a time, this myth goes, the *mūrti* of Morzai emerged from the sea and was found by local fishermen in Morjim. This extraordinary event came to the attention of the king of neighboring Sawantwadi (Maharashtra), who came to inspect the curious happening. When he arrived in Morjim, he showed himself to be skeptical about the alleged divinity of the *mūrti* and asked the people for proof. The villagers prayed to the goddess to reveal her divine qualities. She fulfilled their wishes and, in front of the king's eyes, miraculously filled a tidal inlet with fish. Facing the power of the goddess, however, the simple people were gripped by fear and left the place in a panic, whereupon the king laid his hand on the goddess, granted the fisher folk a subordinate ritual function in her cult, and annexed Morjim to his kingdom. Even though this myth does not reflect the actual distribution of rights and privileges in Morjim's temple today, it can be seen as an evidence of the sociopolitical dynamic in the Pernem province, which was for a long time the frontier between Portuguese Goa and the Hindu kingdoms of Kshatriya dynasties such as Maratha and Rane ruling in Maharashtra's southernmost province of Sawantwadi.

Other, more indirect indications of historical transformations can be seen in the fact that many local village deities of Goa are also considered manifestations of great Hindu gods worshipped throughout India. Particularly widespread cases in point are the many Goan village goddesses who, next to their local names— Sateri, Bhumika, Bharadi, Kelbai, and so on—are also known and worshipped as Shanta Durga, a manifestation of the great Durga. Notably, this Goan adoption or appropriation of the puranic Durga does not leave her identity and image completely untouched but adds the distinct title "Shanta" to it, thereby producing debates over her true nature among Goan scholars. Shenoi Vahman Ragunat Varde Valaulikar, that is, Shennoi Goembab, the great "Goan Master" of Konkan folklore, culture, and language, argued that "Shanta" stands for śānti, "peaceful," and thus contrasts distinctly with the ferocious image of the puranic Durga and, in particular, her identity as Mahishasuramardini, the warrior goddess who successfully overwhelmed and killed the demon Mahishasura (Valaulikar [1945] 1977). Instead, Valaulikar argues, the Goan Shanta Durga marks a celebrated aspect of the Devi or Great Goddess of Indian mythology that shows her interfering in and pacifying a terrible fight between Vishnu and Shiva, thereby salvaging and restoring the order of the universe. Suspecting too much romanticism in Valaulikar's image of the goddess and by implication Goa at large, and yet confirming the local peculiarity of the universal goddess, modern scholars V. R. Mitragotri and K. M. Mathew (1991) argue that her name refers to her mythical apparition to Shantamuni, a sage who once lived in Goa. In general, Saibini Sateri–Shanta Durga's multiple identities are presumably the result of historical transformations. A most palpable iconographic evidence of this transformation can be found at places where the goddess is represented by her most ancient manifestations, natural anthills (roen). Throughout Goa and the Konkan, many anthills are worshipped wherever they are found in the forests and wilderness. Many are also parts of shrines and temples, and are embellished by elaborate iconographic decor. And it is in these places that one can find anthropomorphic masks or icons showing Shanta Durga in aristocratic posture armed with shield and sword being placed right over the roen or sacred anthills of Sateri, indicating the superimposition of the ancient earth goddess by the puranic deity.

Other indications of historical transformations can be found among male village gods, whose original names have been extended, for instance, by suffixes like -nāth or -iśvar, transforming Raval into Ravalnath, Buth into Buthnath, or Vetal into Vetaleshvar (Mitragotri 1989). Not all such transformations, however, need to be attributed to processes of political usurpation. Obviously, the processes described by scholars as "sanskritization" (Srinivas 1967)[4] are quite common in Goa and the Konkan. A case in point is the story of the changes in the icon for the local god Vetal that I was told by the people in the village Azgaon in Sindudhurg (Maharastra). Earlier, the people recall, their Vetal was represented by a wooden mūrti, which showed the god in the typical posture of a standing bearded male fully naked. One day though, it was decided that the god, who was known as Agya-Vetal, literally "Fire-Vetal," was to be "cooled." For this purpose, the villagers buried the deity-icon head down and a new icon, again made from wood but showing the god in a white *dhotī*, or loin cloth, was ritually consecrated and installed. Years later, the people again decided to change the deity-icon, this time into a Shiva-*rūpa*, that is, a form of the great Shiva. For that purpose, people performed the full range of cremation ceremonies, as would be done for a high-ranking Brahman, during which Vetal's *mūrti* was burned and its ashes dispersed in the nearby river. Thereupon a new icon of metal was installed in the temple and, henceforth, the god was addressed by the honorific name of Vetaleshvar. While the exact circumstances of these transformations are not known, it is clear that they happened in recent times, probably the twentieth century, and were brought about by internal village politics.

The plasticity of Hindu religiosity in Goa thus becomes clear. Although Gaud Saraswat, Maratha, and Vani control the largest number of temples whose *mahājān* all come from a single caste in Goa, the largest number of registered Goan temples are controlled by *mahājān* from various castes and administered by village communities. A further challenge to the impression of twice-born supremacy in Goan temples comes from the fact that, in a great number of community-administered temples, clans ranked according to the *varnā* system as Sudra or Dalit either hold *mān* or otherwise play essential roles, for instance by playing the ritual drums, whose leather skins are taboo to be touched by caste Hindus (Pereira 1981: 9). Other irregularities from a strictly caste-based perspective include the fact that the hierarchical order of *vangod* or *mānkari* sometimes does not follow the order of thè *varnā* system, which means that members from lower castes hold higher *mān* than members from higher castes (Thomaz 1981–1982: 33; Pereira 1978: 163, 1981: 118; Rubinoff 1988: 195). While scholars still wrestle with such "irregularities" (Robinson 1998: 68), suggesting for instance that the *mānkari* hierarchy reflects seniority claims or acquired merits rather than strictly speaking social status (De Souza 1979: 62), one especially intriguing hypothesis emerging from the Goan material is that the *varnā* hierarchy might have historically been superimposed over the *mānkari* hierarchy without the latter fully losing its authority. In particular, Gaude, Kunbi, and Velip—Goa's largest groups with tribal origins, which claim to be *adīvasi*, or aboriginal settlers of Goa—constitute *vangod* and hold *mān* in many community-administered temples. Their claim of seniority is supported not only by the fact that a considerable number of Gaude, Kunbi, and Velip living in the New Conquests have *ganvkār* as their family name; ancient privileges, such as the right to seasonally initiate the ritual sowing of the fields or the ceremony of *devakāria*, that is, the ritual feeding of Kunbi dignitaries during temple festivals, also buttress their special status in the ancient village organization (Pereira 1981: 8ff.).

The completion of the sociological picture of Hindu religiosity in Goa requires mention of the great number of temples that are too insignificant or simply too poor to be registered,[5] and therefore do not show in any official list. These are the temples administered by land laborer, fishing, and artisan communities that are ranked as Sudra or Dalit in the *varnā* system, and also the tribal communities of Gaude, Kunbi, and Velip. Apart from not being registered or being registered only in small numbers, the temples administered by Goa's laboring and tribal communities differ significantly in the religiosity displayed from temples administered by twice-born castes. As mentioned before, deities of Gaud Saraswat, Maratha, and Vani such as Mangesh, Maruti, Mahalakshmi, and Shanta Durga are considered sanskritic, meaning they are embedded in some kind of *purāṇa* or textual tradition, receive vegetarian offerings, and are served by Brahmanical priests. Deities of many village temples or temples administered by Sudra, Gaude, Kunbi, and Velip communities such as Sateri, Vetal, and Ravalnath, in contrast, are considered "fierce deities," which means their traditions are orally transmitted, receive at least occasionally nonvegetarian offerings such as cocks or fish and are served by *ghaddi* or *guranv*, that is, non-Brahmanical priests. Notably, though, fierce deities as a rule keep their ancient identity even after they have been superimposed on and transformed by sanskritic deities. As with Sateri's anthill that continues to be worshipped under the icon of Shanta Durga, fierce deities thus often continue to be served by *guranv* and receive bloody sacrifices after they have taken on the name and identity of a sanskritic deity. Frequently, Brahmanical and non-Brahmanical services are separated though and performed at different times or different places, so that Sateri–Shanta Durga, at her festival, may receive *nayvedia,* or vegetarian, offerings inside, and *bali,* or bloody, offerings outside her temple.

Comunidade

When turning to the *comunidade,* that is, the Goan *ganv* after its transformation by the Portuguese conquest and Catholic domination, the question arises as to how much the ancient village organization has actually been changed by the coming of colonialism and conversion. Given the rather meager sources on precolonial Goa, scholarly opinions regarding the extent of Goa's colonial transformation vary substantively. A long-standing school of researchers dating from Baden Powel (1900) to Michael Pearson (1987, [1984] 2005a)[6] argues that the Goan *ganvkārī* marks an exceptionally archaic and autonomous form of village organization in India, often labeled a "village republic" for its collective ownership of land and egalitarian redistribution of profits among the villagers, that was comparatively little affected by the Portuguese. This school commonly refers to the *Foral de usos e costumes dos Gauncares,* that is, the Charter of Rights and Duties of the Gaunkars, that was compiled by the Portuguese revenue superintendent Afonso Mexia in 1526 as an early source (Mexia [1526] 1992), and holds that Goa's village organization was spared major feudal interventions by the various premodern Muslim and Hindu dynasties ruling in the Deccan. Apart from changing people's religious orientation, this school argues, even the Portuguese intervened only little into the social structures and modes of production of the old *ganvkārī* organization. Various reasons are given for this view. D. Kosambi attributes the resilience of Goa's rural traditions to its "marginal location" in relation to the Deccan Hindu kingdoms and Muslim sultanates, from which it was separated by a "mountain barrier ([1962] 1992: 159). Pearson argues that "premodern states, whether Bijapur, Portugal or any other in general interfered very little in the everyday lives of most of their subjects," and in particular, "the village administration was left strictly alone by the Portuguese" in Goa (1987: 108).

Other scholars see things differently. They consider Afonso Mexia "the first Portuguese Orientalist" whose description was uncritically taken to prove the idea of an archaic and pristine India (Axelrod and Fuerch 1998: 453) and challenge "the myth of Portuguese tradition-preserving intervention in its colonies" (Subrahmanyam 1997b: 30). While generally criticizing romanticizing tendencies in the historical scholarship on Goa, these scholars accentuate different types of changes effected by the Portuguese. Subrahmanyam specifically questions the assumption that the absence of feudal intermediaries was intrinsic to Goan villages and argues that "it is hard to escape the suspicion that this situation was largely the consequence of the fact that a fiscal elite class (both Muslim and Hindu) that had existed in the fifteenth and sixteenth centuries had been deliberately wiped out, delegitimized or swept aside in the transition to Portuguese rule" (ibid.: 36). P. Axelrod and M. A. Fuerch see Portuguese interventions above all in processes emphasizing "land ownership, revenue and the relationship between the village and the state," thereby interfering with an indigenous mode of "Hindu thinking which connects individuals in complex substantive ways to their deities and, in turn, individuals and deities to the soil of a particular village" (1998: 456, 468). Janet Ahner Rubinoff (1988: 201ff.) and Teotonio De Souza (1990: 71ff.) argue that the Portuguese did undermine the communitarian character of the Goan village organization in many ways, in particular by infringing on the rights of *ganvkār* and fragmenting their clans, facilitating the alienation and confiscation of village land, and weakening indigenous support systems for widows and orphans.

However one assesses the colonial impact on Goan villages, it is evident that the early-modern Portuguese-Catholic regime pursued policies that reproduced a good deal of the ancient *ganvkārī*. As mentioned before, the backgrounds and rationales of this "reproduction" vary substantively, ranging from political and technical limitations to the effective control of the colonial administration and society, through self-consciously drafted assimilative strategies of conquest and conversion, to epistemic commonalities regarding the status of signs and images. The question whether the transition from *ganvkārī* to *comunidade* should be called a conservative continuation or an aggressive assimilation or a radical rupture needs to be relegated, therefore, to individual case-by-case explorations. Arguably, these limitations do not alter the fact though that the Portuguese-Catholic regime did, to a large extent, reproduce major social structures and hierarchies of Hindu society among Christians in Goa.

Continuing the important division between *ganvkār*, that is, communal land ownership, and *mundkār* or *render*, that is, land tenants and agricultural laborers, seems to be part of the general strategy of the early-modern conquest to combine carrot and stick, reward and punishment. It granted *ganvkār* who converted to Christianity all their traditional privileges and forced *mundkār* and laboring castes to convert, because this was the only way for them to continue their contracts and employment with their traditional patrons. Continuing the *ganvkār* system arguably also reflects the dual colonial-clerical agenda of the early-modern conquest, since it secured revenue for both parts of the Padroado agreement: tax revenue from the *ganvkār* income for the Portuguese Crown and land usufruct from the *ganvkār* land for the Catholic Church. Interestingly, not only was a good part of the best village land thus reserved for the local churches and their feasts and services, but Catholic patron saints were also formally registered to receive *jon*, shares in the annual village surplus (Pereira 1981: 43). Like the Hindu deities in the *ganvkāri* system whom they replaced, some Catholic patron saints thereby gained the status of legal persons in the *comunidade* system.

While the transition from *ganvkāri* to *comunidade* thus continued and reproduced major socioeconomic structures of the Goan *ganv*, closer inspection also reveals important changes. In particular, archival evidence indicates the ancient significance of castes and communities not based on agricultural production and without land, which are not mentioned anymore in Mexia's codification of the *comunidades*. Hence, Cunha Rivara identifies in his footnotes to the publication of Mexia's *Foral* of 1526 one of the villages as "Pescadores d'Ambarim," that is, a fishing community (Mexia [1526] 1992: 122). Likewise, Francisco Pais lists in his *Tombo das Rendas* for Salcete and Bardes of 1595 that among the sixty-six villages from which Salcete draws its name (Sanskrit *ṣāṣṭi* for "sixty" is taken to be an old name for Salcete), some are specified as having *bois*, that is, fish sellers; *chaudarins*, that is, toddy tappers (collectors of palm sap); and *pescadores*, that is, fishermen, as their founders (Pais [1595] 1952: 101; Pereira 1981: 17). These nonlanded villages were obviously of significant size and resources and constituted independent *ganv* in their own right. In the same fashion, Kosambi states that *comunidade* built on an idea of economic cooperation that was not only realized among agriculturists but also shows that the cooperative idea spread among the Khazans, or salt-pen workers, and was generally taken up by workers' groups on the same profit-sharing basis as the "now extinct industrial associations that took the same form in particular of fisherman and weavers" (Kosambi [1962] 1992: 169; see also Xavier 1903–1907: 2:410ff.). The hypothesis here is that the ancient pre-Portuguese constitution of the *ganv*, as found in these extinct villages of nonlanded communities and in the appreciation of tribal communities practicing *kumeri* or shifting cultivation, was based on a conceptual and practical relationship among people, land, and the divine in which land was not reduced to economically defined agricultural land. Rather, the soil of the *ganv*, as I will elaborate below, was defined as an embodiment of the village goddess and thereby constituted and reaffirmed in a ritualistic way. Defining the *comunidade*, then, as *"associação agricola estabelecida em cada aldèa desde a sua fundação"* (agricultural association established in every village since its beginning; Xavier 1852: 1), arguably reduced the land to the juridico-economical category of taxable agricultural land and, by implication, excluded the villages of communities that were not based on agriculture. Accordingly, the communities that did not need to pay taxes were excluded from the Foral and the Tombos, and were declared extinct in the records, even while they continued in practice (Siqueira and Henn 2001).

Why the Portuguese-Catholic regime reproduced among Goan Christians the complex stratification that it was the first European voice to call *casta* or caste is less clear, especially assuming the thesis elaborated earlier that, at the time of the Portuguese conquest, the *varnā* system was neither as consistent nor as homogeneous in Goa as it became in the course of colonial history. As mentioned before, systematic research of the Portuguese origins of the early-modern European terminology and meaning of "caste" remains a pressing scholarly project. One important question to explore would be whether the combination of bodily and religious criteria inherent in the *varnā* stratification was resonating with similar distinctions made in the early-modern Lusitan world. More precisely, it would be interesting to compare how Hindu notions of graduated "pollution" among castes were related to Portuguese notions of graduated "blood purity" among the various ranks of Portuguese-Goan colonial society (Boxer 1963). As historians point out, the Portuguese-Goan society was ranked, from top to down, into *reinos*, that is, Portuguese-born from Portuguese parents in Portugal; *castiços*, that is, Portuguese-born from Portuguese parents in India; *soldados*, that is, unmarried Portuguese men living in India; *casados*, that is, Portuguese men living in India who had married Indian women; and finally *mestiços*, that is, persons born from Portuguese and Indian parents. These rankings were complemented by religious criteria distinguishing and ranking, again from the top down, *velhos cristãos*, that is, "old Christians"; *novos cristãos*, that is, converted Jews or Muslims; *cristãos da terra*, that is, converted Indians; and finally *gentios*, heathens (Pearson 1987: 95; Boxer [1969] 1991: 250; De Silva 1994: 306). In particular, the religious rankings followed comparable criteria in the context of the Reconquista in Portugal and at the colonial frontier in Goa. Parallels and convergences may also have been encouraged by the fact that the colonial encounter generated certain comparable forms of social dynamism. Hence, while Charles R. Boxer notes

that the passage from Portugal to India transformed many a Portuguese common man into a *fildalgo* or aristocrat (Boxer 1991), Rowena Robinson and Caroline Ifeka point out that conversion to Christianity was a welcome occasion for
uplifting the status of Sudra to Chardo, or Kshatriya to Bahmon (Robinson 1998:
77; Ifeka 1989: 263).

Regardless of the background and rationale of the Portuguese-Catholic
adoption of the caste system, it is a matter of fact that the early-modern colonial
regime continued, albeit with some modifications, the Hindu *varnā* stratification among the converted Catholic population of Goa. Hence, the caste status
of converts was routinely marked in baptismal records in Goa (Wicki 1969: 20)
and caste privileges played an important role in the organization of *comunidades*
and local churches allowing, for instance, only Catholic Brahmans in the semi-
naries of Goa (Borghes 1993). Writing about modern Goa, Adelyn D'Costa distinguishes six castes or caste-like divisions among Catholics: "Bahmon, Chaddi,
Gaudde, Sudir, Mahar/Chamar and Kunbi." Of these, she qualifies Bahmon as
equivalent to Brahman, Chaddi to Kshatriya, Gaudde as an amorphous group
split between Brahman and Sudra, Sudir as Sudra, Mahar/Chamar as "closely
correspond[ing] to the Hindu untouchable groups," and Kunbi "as a distinct
tribal group" (D'Costa 1977: 285). Luís Filipe Thomaz lists four Catholic caste
ranks in Goa—"Brahman, Chardos, Sudras and inferior castes" (Thomaz 1981–
1982: 34). D'Costa and Ifeka note that the two highest-ranking Catholic castes are
subdivided by further rankings indicating high (*oontz pounde, morgad*) and low
(*sokol, foscotto, saddula*) status (Ifeka 1989: 262; D'Costa 1977: 285). D'Costa adds
that the Gaudde and Sudir ranks are also subdivided: Gaudde into *bhadkara* and
non-*bhadkara,* that is, land-owning and non-land-owning sections, and Sudir
into *kamdars, vauraddi,* and *nistenkar,* that is, artisan, land-laboring, and fishing
communities. As already mentioned, there are some modifications between the
Hindu and Catholic systems, the most obvious being that there is no Christian
caste that reproduces the Hindu Vaishya rank and that the Christian ranking
tentatively agglomerates Hindu *jāt* groups thereby arguably essentializing the
Hindu *varnā* system.

One question that receives considerable attention in the literature is whether
Christian castes in Goa continue Hindu notions and practices of purity and pollution. A first inspection seems to largely reject this assumption insofar as restrictions of food-sharing and the segregation of pollution-removing groups are,
if not totally absent, at least less important in Goa's Catholic society. One major
argument in the literature therefore has been that,

> on converting to Catholicism over four hundred years ago, Hindus learned to
> conceive caste less in terms of inequality prescribed by an all-encompassing
> religious ideal of freedom from pollution, and more in terms of inequality of
> strata, each distinguished by a caste name (i.e. Bahmon, Chardo, Sudir), in-
> herited occupational function, caste endogamy and degree of cleanliness (*lim-*

peza, Port.)—implicitly "fairness" as distinct from "darkness" and dirt (*suje*): Christian castes are thus ranked high (*oontz*) and low (*sokol*) on a scale of moral value of goodness (*boren rupem*) and beauty (*sobitai*). (Ifeka 1989: 262)

What Caroline Ifeka's observation emphasizes is thus, on the one hand, that stratification in Goan Catholic society has to a large degree produced and is producing what the Portuguese sociologist E. J. Barros called "casteified classes" (Ifeka 1989: 265), that is, castes defined by socioeconomic differences such as land ownership, income, education, dowry gifts, and so on. And it is this modern economization of Christian castes in Goa that arguably enhances the essentialization of *varnā* at the expense of *jāti* principles, by diminishing the political, social, and ritual aspects of the latter. One notable general observation is thus that early-modern Portuguese colonialism preceded and possibly initiated the colonial essentialization or "invention" of caste that has become a major point in postcolonial theories of later periods (Dirks 1989, 1993; Inden 1986). On the other hand, Ifeka's quotation also reveals that the historical concept of caste among Goan Catholics still has much to do with criteria of blood purity, skin color, and cleanliness, which, although not identical with Hindu notions of purity and pollution, do clearly resonate with the ideological and, in historical perspective, religious evaluation of corporeal qualities and substances. It is therefore not a coincidence but a coherent logic that distinctly connects premodern and modern values that, to this day, Goans, Catholics as well as Hindus, define caste endogamy not only by reference to *varnā* rank and socioeconomic status but also by reference to skin color and religion.

Returning to the *comunidade,* it is notable that Goa's Christian population not only reproduced the *ganvkār* and *varnā* systems of the old Hindu village organization but also the stratification of *vangod,* or *vangor* as it is pronounced by Goan Catholics. Christian *ganvkār* too were stratified in *vangor* whose differing social statuses were reflected in social and ritual honors and privileges. Old *comunidade* records show, for instance, that *vangor* honors entitled their holders to offices in the village administration, were endowed with additional shares in the village profits, and played a role in the ritual order of religious ceremonies. As Janet Rubinoff notes,

> For example, during the "Corn Feast," the annual blessing of the new paddy in late August, representatives of the various *vangor* carried the palanquin with the statue of St. John, patron saint of the village, while lesser ranked *vangor,* non-*ganvkār,* and finally women and children followed behind. When the village priest cut and blessed the new paddy in the fields, each *vangor* was called forward by order of its numerical rank to receive its bundle to decorate the church and to distribute among family members. (1988: 197)

The formal rights of the Hindu *mahājān,* finally, found their equivalent in the Catholic *confrarias* or confraternities. Modeled originally after the religious organizations that represented the feudal classes and artisanal guilds during church ceremonies in Portugal (Oliveira Marques 1971: 205), the *confrarias* became in Goa a powerful means to publicly express and display social distinctions and hierarchy. Examples of occasions of such display were and to some extent still are religious ceremonies, in particular the various processions at the patron saints' feast days, Corpus Christi, Good Friday, and so on, at which the members of different confraternities distinguished themselves by differently colored ceremonious capes; performed different functions such as carrying banners, lanterns, or statues of saints; and walked at privileged positions in front of or next to the figures of Christ or Our Lady. From the very beginning, different confraternities distinguished in this way *descendentes*, that is, people of Portuguese descent, from *gente da terra*, that is Indian natives, and marked the various rankings among the local population. Members of different *confrarias* come from different strata of society, distinguishing, for instance, a *confraria maior* that was exclusively reserved for *ganvkār* from a *confraria menor* whose members were non-*ganvkār* or came from "lower" *varnā* or *vangor* ranks. Interestingly, the modalities of these public distinctions vary in the different parts of Goa. Hence, caste divisions are generally stronger in the villages in Salcete where historically the Jesuits worked and where the most Bahmon-administered *comunidades* can be found. A typical example is the town of Margao where the highest-ranking Confraternity of the Immaculate Conception is reserved for Bahmons and distinguished from two lower-ranking confraternities dedicated to St. Michael and to All Souls formed by Catholic Chardo, Sudir, and Kunbi (Thomaz 1981–1982: 38ff.). In the villages in Bardes, on the other hand, where historically the Franciscans worked and where more Chardo-administered and mixed *comunidades* can be found, *ganvkār* divisions are stronger. An interesting example here is the town of Mapusa, where the high-ranking Confraternity of the Blessed Souls was reserved for local *ganvkār* and the lower-ranking Confraternity of Our Lady of the Miracles was open to people from the entire community until both confraternities were fused in 1898 (Azevedo 1985: 101). In general, the Catholic *confraria* system essentializes the hierarchies borrowed from Hindu society. This observation is substantiated by the fact that the notable occasional rank-reversal within the Hindu *vangod* system, and the privileges enjoyed by Goa's tribal communities in Hindu temples, cannot be found in the Catholic *vangor*, *confraria*, and, in general, *comunidade* systems.

In summary, it is clear that the transition from *ganvkārī* to *comunidade* did not pass without major changes, and that the *ganv* was never a pristine or static unit. The most incisive change induced by the Portuguese was arguably to redefine the judicial and economic constitution of the *ganv* in such a way that tribal, Dalit, and non-twice-born caste communities were no longer acknowledged as independent villages. Similarly, the Catholic caste and *vangor* system did not reproduce the *mān* or ritual honors for the tribal and laboring population that held a functional place in the ancient Hindu system. At the same time, the histori-cal transition reveals tendencies toward an essentialization of the *varnā* system, both by removing the various inconsistencies and rank-reversals recognizable in the Hindu system and by strengthening the status and power of "higher" and in particular twice-born castes vis-à-vis the "lower castes," Dalit, and tribal popu-lation. These circumstances notwithstanding, the *comunidade* nonetheless con-tinued to reproduce many important features of the old *ganvkārī* organization. Backgrounds and rationales of this continuation arguably had to do with both the facilitation of conversion and similarities resonating between the ranking systems of the reconquistadorial Iberian society and the Portuguese-Goan co-lonial society. Most importantly, the *comunidade* did reproduce among the con-verted Goan Catholics the three major hierarchical systems of the old *ganvkārī*—the division and ranking of *ganvkār, mundkār,* and service groups in *vangod* or *vangor;* the *varnā* ranking and *jāti* differentiation of castes and subcastes; and the ranking of *mān* or ritual honors reflecting the socioeconomic hierarchies. The impression of a continuation of the social, economic, and ritual hierarchies that, eventually, after the "return" of Hindus to the areas of the Old Conquests, generated a formidable parallelism between the Catholic and Hindu societies of Goa, prevails even beyond the various modifications of the Catholic caste system, such as the abolishment of the Vani rank and the tentative agglomeration of the *jāti.* Reason for this impression is arguably that the modifications and changes effected in the Catholic system did in fact take on and reinforce dynamics that were prevalent already in the Hindu system. In particular, did the replacement of Hindu gods by Catholic saints, from a local perspective, repeat the transforma-tions effected by the immigration or emergence of politically dominant Hindu castes that had traditionally replaced and superimposed ancient local deities with pan-Indian sanskritic deities? To some extent, Robinson therefore may indeed be right to summarize her chapter on "the socio-political context of conversion" with the observation that "Hindus may not have perceived Catholicism as a com-pletely alien religious tradition" (1998: 32).

Ganvdevāta

Are coexistence and syncretistic intersections between Hindus and Catholics thus grounded in the similarities of their socioeconomic organization, as a num-ber of scholars working on South India have argued (Appadurai and Appadurai Breckenridge 1976; Stein 1975; Bayly 1989; Mosse 1994, 1997; Kaufmann 1982)? Was it, after the historical "return" of Hindus to the Old Conquests in Goa, the paral-lelism of Hindu and Catholic *varnā, vangod/vangor,* and *mānkari* ranking that motivated the villagers to transgress their doctrinal religious divisions? Is caste indeed the essential feature that constitutes and buttresses all noteworthy so-cial relationship in Indian society? As obvious as these conclusions seem to be, a closer look reveals serious objections. Nowhere can one find Hindu and Catholic *ganvkār* or Hindu and Catholic castes involved in any actual caste-based interaction, *Gemeinschaft*, or syncretism. In fact, unlike South India where Christians, to some extent, are integrated into Hindu society by constituting a kind of caste, it seems that in Goa, it is precisely the existence of a full-fledged Catholic caste society that prevents such integration by producing two similar but separate communities whose public and private affairs, social and religious expressions, gatherings and activities, for the most part, are quite aloof and distanced from each other. In order to understand what actually facilitates coexistence and syncretism between Hindus and Catholics in Goa, it therefore becomes necessary to search for deeper principles constituting the Goan *ganv*. These can arguably be found in the conceptual and practical connection that brings people, village, and patron gods and saints together.

In order to appreciate this perspective, it is important to reiterate that Hindu *ganvdevāta*, or village gods, do not just represent but embody their villages. The strongest expression of this principle can be found in the widespread idea that the soil of the village is actually the body of its goddess. This concept finds most palpable expression in iconography that manifests the village goddesses in a single stone head placed on the bare ground, thereby vividly evoking an image of the subterranean extension of the rest of her body. This iconic equation of villages and gods has the strongest association with ancient Goan and Konkan goddesses such as Sateri, Bhumika, Kelbai, Morzai, Mauli, Bharadi, and Mhalsa and their male spouses and consorts Vetal, Ravalnath, Kshetrapal, and Buthnath. Sateri and Bhumika are commonly seen as "earth goddesses" since, in their most basic form, they manifest themselves as *roen* (see figure 4.1).

Since abandoned anthills are often the natural habitat of snakes, the use of images and icons of snakes representing male village gods marks a consistent iconographic complement of the divine feminine anthill. Especially among Goa's tribal population, it is common to worship anthills and certain snakes wherever they are found in the forests and wilderness. In many villages, anthills have been given elaborate iconographic decor. They are marked by colors and flags, surrounded by gated walls or structures of shrines, and quite a number have become part of full-fledged temples. Here, anthropomorphic images or icons complement aniconic manifestations, often indicating the superimposition of ancient goddesses such as Sateri and Bhumika with puranic deities such as Shanta Durga. Next to their manifestation as anthills and snakes, ancient *ganvdevāta* are represented by rocks or trees, something that is commonly interpreted as evidence that they have "grown out of the earth," that is, they have manifested themselves without human interference. Many local myths and legends tell about images, icons, or other tokens of village gods that have emerged from the ground, appeared from nowhere, or been washed ashore by the sea.

Figure 4.1. *Roen* (sacred anthill), Goa. Photograph by Gabriele Henn.

Aniconic representations are embellished by anthropomorphic or otherwise figurative images, icons, monograms, and tokens of village gods and tutelary beings. Altogether, the aniconic and iconic presence of village gods is overwhelming in Goan villages marking myriad public and private places. Typical locations for the manifestation of local gods are either right in the center, that is, at village and town plazas and marketplaces, or at the peripheries and liminal sites, such as borders between villages, boundaries between settlements and wilderness, or at seashores, riverbanks, dams, crossroads, and hilltops. The most gorgeous iconographic representation of local deities can be found in the village temples. Here, the icons and images of the *ganvdevāta* are complemented by shrines and images of *purvoj* or *vodil,* that is, ancestors who might be represented by anthropomorphic icons or simply by *nāḷ,* coconuts. Temples are complemented by wayside shrines marking numerous locations that represent village gods, ancestors, and minor gods or tutelary beings. Sometimes, shrines are also dedicated to one of the great pan-Indian gods, especially Ganesha, Shiva, or Durga, most of whom, however, also have another local identity. The structures of shrines are manifold. A widespread form is *gumpti,* a small usually whitewashed grotto-shaped shelter with an opening in front that may be placed right on the ground or elevated on a sort of table, and may or may not contain icons or tokens of a god or tutelary being. Shrines are typically looked after by people living in the vicinity, and it depends on their patrons, their status, and their means how elaborate a shrine and its iconic decor is. Goa's postcolonial prosperity and the current economic boom in India at large has led to the general aggrandizement and embellishment of wayside shrines, many of which have been turned into solid structures today with roofs and gates, decorated by colorful tiles, images, and icons. In some cases, as with the tutelary god Bodgeshvar who has his abode at the boundary of the city of Mapusa and who is patronized by a large and newly emerging urban middle class, shrines may grow into major structures that compete with established temples in size and popularity. Just like temples, shrines have a fixed devotional program and, apart from the individual daily worship, usually have one day every week, and one or several days per year, when patrons come together in larger number to worship or celebrate festive events.

The iconic presence of gods and tutelary beings is also overwhelming in the private sphere. Typically, one finds in the front yard of a Hindu home a colorful Tulsi Vrindavan, that is, a shrine holding a Holy Basil plant (*Ocium Sanctum*) that represents Tulsi, the wife of Vishnu, whose various puranic stories flow together to become a popular symbol and token for domestic harmony and bodily healing. Inside the home, as well as in shops and workshops, many Hindus have a house altar that presents a combination of images from their village gods, tutelary beings, and *kuladevatā*. For all *ganvkār* who live in their traditional village, these *kuladevatā* are the same as the *ganvdevātā*, something that qualifies *ganvkār* to belong to the group of *mahājān*. Where *ganvkār* do not live in their traditional village and for all people who do not belong to the group of *ganvkār*, the *kuladevatā* are associated with another village from which the family claims its origin. It is not rare in Goa that families remember and regularly worship family gods that are associated with faraway places from where their great-grandparents or even further-distant ancestors once originated.

Ganvdevātā are typically seen as protectors or patrons of their villages and are praised for shielding the village community from natural disasters, illnesses, and social conflict. While the lordship and protective forces of village goddesses such as Sateri and Shanta Durga are usually associated with their iconographic display as "queens" armed with shields and swords, village gods such as Ravalnath and Buthnath are often seen as the "lords of the ghosts" and are praised for their control of *bhūta*, that is, "evil spirits." An especially notable iconography of Vetal shows him as an upright, larger-than-life naked male with explicit genitalia arguably symbolizing his procreative powers. Village gods are complemented and "assisted" in their protective functions by minor gods and tutelary beings. These are generically called *rakhne*, that is, "guardians," and are, as mentioned before, associated with locations in the village that are considered precarious or dangerous. Often marked by trees, rocks, images, or icons, the sites and shrines of *rakhne* usually show traces of the devotion that is paid to their divine residents, such as oil bottles, flowers, incense, rice grains, or flatbreads. Sometimes offerings reveal something about the identity of a deity that is not represented by any anthropomorphic image. Hence, bangles indicate a female deity and *vidī*, or local cigarettes, indicate a male one. Shrines may show a myriad of walking sticks indicating a minor gods that is known to be lame, or leather sandals indicating a god that constantly walks the territory with which he is associated. Some of the offerings also tell something about the particular powers attributed to the deities and about mimetic ways of evoking or acknowledging these powers. Hence, one can find shrines that display myriad miniature wooden cradles indicating that their deity is renowned for granting children, and others that show miniature replicas of specific body parts indicating that the deity is popular for healing arms, legs, or so on. Most commonly these replicas are part of mimetic practices by which people either try to evoke or, often after making respective vows, thank the deities for divine cures or the boon of children. Apart from the day-to-day and weekly routine of worship, the protective and therapeutic power of *ganvdevāta* is especially evoked and renewed at annual *jātra* or *utsav* festivals. These festivals are celebrated in grand style every year at a fixed date, combining elaborate rituals and ceremonies inside and outside the temple with a colorful fair offering paraphernalia, food and drink, simple consumer goods for sale, and various entertainments for children and adults. On these occasions, crowds of people come to the gorgeously decorated temple to pay homage and present their offerings to the village deities, often taking vows and asking the gods for blessings, oracles, and boons. As indicated by the name *jātra*, that is, "journey," temple festivals, as a rule, also suggest that the *ganvdevāta*—represented by a special *utsāvmūrti*, that is, a small portable image or icon; *tarang*, one or several richly decorated ritual batons; or *kolso*, that is, an earthen or copper vessel—are carried in festive chariots or palanquins through the village territory. Typically the *ganvdevāta* are visiting *śīmeveiḷe*, that is, tutelary beings associated with the village borders and shrines of ancestors and village gods in other parts of the village and, occasionally, in other villages, so their *jātra* can be seen as a bodily ritual assertion of the village territory and genealogical memory, as well as its social and family ties with other villages.

The Mahotsav festival in the town of Pernem (Pernem), which is annually performed at the occasion of Dusserah in the Hindu month of Ashvin (September-October), gives an idea of how *ganvdevāta* reflect the social organization of a village, mark its territory, and provide protection and healing to its population. This festival, which I attended in 1992, centers around three local deities—Bhagavati, Ravalnath, and Buthnath—who are honored and celebrated in grand style by the seven *ganvkār vangod* of the town. The *ganvkār* all belong to the local Kshatriya dynasty of Dessai, whose Dessai Deshprahbhu clan claims royal descent from the region of Sindudhurg in South Mahrarashtra and holds the first and highest *mān* in Pernem. After receiving offerings from each of the *ganvkār* families in the temple, the icons of the deities are carried in solemn procession through the town visiting various temples and shrines of associated deities and *purusha* (ancestors), as well as stopping at private houses for devotees to take their *darśana*, or blessing. After the Dessai *ganvkār*, members of the local castes of Sutar (carpenters) and Kumbar (potters) have the right to present offerings to the deities. On the night of the last day of the festival, the ceremonies are then taken over completely by members of the two artisanal castes who, acting as *guranv* or non-Brahmanical priests, perform a ritual known as *Tin Combeachen Devpon*, literally the "Three Cocks Ritual." This ritual takes its name from the fact that three small cocks are immolated and their blood is spilled over cooked rice that is offered to the *tarang* of Ravalnath and Buthnath. At the moment of the offering, the *guranv* get the *bhār* and are possessed by the two deities, then take their *taranga* and carry them in a long procession through the streets, again visiting associated deities and ancestors and stopping at people's houses. Interestingly, among the sites visited this second time is the house of a former Muslim ruler of Pernem who, according to local myth, was defeated by the warrior god Ravalnath who nevertheless pays ritual homage to his former adversary every year. The journey of the deities lies at the heart of a story that suggests that the *taranga* of Bhagavati, the *ganvdevī* of Pernem and sister of Ravalnath, was also originally part of it. Conflict arose between the divine siblings about their ranking, however, in the course of which Ravalnath, who is said to have come with a group of Maratha from Maharashtra, banned his sister from the *jātra* by throwing her baton into a well. Although Bhagavati thus no longer takes part in the annual procession, the popular version of this story has it that each time the procession passes the well, the sounds of a drum can be heard from below. The ceremony ends when the deities return to their temple, at which point crowds of people are waiting to present to them persons, mostly women, who are allegedly haunted or possessed by "evil spirits." A dramatic scene develops during which the *guranv*—accompanied by fierce drum beating—rather rudely address the "patients," asking them to reveal the names of their spiritual tormentors. Eventually, the "patients" are permitted to eat from the sacrificial rice and released.

Another feature of *ganvdevāta* is that they are treated like social persons. Typically, village gods are seen as legal members of the village community and officially "own" the *devache bhat*, or "god's land," that is set aside for the building and maintenance of the temple. The gods also receive *jon*, that is, they partake like human *ganvkār* in the annual surplus achieved from the *ganvkārī* land and product. Village gods and tutelary beings are interrelated, thereby reproducing all kinds of hierarchical, functional, kinship, and neighborhood relationships common for the *ganv*. Social ranks and relationships of deities are usually reflected in their iconography and the differentiated ritual treatments they receive. While the icons of the *ganvdevāta* show the deities typically in the postures of kings, queens, or warriors, the iconic representation of minor tutelary beings portrays *rakhne* and *deunchār* typically dressed like herders or farmers equipped with torches, blankets, leather sandals, and walking sticks. This goes together with the widespread understanding that *ganvdevāta* act as "lords" or "village chiefs" who are said to "command" *rakhne* like "soldiers" or subordinates. Sometimes, relationships among deities may also be just functional, as in the case of a god who is said to be "mute," that is, who does not communicate with his devotees by way of an oracle or a possessed medium, and therefore talks through the oracle or medium of another god. Or relationships may be based on neighborhood, with deities in adjacent villages or territories honoring each other through visits or gifts on the occasion of festivals.

As we have seen in previous chapters, deities may also have "historical relationships" with each other, as in the case of deities who, in the sixteenth century, had been displaced from the areas of the Old Conquests to the New Conquests and today entertain relationships to deities in their old village. Very commonly, village deities are kin related and thus presented in their iconography and mythology as married couples, parents, offspring, or siblings. Most often, the ancient goddesses Sateri and Bhumika are seen as spouses or consorts of Vetal, Ravalnath, or Bhutnath. Usually, these kin relationships indicate regular and amicable interactions among the divine relatives, who pay ritual visits and send gifts to each other honoring each other's festivals and anniversaries. As the ceremonies in Pernem showed, however, it is also not at all rare that rituals and mythologies twining around divine kinship relations reveal and manifest animosities and conflict among the relatives. Hence, divine siblings, couples, fathers, and sons may be engaged in conflicts over their ranking, resent alleged neglect, or get into seemingly trivial domestic disputes that lead to permanent tensions, mutual sanctions, and even physical abuse. In fact, as Corinne Dempsey has suggested, the images and stories about the "rivalry and reliance" among divine siblings precisely epitomize the tragic ambiguity that characterizes especially the relations among people who are close to each other (1998). As is all too common among family members, neighbors, and people who share common interests and concerns, love and hate, friendship and hostility, care and ignorance are most closely related, and become more intense the closer people are.

There are many ways for *ganvdevāta* and their devotees to communicate with each other. One of the most dramatic is known as *bhār*, indicating that a god takes possession of a human medium. Here, too, images and icons play an important role insofar as they often trigger the possession, for instance, when a person is possessed by touching the *nāḷ* embodying an ancestor, or by placing the *kolso* that stands for a goddess on its head, or by carrying the *tarang* that represents a village god. The actual communication among deities and devotees is here usually carried out through *bharbharī bhāsā,* that is, the speaking in tongues of the possessed individual. Quite often this speech is not or only partially intelligible and therefore requires the interpretation of ritual specialists, priests, or village elders. The invocation of the *bhār* is therefore a common way of publicly taking on communal problems and finding reasons and solutions for conflicts or queries in the village. An illustrative case in point is a *bhār* possession that I witnessed in 1996 in a village in Bardez. The divine agent of this possession was a minor tutelary deity whose name indicates that he is associated with the productive but also ecologically precarious *khazān* land. The god has no particular icon but has manifested himself in an old tree, next to which he is venerated today in a small one-room temple. The coming of his *bhār* was part of a larger Satya Narayana *pujā* for the execution of which the people of the village had hired a number of *pujāri,* that is, Brahmanical priests. At the end of this ceremony, the *pujāri* stepped aside and the tutelary god was invoked by one of the villagers who for that purpose simply circled the tree. As a sign that the *bhār* has arrived, the medium beat his chest, raised his arms high in the air, and began to talk in a high voice. Then he took up a basket with rice and some coconuts and ran to one of the nearby lagoons. A couple of men ran behind him. Interestingly, the people called the basket with the rice and coconut offerings *bali,* which means "animal sacrifice" and may indicate that the tutelary god had earlier or at other occasions received blood offerings. After a while, the *bhār* returned and requested, again in a high voice, five more coconuts and *vido,* chewing tobacco. After receiving the requested gifts he climbed the tree and placed the tobacco there. A loud dialogue between the *bhār* and some village men began during which the deity complained about certain unwanted factions in the village community that had allegedly tried to establish separate meetings and rituals. He also complained that some people were not present at the ceremony. The dialogue became heated, and the *bhār* made indications that he wanted to run away, but was held back by some of the villagers. The god asked for yet more coconuts and, beating his chest violently, circled the tree a number of times. After that, the villagers brought in an elderly, frail-looking man who sat down under the tree. People took off the man's shirt, then the *bhār* placed a coconut in his trembling hands and firmly knocked his head while engaging him in a loud dialogue. The old man could be heard saying repeatedly *bandele, bandele,* "I am bound, I am bound," indicating that he was under the influence of some evil spirit. Then, on the command of the *bhār,* people tossed rice on the old man and gave him water to drink, after which he leaned backward with a perceptible gesture of relief, as if he wanted to fall asleep. After a while people helped the old man to get up and took him back to his house. The *bhār,* for his part, circled the tree one more time then threw himself onto the ground, and the possession was over. After the session, the villagers, men and women, were quite agitated and talked at length about the happening. The fact that the deity had asked for more coconuts and attempted to run away was considered a sign that he was seriously discontented, and they expressed concern that this might have unwanted consequences for the village. It was considered a good sign, though, that the god had freed the old man from "a bad spirit" troubling him. Eventually the people agreed that in the near future, the *dhājan,* literally "the ten," that is, the village council, should meet and talk.

Patron Saints

Although imported from, if not imposed by, Christian missionaries and, for the most part, originating from the list of canonizations authorized by the Catholic Church in Rome, patron saints have become an intrinsic part of Goan religiosity. The story of St. Anthony of Siolim who, through his intricate encounter with the local god Vetal, gained an entirely new and local iconography and identity is an expressive case of local adaptation, but certainly not a singular one. The most widespread and popular Goan adaptation of Catholic sainthood is arguably related to the name or title Saibini Mai. Combining the Arabic-Persian notion of *sahiba* for "mistress" with the Konkani-Portuguese term *mai* for "mother," Saibini Mai is in Goa not only a honorific title and a common form of address for every incorporation of the Virgin Mary or Mother of God but also one for every Devi or Hindu goddess. It is outmatched in intimacy of devotional address only by local devotees' addressing the Catholic Mary or Hindu Devi simply as *tu,* "you," or *ti,* "she," thereby articulating her status as a member of the village community. All over Goa, the Catholic Mary in her multiple incorporations as Our Lady of the Rosary, Our Lady of the Mount, Our Lady of Good Guidance, Our Lady of Miracles, and so on, is thus addressed and worshipped under the same title of Saibini Mai that is used to call upon and pay homage to the Hindu Devi under her multiple manifestations as Sateri, Bhumika, Kelbai, Shanta Durga, and so forth. The mediating principle is arguably a common conceptualization and embodiment of female divinity or sainthood that renders comparable and even interchangeable the Virgin Mary and the Independent Durga, the Loving Mother of Christ and the Devoted Wife of Mahadev, the Catholic village patroness whose personal intercession before God guarantees grace for her villagers and the Hindu *ganvdevi* whose embodiment of the village soil stands for the protection and well-being of the entire village.

What *ganvdevāta* are thus to Goan Hindus, patron saints are to Goan Catholics. Similarities and affinities among gods and saints are most notable in the nature of their manifestation and in the material substances, bodily attitudes, and ritual practices used in their worship and devotion. If Sateri–Shanta Durga–Saibini Mai, whose body, the anthill, embodies the soil of her village, is considered the archetypical Hindu village goddess of Goa, then St. Francis Xavier, also known as Goencho Saib, the Lord of Goa, whose mummified body is kept in the

Basilica of Bom Jesus in Old Goa, is the archetypical Catholic patron saint. From the myriad manifestations, images, statues, and monograms of patron saints that can be seen all over Goa, St. Francis Xavier's manifestation is certainly the most significant, because it is the most authentic of all religious icons, that is, a relic. Like the face of Christ imprinted on the celebrated Veil of Veronica that gave the pious lady the name of *vera iconica,* "true icon," the trace left behind by St. Francis Xavier marks the most genuine of all Catholic icons in Goa, which his devotees simply refer to as *kudh,* the body, thereby implying that the corporeal presence of the saint stands for the protection and well-being of all Goa (see figure 4.2).

"Xavier's holy presence in Asia . . . was particularly propitious to the Portuguese," notes Ines Županov. "Whatever he touched became a mark on the map of Portuguese possessions" (1995: 149). Not surprisingly, the belief in the miraculous power of St. Francis Xavier's body has been nurtured by the agents of the Padroado themselves. After his death and burial on Shangchuan Island in China in 1552, Francis Xavier's canonization was promoted by the Jesuits (Gade 1996). Apart from a series of miracles attributed to the saint *in spe* during his lifetime, the central theological argument for his canonization was that his dead body, which was exhumed a couple of months after his burial, miraculously resisted decay. It had "the semblance more of life than of death," Jose de Lucena, his first biographer, reported about the official examination of the sacred relic in 1600 (Azevedo 1984: 11). The miraculous fame of the so-called incorruptible body of Francis Xavier was reasserted once more when this body, after having been interred for another couple of months in a church in Malacca and exhumed for a second time, arrived in Goa in 1554. A letter written by Nunes Barreto, the Jesuit vice-provincial, describing to Ignatius of Loyola the arrival of the body in Old Goa transmits an idea of the effect this had on Goans:

> All the people, I think more than five or six thousand, did not want to leave the church without being shown the body and we showed it to them. People's devotion and admiration was huge: some were weeping, others beat themselves asking God for forgiveness of their sins, others made all efforts to touch . . . the body of the benevolent Father. . . . Before Sunday night we had to take [the body] inside because we were anxious of [so much] devotion of people, but even there we could not close the doors of the church till the middle of the night. (Schrimpf 1996: 120)

In Goa, the fame of the miraculous relic grew and led to a series of official mutilations executed to facilitate the distribution of parts of the sacred body to various places in the world. Thus, Claudio Aquaviva (1543–1615), the Superior General of the Society of Jesus, ordered in 1614 to sever Francis Xavier's entire right arm and to send the lower arm and hand to Rome, where it went to the

Figure 4.2. St. Francis Xavier, Old Goa. Photograph by Gasper D'Souza.

mother church of the Jesuits, while three other parts were sent to Jesuit churches in Cochin, Malacca, and Macau. The event became notorious above all through legends reporting that the amputation had caused profuse bleeding of the mummy. Twelve years later, the body was mutilated again, when all its internal organs were removed and apportioned to churches all over the globe. After 1622, the year of Francis Xavier's canonization, his body became the object of more or less regular exhibitions, at which it was openly presented to worshippers in Goa. At one of these occasions, the body was mutilated yet another time when a pious Portuguese lady, whose name is handed down as Dona Isabel Caron, obviously eager to possess a part of the precious relic herself, bit off the small toe of his right foot while pretending to kiss the feet of the mummified saint (Azevedo 1984). Since 1952, the body is no longer openly presented to worshippers but only shown behind the glass of a silver sarcophagus. Even then and to this day, thousands of devotees, both Catholic and Hindu, regularly come to see the saint at his annual feast day and especially his ten-year death anniversary, expressing their faith in the miraculous power of *kudh,* the body. Stories abound in Goa of people who have been miraculously healed or received boons after making a vow to St. Francis Xavier and touching the shrine of his sacred body. In one celebrated miracle, he saved Goa from destruction at the moment of its liberation by the Indian army in 1961, as told by Nora Seco de Souza: "If General Vassalo de Silva, the last Governor General of Goa, did not obey Salazar's orders, at the peril of his own life, and raze this territory to the ground, it was due to the intervention of St. Francis who saved us all from death and destruction" (De Souza n.d.: 8).

Every ten years, at the occasion of the annual death anniversary of the saint in December, the relic is presented for a special exhibition. In 1994, the sarcophagus with the saint's body was lowered from its elevated position in the Basilica of Bom Jesus for that purpose and was transferred to the more spacious Se Cathedral in Old Goa, where it was accessible for devotees for a period of one month. The Goan archdiocese styled the event as a special instance of India's "unity in diversity" and invited representatives from all regions and religious communities of India to take part in the solemn procession that carried the relic to its temporary abode. For the more than 100,000 pilgrims, most of them Goan Catholics and Hindus, who in the following days and weeks came to patiently line up in order to use the rare opportunity to come close, touch, and kiss the precious container with the relic, the event was clearly a touching experience associated with the idea of partaking in the blessing and protection of Goench Saib, the Lord of Goa (Dias 1993). "The passionate love of Goans, mainly but not exclusively Christian, for *Amcho Saib*, is there for all to see and taste. The Saint does indeed lord it over the minds and hearts of all those who claim any kind of association with this tiny parcel of land in the western coast of India," writes the Goan Lucia da Veiga Coutinho but, then, pauses and ponders where this particular local sympathy may come from, given the fact that the celebrated "Apostle of the East" had actually spent only a few months in Goa. "It is not the living Xavier," he eventually concludes, "but rather his dead body that seems to have built up the unbreakable relationship between him and us" (Veiga Coutinho 1994: 23).

Not all Goan villages have relics of their patron saints, but in all villages the patron saints are related in a special way to the village and its people. As mentioned earlier, popular Catholic religiosity was and is guided in Goa by a "localistic principle" that closely associates saints with the territories and localities of their villages. Following this principle, two categories of saints are distinguished: *santos titulares,* the actual patron saints, whose major iconographic representation can be found in the main village church, and *santos minores,* other saints, whose images and icons are placed in chapels that are associated with the main church and scattered in the various wards of the village or town. As a rule, the social patronage of patron saints and other saints for churches and chapels reflects, to some extent, the social hierarchies in the villages. The number of associated saints and chapels, though, depends not only on the prosperity of their patrons but also on the popularity of the saints themselves. Hence, Mapusa, the capital of Bardez, for instance, whose main church is dedicated to the arguably most popular Goan saint after St. Francis Xavier, Our Lady of the Miracles, has eight associated chapels. These are Flight of Our Lady to Egypt in Cuchelim, St. Sebastian in Corlim, Our Lady of Carmel in Camarcassana, Our Lady of Miracles in Horta, Holy Cross or Jesus the Redeemer in Angod, St. Joseph in Ansabhat, Holy Cross in Gauncavaddo, and St. Francis Xavier in Duler (Azevedo 1985: 100).

Both patron saints and other saints are also represented in myriad wayside crosses and shrines located inside and outside of villages. Like their counterparts the Hindu shrines, these Catholic markers and shrines vary widely in shape and are predominantly placed at central locations, such as village plazas and marketplaces, and peripheral and liminal locations, such as the borders between villages or between the settled and cultivated land and the forests, as well as at riverbanks, seashores, bridges, dams, crossroads, and hilltops. The most common and widespread Catholic landmarks are *khuris,* crosses. *Khuris* may vary from simple whitewashed stone crosses to gated and roofed structures of metal or stone housing crosses that may be elevated on altarlike tables and are usually richly ornamented with tiles, colors, images, and icons. Typically patronized and maintained by people from the vicinity, the architectural equipment of *khuris* depends again on their popularity and may in some cases compete in size even with established churches. A case in point is Fulancho Khuris, the Flower Cross, which is located next to Goa's Highway Number 17 at the entrance of Pajim city. Patronized by well-to-do middle-class urban and labor migrant groups, Fulancho Khuris gained its fame for working miracles from its location at Goa's major traffic artery and near the largest hospital of the state. Having been continuously remodeled and enlarged since 1990, it today is the size of a basilica with room for several hundred worshippers. While many *khuris* are associated with particular saints, certain crosses carry their own agency. Fulancho Khuris is one example, as is Santa Cruz, the holy cross that figures as the patron saint of a large village of the same name near Panjim. Interestingly, devotees also address these crosses with personalized salutations, calling them, for instance, *tu,* you, or *to,* him, thereby acknowledging both their intimate status as a member of the community and their independent agency. Frequently marking conspicuous and liminal locations, Catholic crosses and shrines are often located in close vicinity, side by side, or back to back with Hindu *gumpti* and shrines, and, not rarely, icons and images of Hindu gods and Catholic saints can be found in one and the same shrine. Interestingly, though, people's offerings, as a rule, unmistakably indicate the religious identity of the divine or saintly beings to whom they are addressed. Hence, candles, fruits, and cigarettes mostly indicate Catholic saints, and oil-lamps, incense sticks, rice grains, *vidī,* and *vido* usually indicate Hindu gods and tutelary beings.

Again, copying and paralleling Hindu *ganvdevāta* and tutelary beings, Catholic *santos titulares* and *santos minores* are seen as protectors and benefactors of their villages, and in general are associated with the well-being of the villagers. Some saints, such as St. Francis Xavier in Old Goa and Our Lady of the Miracles in

Mapusa, are famed for their miraculous powers far beyond their regions. Others, such as Nossa Senhora da Boa Viagem, Our Lady of Safe Journey, in Margao or Nossa Senhora da Saude, Our Lady of Health, in Cortalim, are known for specific forms of protection or healing. Apart from day-to-day and weekly veneration, the protective and therapeutic powers of saints are most emphatically evoked during the annual feast days of the local churches. At these occasions, the icons and images of Christ, the Virgin Mary, and saints are usually made accessible to be touched, kissed, and receive offerings, and are carried through the streets to bless the people standing in front of their houses offering candles and flowers. These are also occasions when many Hindus salute the Catholic saints with oil-lamps, flowers, and devotional gestures. In autumn, Novi Konchi marks a special festival when the patron saints' icons are carried into the fields to bless the new rice, which is cut by the priest and the *ganvkār,* thereby initiating the harvesting season. The iconic presence of Catholic saints is as overwhelming in the public and private spheres of villages and towns as the presence of Hindu gods. Typically, Catholic homes, shops, and workshops are marked by crosses and house altars displaying saints' icons, and the monograms and images of saints can also be found on and in countless cars, taxis, buses, and boats. Obviously relying on a common principle of spaces and locations that are to be marked and protected by divine or saintly forces, Hindu and Catholic icons and monuments can indeed be said to compete over space and place in the Goan village.

The icons, images, crosses, shrines, and other manifestations of the saints are thus directly involved in the expression and transference of the agency of their saintly prototypes. Many manifestations are said to be self-generated, like the ever-recurring apparitions of the Virgin Mary in Goa, or invested with miraculous powers in their own right, like Fulancho Khuris, the miracle-working cross, or the image of St. Anthony of Siolim that killed the snake. As a rule, images and manifestations of saints are sensually consumed rather than intellectually comprehended, and the trust, devotion, respect, and fear that people have for them are enacted in palpable gestures more than articulated in abstract expressions of belief or faith. In other words, the icons and manifestations need to be seen, heard, smelled, touched, carried around, possibly eaten, and involved in mimetic actions, such as the offering of wax replicas of body parts and baby dolls, in order to become effective and induce blessings, prosperity, healing, and children. In fact, Catholic saints in Goa may even interact with their devotees, just like Hindu deities, by taking possession of a medium, as Robert Newman reported in the context of a Marian apparition in the home of Antonio, a poor laborer in the village Velim (Salcete) in 1987:

> When Antonio [the man who had the vision of Mary] complained to two women that people made fun of the Holy Mother and did not believe in her, the older woman suddenly fell on her knees, folded her hands and said aloud in Konkani, "Who is making fun of me? They do not know who I am. I am

Our Lady of Vailankanni!" Onlookers were "dumbfounded and terrified." The woman trembling violently, spoke again, demanding all should kneel and pray with her. Finally she commanded, "I am tired. Anyone among you recite the remaining Hail Marys." When that was done she repeatedly told them to pray to her and collapsed on the floor. When the woman was revived she could not recall her experience. (Newman 2001: 155)

Our Lady of Miracles in Mapusa

Syncretistic practices between Hindus and Catholics are most explicit and articulate at the annual apex of local religiosity during temple and church festivals. In this final section, I analyze two local festivals that have become especially well-known and popular, regularly drawing large crowds from both the Hindu and Catholic communities. These are the church feast of Nossa Senhora dos Milagres in the town of Mapusa (Bardes) and the village festival called Jagar/Zagor in the village of Siolim (Bardes).

The annual feast of Nossa Senhora dos Milagres, also known as Our Lady of the Miracles, the Catholic Mary of Mapusa, falls on the Monday after the second Sunday after Easter. On this day, thousands of people, Catholics as well as Hindus, come to Mapusa to receive blessings from Milagres, as most people simply call her, and to visit the big fair that traditionally accompanies the feast. At the fair, which is set up right at Igroz Vado, the Church Ward, several dozen stalls hawk cheap garments, kitchenware, toys, music, trendy "oil paintings," video discs, cell phone covers, soft drinks, milk tea, and sweets. Grinding stones from Bicholim and Portuguese-style furniture from Salcete are at a special sale during the Milagres feast. Another commodity sold in grand style are Catholic devotional images and paraphernalia showing the Sacred Heart of Jesus, the Virgin Mary of Lourdes, the Mother of God with Baby Jesus, Our Lady of Vailankanni, and other popular saints such as Sebastian, Michael, and Francis Xavier. A notable curiosity here and at other Catholic church feasts is the fact that the image stalls always also offer some images of Hindu saints or gods that are either especially popular, such as Shirdi Sai Baba, or show iconographic motifs that resonate in the Catholic tradition, such as Baby Krishna. The devotion for Milagres culminates when hundreds of people attend the masses that are read throughout the day in the church, and thousands patiently queue in long lines before the statues of the saint displayed in the churchyard to offer their individual prayers, vows, and offerings. Known especially for her power and readiness to heal people, grant them children, and respond to their personal requests, Milagres is one of the most popular saints in Goa today, next only to St. Francis Xavier and Our Lady of Vailankanni. Most commonly, devotees pose requests for her by making a *promesa* or *angon*, that is, a vow. A traditional formula for making a vow to the saint is *Hanv borim zalim zalear bhik magaon tuji angon farik kortelim,* which translates as, "If I get cured, I vow to beg alms for you" (De Souza and D'Souza 1987). This meant in the old days that a devotee whose request was fulfilled would compensate the favor by placing him- or herself in the churchyard and beg with a *kotti* or coconut shell for alms, which were then given to the church. In modern days, though, begging has become a less popular compensation for received boons, and people are more likely to oblige Milagres either by performing certain devotional services or ascetic exercises, such as praying rosaries or keeping periods of fasting, or by making offerings, such as candles, oil, or money.

A particular offering that illustrates, once again, the mimetic relationship that is so common in interactions with Hindu deities and that is therefore presented to Milagres by both Catholics and Hindus, is miniature wax replicas of human bodies, body parts, or babies given to plead or thank for the healing of specified illnesses or the granting of children. Other offerings, however, show that, notwithstanding their common worship of the saint, Hindus and Catholics do traditionally keep certain distinctions and distances between each other. Hence, there are two statues of the saint placed in the churchyard for personal worship, one for Catholics who offer and burn candles and another for Hindus who present small cups of coconut oil that is then poured over the saint's icon. The two statues of Milagres show the same iconography—the Mother of God holding Baby Jesus in her arms—but for obvious technical reasons have slightly different forms and arrangements. Thus, the statue for Catholics has an adjacent candle stand, while the one for Hindus has a special device to gather the oil poured over it. A notable recent observation is that, while this division between Catholics and Hindus was strictly observed in the past, today one can occasionally also see a Catholic offering oil or a Hindu presenting candles to Milagres.

Milagres's fame as a great miracle worker is of course expressed in her very name. In fact, there is historical evidence that she was first known as Nossa Senhora de Todos os Bens, that is, Our Lady of All Blessings, but in response to her frequent miraculous interventions on behalf of her devotees, she was renamed Nossa Senhora dos Milagres. It is also said that after becoming Milagres, she outdid in popularity St. Jerome, the official patron saint of Mapusa (Furtado 1985). The earliest historical mentions of Milagres go back to Henrique Bravo de Morais, Dean of the Se Cathedral of Old Goa, who, in his *Noticias do Arcebispado de Goa* of 1722, wrote about the great devotion that was paid to Mary of Mapusa (Azevedo 1985: 96). Like other churches in the provinces of the Old Conquests, there are indications that the oldest church of Mapusa, which was built by Franciscan monks in 1594, was located on or near the site of an ancient Hindu shrine or temple, which is said to have been dedicated to the goddess Tulsi. Archaeologist Ricardo Michael reports finding ancient architectonical fragments in the church showing "carvings of figures of Indian mythology" and even a golden necklace in the form of a lotus flower. The necklace, it is said, adorned until recently the statue of Milagres at her annual feast day (quoted in De Souza and D'Souza 1987: 33).

For Goans the reason for the syncretistic worship dedicated to Milagres becomes self-evident through a local myth. This myth relates that Milagres is one of seven divine sisters, six of whom are identified as the Hindu goddesses Lahirai, Mahamai, Kelbai, Adipai, Morzai, and Sita. The seventh, the goddess Mirabai, it is said, was converted to Christianity by the *firanghis,* that is, "foreigners" and became the Milagres of Mapusa. Five of Milagres's Hindu sisters are venerated in Goan temples today: Lahirai in Shirgao (Bicholim), Mahamai in Mulgao (Bicholim), Kelbai in Mayem (Bicholim), Adipai on the Island of Anjediva, and Morzai in Morjim (Pernem), while Sita, the sixth sister, is said to have disappeared into *patal,* the Hindu netherworld. The seven sisters, the myth goes on, have one brother, Khetoba or Khetro, who in a domestic conflict was kicked so hard by one of his sisters that he became lame. He is venerated today as a minor deity in the village of Chopdem (Pernem) (Saldanha 1912). Milagres has a special relationship with her sister Lahirai, from whom she traditionally receives one *kolso,* that is, one copper vessel of oil, on the day of her feast. Lahirai is the village goddess of Shirgao who, for her part, has the widespread fame of being *jāgṛit,* that is, responsive to her devotees' requests, and therefore is celebrated in grand style at the day of her annual festival on the fifth day of the Hindu month of Vaishaka (April-May). On this day, Lahirai is worshipped by thousands of devotees, mostly Hindus and a few Catholics, who seek the blessing of the deity not only through prayers and offerings but also and more dramatically by participating in a nightly ceremony of fire walking described by R. G. Pereira:

> The Dhonds [devotees] dance around the pyre with mounting enthusiasm, shouting loudly to the rhythm of the drums, drenched in sweat, like real possessed beings. It is a moment of great frenzy and general excitement.... At a given time and signal, all the Dhonds jump into the pyres . . . and they run through it in large strides, one followed by another, exhausted by the fatigue and excitement which overcome them. The last to pass it is the Modd [non-Brahmanical priest] with the Kollos [insignia of the goddess Lahirai] and thus ends the great sacrifice. (Pereira 1978: 144ff.)

The family relationship between the saint and goddess is reaffirmed when Milagres, on the occasion of the Shirgao festival, traditionally sends a basket of Mogari (jasmine) flowers to Lahirai.

The formula of the Seven Divine Hindu Sisters, one of whom converts and becomes the Catholic Mary of Mapusa, gives the closest insight into how the local people conceptualize the syncretistic worship of Milagres Saibini. This formula is widespread in Hindu mythology and resonates with the puranic theme of Saptamatrikas, or "Seven Mothers," who, according to legend, helped the Great Goddess to defeat two demons named Sumbha and Nisumbha. Taunted by her adversaries that she needed the power of so many other women to fight them, the Goddess answers, "I am one. Where in this world is there another besides me? Look, o evil one, as these manifestations of mine enter back into me. Then all the *śakthīs* disappear into the body of the goddess and she alone defeats Sumbha" (Erndl 1993: 27). The formula of the Seven Sisters, in other words, stands for the idea of the formless and all-embracing nature of the Goddess who manifests herself in many *śakthī pīṭhās,* that is, "places of power." In Goa, though, and arguably in local contexts and myth in other parts of India too, the formula of the Seven Sisters also expresses a more reified and palpable notion of togetherness that finds its articulation in the idiom of genealogy, kinship, and family relations. Here, the formula stands for the idea that gods, like people, are kin related with each other; that kin-groups trace their relationships and descent from genealogical ties with common ancestors; and that families hold together by blood ties and family solidarity. The formula of the Seven Sisters is arguably embedded not only in the notion of the Hindu Devi as Mother, Independent Women, and Loving Wife, but also has its mythological grounding in the common theme of God as King whose dynasty is carried on and defended by clans of sons, brothers, and cousins. The story of Milagres Saibini of Mapusa is buttressed here by Corinne Dempsey's work on the relationship and syncretistic intersection between Hindus and Syrian Christians in Kerala showing that the idiom of kinship, genealogy, and family relations expands beyond Hinduism and constitutes commonality and syncretism on an interreligious level (1998). Interestingly, though, family relationship does not only stand for harmony and solidarity, but also expresses tensions, conflicts, and at times even rupture. As in the case of Bhagavati of Pernem, who is kicked out of the local pantheon by her brother Ravalnath, the story of the Seven Sisters of Mapusa mentions conflict among the sisters and their brother Khetro that even leads to violence and physical damage. Notably, tension can also be felt in the relationship between Milagres and her sister Lahirai. Hence, it is considered a dangerous omen that requires particular ritual precautions if the feast days of Milagres and Lahirai happen to fall on the same day. Whenever this occurred in the past, local mythology reports, something bad happened such as in 1910 with a fire breaking out in the church. As Dempsey's title—"Rivalry, Reliance, and Resemblance: Siblings as Metaphor for Hindu-Christian Relations in Kerala State"—cogently articulates, the family relationship that binds the gods together entails both harmony and conflict.

The Siolim Jagar/Zagor

Another festival that enjoys great popularity among Hindus and Catholics in Goa is the Jagar/Zagor festival of the village of Siolim (Bardes). This festival—to which Hindus refer as Jagar and Catholics as Zagor—marks a form of festive night vigil that combines religious ritual, invocation, and sacrifice, with joyful entertainment, singing, dancing, and acting on a kind of stage. Its practitioners come from two caste (*jāti*) groups: *mundkār* or *render*, that is, (former) agricultural tenants, and *kharvi*, that is, fishermen, both of which are ranked as Sudra in the classical *varnā* system. Today, most of them earn their livelihoods partly from traditional occupations such as toddy-tapping, agriculture, and fishing and partly from jobs or small businesses in the modern sector or as migrant workers in the Arabian Gulf countries. The central focus of the devotion and ludic performances of the festival are Jagoryo, a local Hindu tutelary god, and St. Anthony, the patron saint of Siolim. The simultaneous invocation of Catholic saints and Hindu deities is not unusual and can be found in Jagar ceremonies in other Goan villages too. What makes the Siolim Jagar special and unique is that, here, Hindus and Catholics jointly participate in the religious functions and ludic performances and also constitute the interreligious crowd of devotees and spectators that come for the festival every year. More precisely, until the mid-1990s, the ritual and ludic functions were subdivided and shared by two Hindu and seven Catholic families giving roughly equal rights to both communities in that the function of the main singer was performed by a member of a Hindu family and the function of the main actor was performed by a member of a Catholic family. After that time, though, the nationwide political upswing of Hindu nationalism made itself felt in Goa and Siolim and affected the ceremonies, which, though still jointly organized and performed by Hindus and Catholics, became more controlled by Hindus. Hence, today, Hindus are in the lead of the ceremonies and also have assumed two more of the stage characters that traditionally had been performed by Catholics.

Nonetheless, the Hindu-Catholic collaboration in the Siolim ceremonies has always been dynamic and looks back to a complex history. Historical and ethnographical evidence shows that the "Hindu origins" of the festival, which arguably were themselves part of longstanding tensions between demotic and sanskritic trends in the formation of Hinduism, underwent crucial changes in the sixteenth and seventeenth centuries, when Jesuit missionaries replaced the references made in the central ritual invocation to Hindu gods with ones to the Christian Trinity and Catholic saints, thereby assimilating the festival into Catholic liturgy. To this day, the ceremony is associated with the feast day of the local Catholic patron saint Our Lady of Guidance, which falls on the Monday after the first Sunday after Christmas. In the mid-eighteenth century, the Jesuit assimilation policy was dropped, however, and the Zagor ceremony was banned as allegedly a "barbaric entertainment" and "pagan reminiscence." Following this time, the ceremony turned into a clandestine and subversive spectacle, which successfully resisted attempts at its suppression and eradication by the Portuguese-Catholic regime and, finally, in the early twentieth century, after the "return of Hindus" to the Old Conquests, was revived and henceforth jointly celebrated by Hindus and

Catholics (Henn 2003). Chapter 5 provides a more detailed elaboration of this larger historical background; here we focus on the peculiar circumstances that frame and facilitate its syncretistic expressions and practices today.

In recent years, the popularity of the Siolim Jagar has grown continuously, to the point that today the festival is famed far beyond Siolim's boundaries and attracts thousands of pilgrims and spectators every year. Various circumstances contribute to this enormous popularity. One is that, unique among all Jagar festivals in Goa, the ceremony in Siolim focuses on a local tutelary deity who, famous for his responsiveness to his devotees and willingness to fulfill their requests for protection, healing, and prosperity, is known as Jagoryo, a name that may be translated as the "Awaken" or the "Alert." In Siolim, in other words, the Jagar has been reified into a unique Jagar god. Historical evidence suggests that this happened around the year 1930, when local Hindus became part of the then-Catholic festival, thereby helping it to resist the attempts of eradication by the local church. Today, devotees come long before the actual night ceremony starts and line up in long queues before Jagoryo's shrine, a typical *gumpti* or grotto-shaped shelter adorned by a simple oil lamp and the Om sign. The shrine is placed on an altarlike table that itself is located on an elevated plateau in the spacious roofed hall, which is open at three sides and also functions as the stage for the performance. Devotees come to present offerings, ask for boons, and receive blessings from the famed local god. Offerings entail myriads of bottles of coconut oil, candles, flowers, and gifts of mostly minor sums of money, which are accepted by *ghaddi* or local priests who also mediate the devotees' requests by uttering short prayerlike invocations to the god. Demonstrating again that common worship and syncretism in no way means that people are uncertain about or even blur their religious identities, it is important to note that Hindus and Catholics as a rule make different offerings—oil for the former and candles for the latter—and, in general, act as distinct groups. In fact, it is against the background of a politically and demographically strengthening Hinduism in contemporary Goa that even certain tensions between the two religious groups can be felt in recent times.

Starting around midnight and lasting until daybreak, the performances present a series of five *songe*, that is, dramatic characters, whose songs, costumes, and, to some extent, dance steps are prescribed by *kaido*, that is, tradition. These are *Sayeed*, the town-crier and clown; *Firanghi Raja*, the foreign king; *Maloni*, the gardeners; *Bhovor*, the tutelary god himself; and *Mhar ani Mharin*, the Dalit and his wife. Unique again among Goan Jagar ceremonies, the performance of these traditional characters is interrupted in Siolim by several hours of free entertainment. These are filled by an annually changing program of *tiatr*, a Goan genre of commercial folk theater that is especially popular among Catholics and favors tragic-comic skits from everyday life. In the 1990s, when I did most of my research in the region, the Siolim Jagar became especially popular because its entertainment portion included brief guest performances by Remo Fernandes, an internationally renowned rock star, whose ancestral house happens to be located in Siolim.

Although the popularity of its entertainment is not unimportant for the villagers engaged in the Jagar—certainly not least because of the considerable returns it provides in terms of money and media attention—the actual significance of the festival clearly lies in its traditional parts and religious meanings. In order to appreciate these perspectives, it is important to see how the ceremonies generate and stage a village cosmos in which people, supernatural beings, and sacred sites of both the Hindu and the Catholic community are brought together. By tradition, a senior Hindu acts as *ovio munti* or lead singer for the invocation of saints and gods, and, since recently, another Hindu dances *Bhovor*, the tutelary god on stage. Other ritual functions on stage and in the group of musicians and chorus singers are divided more or less equally between Hindus and Catholics. A similar Hindu-Catholic pattern is enacted for the redistribution of the offerings that Jagoryo receives at his shrine, which are divided into four parts. One full part goes to the temple of Sateri, the ancient village goddess of Siolim, and another one to Khazonio, an important Hindu tutelary god whose shrine is located in the ward in which the Jagar is performed and who is looked after by Hindu families that are active in the festival. Half a part goes each to the chapels of St. Anne and St. Francis Xavier, both of which are located in the area and are maintained by Catholic families who are functionaries in the festival. Another full part finally goes to the Christian family on whose property the old Jagoryo shrine is located, at which the rehearsals for the festival traditionally take place.

The complex network of people, supernatural beings, and ritual sites that the Jagar generates and enacts are complemented by the various rituals that are part of the festival. One of these is *parob*, the opening of the Jagar season that is held about a month before the actual festival. This ritual is performed outside in the fields where rustic offerings of *rot* (flatbread), *sorro* (palm-liquor), and *karyaco* (dried fish) are presented to Khazonio, Karoba, Daroba, Musonio, and Mataro Azo, all of whom are tutelary gods or have the status of ancestors, and are known and respected for guarding and protecting the fields and boundaries of Guddem and Dando, the two wards of Siolim, in which the ceremonies take place. Khazonio, the guardian of the diked *khazan* land, has a particular role in the *parob* ritual, since he is the one who speaks for Jagoryo, who himself is said to be voiceless. Hence, it is Khazonio whose *bhar* takes possession of a member of one of the Catholic families and, while calling open the season of the Jagar, may also articulate concerns, conflicts, or other issues of importance for the community.

At the day of the festival, the ceremonies start at Jagoryo's old shrine, a *gumpti* located under an old Banyan tree, where the Hindu leader surrounded by all functionaries makes offerings and invokes Sateri, the village goddess, and the local tutelary deities, asking for success for the festival. Thereafter, the Catholic leader prays and asks St. Anthony and other local saints for their blessing at the house altar of the adjacent Catholic house. Two *zuvari,* or torch-lit processions of functionaries, special guests, and neighbors, then start for Jagoryo's new shrine located in the nearby festival hall, one stopping and performing prayers on its way at a chapel of St. Anne, the other at a chapel of St. Francis Xavier. Once arrived in the festival hall, which by then is filled and surrounded by thousands of spectators, the festival begins with the *nomana,* that is, the invocation of the Christian Trinity and Virgin Mary traditionally sung by the Hindu leader:

> First homage (*noman*) to God Father, first homage to God Father (*devā papa*),
> Second homage to God's Son, second homage to God's Son (*devā sutā*),
> Third homage to the Holy Spirit, third homage to the Holy Spirit (*ispirita santa*),
> God is All One, God is All One (*sarvay devā ekuch re*),
> Hail and homage to the Redeemer, Hail and homage to the Redeemer (*Salvador*),
> Homage to Mary's Son, homage to Mary's Son (*Mariyecya kunvarā*),
> Oh Graceful One, oh Merciful One, oh Graceful One, oh Merciful One (*kṛupānidhe karuṇākarā*),
> Jesus Christ is the King, Jesus Christ is the King (*Jesukrista rāyā re*),
> Gratefulness to You, Our Lady, Gratefulness to You, Our Lady (*ārgā dita tuka Saibini*),
> Heavenly Mother of God, Heavenly Mother of God (*Devāce Māi svargiṇī*),
> You are the Queen of Angels, You are the Queen of Angels (*āṇj bāḍāvān tu re rānī*),
> Virgin Mother, God has come, Virgin Mother, God has come (*āṅkvar māi, iśvar jhāḷā*),
> From heavenly God the Angel has come, From heavenly God the Angel has come (*devā svargico, bāḍāvān jhāḷā*),
> He stands before you, Mother, he stands before you, Mother (*tujyā mukhār māi ubha raula*),
> He announces joy and happiness, Mother, He announces joy and happiness, Mother (*sukh ani saṇtoṣ, māi, saṇgu lāglā re*).

After this invocation, the performances onstage begin with a comic dialogue between Sayeed, the clown and village crier, dressed in frazzled trousers and a tall pointed hat, and Firanghi Raja, the Foreign King, in aristocratic costume with crown and sword. The two abuse and make fun of each other, and the king eventually threats to "shoot" Sayeed. After Sayeed has left the stage, Firanghi Raja starts a serious monologue in which he calls upon Sant Anton, the Portuguese-born Franciscan monk and patron saint of Siolim, alluding to his conventional iconography showing him with the Bible in his arm on which Baby Jesus sits:

> Sant Anton, you saint of the foreign race (*bhaktā Firanghi kuḍīyecyā*),
> On your book, Baby Jesus plays, the King (*tujhya librar menīn Jesu rājā keltā*),
> Oh Lord God, Oh Lord God have mercy (*Senhor Deo, misericordia*).

The prayer to St. Anthony goes on with cryptic allusions to the *padri,* that is, "missionaries," and their coming from the sea, and Firanghi Raja, repeatedly squatting down and crossing himself, calls to "sing and pray," *voresanv kantār korī,* for Sant Anton. The performances continue with Maloni, the gardeners singing about the beautiful flowers in their garden, five garlands of which are eventually said to be prepared and presented, one each to Jesu; Saibā, that is, St. Francis Xavier; Bishpa, the Bishop; Raja, the King; and finally to the *sabhā,* that is, the assembly of all human and superhuman beings coming together and coming alive in the Jagar ritual and play.

The performances reach their apex when, announced by loud firecrackers, Bhovor, who is said to embody Jagoryo himself, comes onto the stage. Alluding in his name to the Konkani word for "rotating," Bhovor, wearing conspicuous headgear that is decorated with burning candles, slowly turns himself to the sound of the drums and cymbals that are winding up to a dramatic height. The song accompanying his appearance is particularly cryptic and enigmatic, and variously calls him *Ghadghadya,* a name that resonates with the Konkani word *ghaddi,* for shaman or priest, or *vācanaslele puruś,* that is, "voiceless ancestor," arguably recalling the fact that Jagoryo is said to be without voice, that is, does not communicate with his devotees through *kaul,* oracle, or *bhār,* possession. Reference is also made to Hindu mythology, in particular the Mahabharata epic, when Bhovor is equated with Bhimadev, one of the five martial brothers of the Pandava dynasty fighting to regain dominance over Bharat, the historical kingdom of India, and, in allusion to the insatiate appetite of the mythical hero, is said to eat "raw as well as cooked things," *harve te bhājūn khate.*

Bhovor's dramatic appearance marks the preliminary end of the traditional and ritually effective part of the ceremonies and is followed by the *tiatr* interlude. After this interlude, the festival—now slowly approaching daybreak—takes up the performance of the last and final of the traditional characters, that is, Mhar ani Mharin, the Dalit and his wife. These two sing about their traditional right to receive *sanna ani vanna,* two types of festive food specially prepared for the occasion, and also about their work removing dead cattle and preparing their hides. After this last performance on stage, the festival comes to its end with the Hindu leader, surrounded by all functionaries, reciting a final prayer in front of Jagoryo's shrine during which he variously addresses the tutelary god as *Swami Samesta,* Lord of the Assembly, and *Siolece Mul Purush,* Ur-Ancestor of Siolim.

> Oh, Lord of the Assembly, many people whose wishes you have granted have offered you flowers, oil, candles, and palm wine. Take these offerings and grant the wishes of those who have brought them. Help those who have to perform tasks and who made vows to you and all others who have gathered today. Your name has great fame and like that it shall be in the future. Forgive us if we have made mistakes. Give us your blessings and give us good health.

Places, Memories, and Bodies

Finally, in summarizing how the Goan *ganv* facilitates coexistence and syncretism between Hindus and Catholics, a striking analogy between Goa and South India comes to the fore. In both regions, it seems, the relationship between religious communities is based above all on an ancient village organization that connects political authority, economic redistribution, and ritual honors (Appadurai and Appadurai Breckenridge 1976; Stein 1975; Bayly 1989; Mosse 1994, 1997; Kaufmann 1982). Hence, David Mosse shows how in Tamil Nadu, the relationship between Hindus and Christians is framed by the interplay of the local caste system and the display of ranked ritual honors "allowing 'Hindu' forms of devotion in the worship of saints" during church festivals (Mosse 1994: 91). The historical model for the syncretistic intersection, Mosse argues, is an eighteenth-century Hindu patronage structure that supported Catholic churches and festivals through grants of land and other gifts. The entire system found its ostentatious display at the Christian Easter Sunday, when "the Hindu king (or his representative) arranged for the final procession of the image of the risen Christ in a huge ceremonial 'temple cart' (or *ter*) . . . and along with regional Maravar caste chiefs received 'first honour' marked by prestations of cloth and betel nut from the hand of the presiding Catholic priest" (ibid.: 88). Mutual ritual appreciations like these continued on and made the local Catholic Church part of a socio-ritual system that was acknowledged by both Hindus and Catholics as a ceremonial context in which caste and power relations were symbolized, validated, and, at times, also contested. This system only changed in the twentieth century when British missionaries imposed a strict separation of religion and politics, whereupon local priests were admonished to refuse the exchange of "betel honors" with Hindu village elders at the occasion of the church festival.

Susan Bayly describes a similar situation among the Christian Paravas on the Coromandel Coast in Tamil Nadu. Converted to Christianity by Portuguese missionaries in the early sixteenth century, she writes, "Christianity became a caste lifestyle" for Paravas, and Our Lady of Tuticorin, an incorporation of the Catholic Virgin whose icon had reached India from Manila in 1555, and Francis Xavier, who had visited the Coromandel Coast around the same time, became their "caste tutelaries" (Bayly 1989: 331). Advancing by the mid-seventeenth century to become a prosperous trading elite, the Parava caste organization developed a complex internal status system whose rankings and privileges closely resembled that of a Hindu "little kingdom":

> The scheme of graded rights and honours (Tam. *mariyātai*) allowed the *jati talaivan* [caste head man] to exercise powers which were directly analogous to those of a Hindu "little king" performing his tasks as chief donor or *yayamāna* in the shrines and temples of his domain. Under this system the Paravas' Pa-

droado missionaries devised an elaborate set of status markers for the [Catholic] *jati talaivan* and his caste notables. These tokens of pre-eminence closely resembled the rights and honors which expressed rank and precedence in south Indian Hindu "honours" systems. (Ibid.: 342)

The rights and privileges were publicly displayed during the festivals at the Tuticorin church, whose symbolism amply borrowed and, to this day, borrows from the region's Hindu festivals. In particular, the ceremonious *ter,* or ritual chariot, in which the Tuticorin is carried through the streets is modeled after the famous processions for Tamil Amman or mother goddesses. It is decorated with flags that show a range of Hindu sacred symbols such as Sesha, the five-headed cobra or vehicle of Vishnu; Nandi, the companion of Shiva; and a peacock, the symbol of the local god Murugan-Subramanha. It stops at the house of the Catholic *jati talaivan* to honor, like Hindus do, the head man of their caste (ibid.: 345).

The similarities between the syncretistic contexts in Tamil Nadu and Goa, that is, their embeddedness in the political, economic, and ritual organizations of the villages, are truly striking. Nonetheless, a closer look reveals important differences. While Catholics in Tamil Nadu were integrated into the local Hindu social structure by constituting one or possibly several castes or castelike communities, Catholics in Goa, as we have seen, were never confined to one specific caste but replicated the entire system of castes (Perez 1997). To directly respond to Bayly's pointed characterization, Goan Catholics thus do not practice "Christianity as a caste style" but rather practice Christianity as a caste system in its own right. Ironically, this peculiarity in Goa creates a coexistence between Hindus and Catholics that arguably is more ambiguous than the one in Tamil Nadu. On the one hand, Catholics in Goa reproduced and, to some extent, still reproduce the caste characteristics and attitudes of their Hindu fellow villagers in much greater detail than is the case in Tamil Nadu. On the other hand, Goan Catholics keep themselves much more aloof from Hindus, something that arguably has to do with the fact that they constitute an entire caste society and not just a single caste. In other words, while certainly fostering a common sense of socioeconomic ranking and ritual privilege, the socio-politico-ritualistic parallelism between Hindu and Catholic communities in Goa is not involved in any actual interaction, *Gemeinschaft,* or syncretism between the two religious communities. Despite their striking organizational similarities, Hindus and Catholics form instead two separate communities whose public and private lives, social and religious expressions, gatherings and activities, for the most part, are quite aloof and distanced from each other. It was and is therefore unthinkable for Goan Catholics to exchange "betel nut honours" with Hindu dignitaries or openly display Hindu symbols at their religious festivals and processions. In fact, as we have seen, Hindus and Catholics carefully maintain their distinction and distance even while coming together in common rituals. In sum, what Christopher John Fuller notes for Kerala does not thus characterize the situation in

Goa, that is, that "Christians and Hindus . . . form one total community" (Fuller 1976: 68).

To be sure, one can certainly find historical evidence for political castes alliances,[7] and also syncretistic gestures across the division between Hindu and Catholic castes or *ganvkār* groups in Goa are not altogether impossible. And where these happen, one is probably right to say, as Mosse and Bayly do, that syncretistic intersections are based on social solidarities and political interests. The point to emphasize, however, is that the vast majority of syncretistic intersections in Goa are obviously not motivated by political interests or facilitated by social solidarities, and it certainly is impossible therefore to characterize them, as Mosse does for Tamil Nadu, as "politics of religious synthesis" (Mosse 1994). The interreligious coexistence and syncretism that comes to the fore in Goa, it becomes clear, is not a matter of domains, that is, functional interactions among the social, economic, and religious, but of semiotic representation, material embodiment, and practical action. The single most important moment of this practical epistemology—which itself is part of an ethos that connects metaphysics and praxis—is the belief that the village is an embodiment of the divine or saintly. Sateri–Shanta Durga–Saibini Mai, the village goddess whose iconic body constitutes the village, and St. Francis Xavier, the patron saint whose body relic stands for the safety and well-being of Goa, epitomize this premodern epistemology and ethos that lies at the bottom of the syncretistic intersection between Hindus and Catholics. Notably, though, speaking of "belief" here does not refer to an abstract idea or state of mind but rather, as Pierre Bourdieu notes, to a "state of the body . . . [that] drags the mind along, without the mind thinking of it" (Bourdieu 1993: 126ff.). The religiosity at stake, in other words, is based on forms of knowledge and signification that are thoroughly anchored in embodiment and praxis. This implies in particular that this religiosity does not mark a domain but rather an aspect of culture and society, something that makes it a reality *sui generis*. Even conquest and superimposition, we have seen, can happen only at the cost of reasserting the intrinsically religious character of what it conquers.

Three paradigms of religious embodiment and praxis crystallize for the Goan *ganv* and for the coexistence and syncretistic intersection between Hindus and Catholics. This is first the religious paradigm of space, contiguity, and neighborhood. The fact that both Hindus and Catholics acknowledge the idea that the village is an embodiment of the divine or saintly, and the fact that myriad iconic landmarks indicate the presence of gods and saints in every village, arguably generate a distinct neighborhood and commonality between the two communities. One of the strongest motivations for Goan Hindus and Catholics to transgress the doctrinal boundaries of their religions is therefore the appreciation of *ganvdevāta*, patron saints, and tutelary beings, that is, distinctly spatial manifestations of the divine and saintly. We have seen considerable iconographic and ethnographic evidence of syncretism based on this principle of "localistic religiosity." In many villages, Hindus pay their respects to the Catholic patron saints and, vice versa, Catholics pay their respects to the Hindu *ganvdevāta* at the occasion of church and temple festivals. Local shrines display icons of both Hindu *ganvdevāta* and Catholic patron saints. Members of both religious communities remember and pay homage to local Hindu gods of *their* village that had been salvaged from destruction by bringing them to other regions. Principles of localistic religiosity come to the fore also at points where the replacement of a Hindu god by a Catholic saint reasserts the religious nature of a locality and where the spatial proximity and syncretistic appreciation of Hindu and Catholic shrines suggests competition over the religious significance of the locality rather than doctrinal harmony or tolerance. One notable general principle when accounting for syncretistic practices in Goan villages is, therefore, that, at times or under certain perspectives, the loyalty to be paid to one's spatial belonging, neighborhood, or locality overrules the loyalty to be paid to one's religious doctrine or identity.[8]

A second paradigm is that of memory, genealogy, and family relationships. This paradigm is based on the idea, common to both Hindus and Catholics, that the village forms a community of people who are holding together through time and, ideally, through genealogy and family bonds. Again, local gods and saints epitomize and embody this idea by being appreciated as founders, ancestors, *ganvkār,* and, in general, clan members of a village community. Both Hindu *ganvdevāta* and Catholic patron saints are acknowledged as legal persons in the old *ganvkārī* system and are formally entitled to own land and partake in the annual distribution of *jon,* that is, the share of the *ganvkārī* product. Associations of family relationships mediate between Hindus and Catholics in situations where Hindu gods and Catholic saints are seen as kin-related, as in the case of Nossa Senora dos Milagres and her Six Divine Hindu Sisters, or through the notion of Saibini Mai, the common title for the Christian Mary and the Hindu Devi, that brings together Hindu and Catholic images of the Divine or Holy Mother, Wife, Sister, Virgin, and Independent Woman. Finally, icons and rituals may constitute cultural memory that counteracts the principles of linear or narrative time. Indicative for the palimpsest that renders past and present coeval include iconographies such as Sateri's anthill under Shanta Durga's mask and Vetal's snake in the image of St. Anthony of Siolim, both of which prove the survival of the superimposed. Ritual nullification of the passage of time and, hence, the oblivion of the historical division that separated Hindus and Catholics through conversion, is also created by the evocation of the *praesentia* of Hindu gods and Catholic saints in ritual. Another notable principle of the syncretistic intersection of Hindus and Catholics therefore is that genealogical bonds and ritual memory, at times and under certain perspectives, overrule the historical divisions that religious conversion and transformation had effected in the village community.

The third and last paradigm is that of health and well-being. This one is based on the idea that Hindu gods and Catholic saints are capable and willing to interfere into mundane affairs in order to protect the villages and regions with which they are associated from natural disasters, and shield and heal their people from illnesses and misfortune. This is probably the most widespread and effective motivation for Hindus and Catholics to transgress the doctrinal boundaries of their formal religions in order to seek protection or healing from sacred or holy agents, or forces that belong to the respective other religious tradition. Outstanding examples are Jagoryo, the tutelary god of Siolim, and Nossa Senhora dos Milagres, the patron saint of Mapusa, whose names epitomize the corresponding ideas that Hindu gods are *jāgrit,* that is, awake and responsive to their devotees' requests, and that Catholic saints work miracles. Both attract thousands of devotees from both religious communities every year. Beyond these examples, the paradigm of health and well-being is probably the one that generates the richest repertoire of iconic manifestations and ritual articulations in Hindu-Catholic syncretism in Goa. Accordingly, the images, substances, and tokens of Hindu gods that are approached by Catholics, and likewise the images, substances, and tokens of Catholic saints that are approached by Hindus, for therapeutic or protective purposes are innumerable. In many regards, popular religiosity thus renders the theological doctrines of Hinduism and Catholicism into two competing healing systems, and it is here the concern for health, protection, and well-being that overrules the loyalty to one's religious doctrine and identity.

5 Demotic Ritual
Religion and Memory

Zagor. Representação cómica em concani por amadores analfabetos; teatro groseiro, em Goa. O Zagor está actualmente proibido pela autoridade eclesiástica, sob pena graves, post que não fosse mais immoral do que muitos teatros europeus.[1]

—(Dalgado [1918] 1988: 2:436)

JAGAR OR *JĀGRĀNA* rituals mark a distinct mode of Hindu religiosity. They are performed in many parts of India (Walker 1983: 1:352) and are especially popular in the western Himalayas (Gaborieau 1975; Leavitt 1985; Krengel 1999), Rajasthan (Thiel-Horstmann 1985), Gujarat and Punjab (Erndl 1993), and Goa (Khedekar 1983; Verenkar 1991; Cabral e Sá 1997; Gomes and Shirodkar 1991; Henn 2003). Their name derives from the Sanskrit term *jāgṛ*, which means "wakefulness" (Turner 1966: 5174) and refers to religious night vigils that are seasonally celebrated in honor of local deities, saints, ancestors, and tutelary beings. The rituals are part of temple, village, or domestic ceremonies, and have a special appeal in that they enact a ludic genre of *bhakti* religiosity that combines religious ritual, such as prayer, invocation, and sacrifice, with joyful entertainment such as music, singing, dancing, and, in some regions, also mask and theater plays. Jagar ceremonies are very popular in Goa. Their performers and audiences belong to the rural population who by tradition earns its livelihood through small farming, agricultural labor, or fishing, or some combination thereof, and, today, often also has some income from small businesses, wage employment, or labor migration. Reflecting the peculiar history of the region, the communities performing the ceremony, and also the religious orientations and cultural styles of the rituals themselves, vary considerably. Three different types of Goan Jagar can be distinguished.

The arguably oldest type was performed—until recently—by members of the Perni community. Perni are an occupational subcaste (*jāti*) who performed the Jagar during various festivals at the local temples in South and East Goa. At these occasions, the Jagar was a traditional part of the ritual program that the Perni held the right (*mān*) to perform and for which they were entitled to be remunerated. Like all Goan Jagar, the Perni Jagar combined the evocation of deities—usually opening with Ganesha and then calling upon the *ganvdevāta* of the respec-

Figure 5.1. Perni Jagar Masks, Vaghurme, Goa. Photograph by Gabriele Henn.

tive villages—with the presentation of a series of allegoric skits. The skits were presented as a cooperation of singers reciting short stories, musicians playing the *dholki* and *jhānj*, that is, handheld wooden drums and brass cymbals, and dancers rhythmically moving their bodies. Two peculiarities distinguished the Perni Jagar play from all other Goan Jagar. First, they used colorful wooden masks that the dancers held in front of their faces or bodies (see figure 5.1), and second, women were allowed among the performers, something that has to do with the particular caste identity of the Perni. The masks, which I saw in the homes of Perni in the villages of Vaghurme and Malkarne (Quepem) in 1994, were treated like sacred objects and showed several gods: Ganesha, Krishna, Mahadev, and typically one or two others representing the respective *ganvdevāta* of the villages where the performances took place. Other masks showed two demons, Madhu and Kitu; some animals—*ghoḍā*, the horse; *vāg*, the tiger; *mor*, the peacock; and *pavṇo*, the bird—and a number of peculiar social and ethnic characters such as *ḍharto*, the runner; *mono*, the dumb; *khozo*, the eunuch; and *gaudo ani muṇḍo*, two caste or tribal figures. In the early 1990s, when I started my fieldwork in Goa, official Perni Jagar performances had almost all ended. So it was not possible for me to hear all the songs and learn the meanings of all the characters of the mask dances. Some of the songs, that I recorded in the homes of Perni are translated in German in my book *Wachheit der Wesen* (Henn 2003) and give an idea of the substance of the performances, which, in a dramatic-comical way, present the encounter with demons and foreign people, caricature the odd behavior of certain marginal characters, and make fun of local authorities like priests, policemen, and tax collectors.

Until the 1970s and 1980s, the Perni practitioners, whose villages are located in the province of Quepem, regularly performed at the temple festivals of about forty villages in South (Salcete, Cancona) and East (Quepem, Ponda) Goa. After that time, the performance of the Perni Jagar steadily diminished and, today, is no longer found anywhere. I myself saw the last official performance of a Perni Jagar at the annual festival of the Shanta Durga temple in Fatorpa in 1992. A number of circumstances contributed to the decline of the Perni Jagar. One has to do with the fact that Perni constitute a subcaste of Devadāsī, that is, temple servants. Like the Kalāvant who traditionally played music and performed dances at temple festivals, and the Bhavinī who decorated and cleaned the temples, Perni were of the subordinate caste rank of Sudra. Nonetheless, they gained their livelihood, like the temple priests, from a distinct part of the *ganvkārī* land that was set aside for the temples and temple rituals. Another traditional custom was that some Devadāsī girls remained unmarried in the conventional sense of the term and, instead, in a special ceremony called *śensa-vidhi,* were symbolically married to one of the major Hindu gods, Vishnu or Mahadev. This predestined Devadāsī women, however, to become concubines of rich priests or local landowners. While this concubinage arguably was a respectful and respected relationship in ancient times, it is said to have deteriorated in modern times into prostitution, causing the colonial government, in accordance with Hindu social reform movements, to formally prohibit the *śensa-vidhi* ceremony around 1930.[2] Socially stigmatized and deprived of part of their traditional function and income, the decline of the Perni Jagar was accelerated in post-colonial times, when twice-born castes, Brahmans, Kshatriya and Vani gained more influence in local temples and the once guaranteed rights of subordinate castes were curtailed and abolished (Sirkar 1983).

A social group that performs the Jagar in Goa to this day are the *mundkār* or *render*. Literally tenants, *mundkār/render* had leased land parcels and palm or areca groves against services or payment from *ganvkār* communities or individual land owners in the old *ganvkārī* system. After 1961, when the new Indian government issued a series of land-reform legislations and "land-to-the-tiller" acts, many former *mundkār/render* were able to purchase the land they had been working for a nominal fee, thereby forming a new class of small farmers, toddy tappers, and horticulturists. Many of them supplement their agricultural incomes today with small businesses and labor migration to other parts of India, the Arabian Gulf region, and Europe. *Mundkār/render* are typically ranked Sudra in the old caste system and are part of the Bahujan Samaj, a political caste formation that organizes small farmers, land laborers, fishermen, and artisans in Goa and the Konkan region.

Mundkār/render can be found among Hindus and Christians and the single most famous Jagar in Goa today is, in fact, jointly performed by two *mundkār/ render* communities, one Hindu and one Catholic, in the village of Siolim (Bardez). The background to this syncretistic peculiarity combines a variety of historical circumstances that range from the early history of the ludic Jagar religiosity that became known as Zagor after it was adopted among local Christians in the seventeenth century, through the history of political change and demographic shifts in Goa in the nineteenth century, to the social history of the village of Siolim in the twentieth century. The most notable effect of these historical processes and circumstances, which I will discuss in more detail below, is that, today, Hindus and Catholics of Siolim jointly perform the ceremonies, worshipping Catholic principles, the Holy Trinity, the Virgin Mary, and St. Anthony, the local patron saint of the village, side by side with Hindu gods, Sateri, Khazonio, and, most importantly, Jagoryo, the local embodiment of the divine wakefulness that the ritual evokes. Archival and ethnographic evidence indicates that, throughout the nineteenth and part of the twentieth centuries, the celebration of the Zagor was quite common among Catholics in the areas of the Old Conquests and was a more or less regular part of the annual feast days of the local churches. For reasons that I will elaborate in more detail later, the Catholic Zagor was never fully accepted and legitimized though by church authorities. Instead, the church and at a later stage the Portuguese colonial government officially banned the Catholic Zagor for its allegedly pagan features and subversive activities. By the 1930s, the ceremonies were therefore either abandoned or drastically truncated in most Catholic villages, except for Siolim, where Hindus joining the Catholic Zagor practitioners not only helped the festival to resist the Portuguese-Catholic ban but, after 1961, even made it into a widely known incident of popular religiosity and Hindu-Catholic harmony.

The third and by far largest group of Jagar practitioners in Goa today are the Gaude. Gaude belong, together with Velip, Kunbi, and Dhangar, to the formerly tribal population of Goa. Previously gaining their livelihood from *kumeri*, a form of seminomadic shifting cultivation, most of them today combine some type of traditional income such as agriculture, fishing, or gardening with wage employment or labor migration. Unlike the Perni Jagar, which was performed by professional specialists on temple festivals, the *mundkār/render* and Gaude Jagar are village festivals in which, ideally, all major families of the village or respective ward in which they take place are involved. They are performed at the village *mand,* that is, the central communal location at which village gatherings and rituals are traditionally held. The *mand* varies in shape and size depending on the wealth of the village and may either be just a village plaza on which a *matto,* that is, a temporary ceremonial house, is built for the Jagar, or part of a village temple hall, or even a small temple hall of its own. The ceremonies mark an important event in the annual calendar of the villages and are celebrated in grand style with beautiful decorations and lavish sound and light systems attracting, as a rule, a couple of hundred visitors. Many of them come from neighboring villages or are relatives and are hosted for dinner at the homes of the Jagar celebrants. During the course of the ceremony, the *mand* is considered a sacred space and cannot be entered with shoes. The most serious ritual of the ceremony is the *nomana*, that is, the invocation by name of all the gods, saints, ancestors, and tutelary beings that are relevant for the village. This is done by the entire assembly of the male dignitaries of the village sitting on the *mand* singing the *nomana*, which has the form of a lyrical hymn, composed in *ovi* or quatrains, the typical poetic meter of *bhakti* songs. The *nomana* opens the ceremonies around midnight and closes them at sunrise.

The ludic part of the Gaude Jagar is performed by gorgeously costumed men and boys, and, occasionally, a few prepuberty girls presenting a series of skits, known as *songe*, that is, "characters." For this purpose, the *mand* becomes a kind of stage with spectators sitting in front and around watching and laughing. The singing, dancing, and rudimentary acting of the performers is accompanied by the chorus of men who are alternating with the songs of the dancers and also play the drums. These are typically one *dhol*, that is, a large wooden drum with a deep sound played with a stick; a number of *ghumat*, small high-sounding earthen drums played by hand; and a couple of *jhānj*, brass cymbals whose metallic sounds sharply contrast with the drums. As part of the aggrandizement of the ceremony, many villages hire professional musicians playing the *tabla* (classical Indian two-set drums) and *bina* (classical Indian harmonium) today, thereby giving their festivals a classy style. Although eclectically alluding to popular Hindu epics such as the *Mahabharata* and *Ramayana,* as well as local Catholic lore such as the stories of *Padri* and *Pakle*, that is, "missionaries" and "foreigners," the skits do not follow any master narrative but enact a series of stories and characters. As a rule, forty to sixty characters are presented, covering a wide variety of themes that range from mythological stories, historical episodes, social and ethnic typologies, to day-to-day scenes from village life. As in the Perni Jagar, serious issues, such as the protection of the village from disaster and the controlling of alien forces and demons, alternate with light themes like the caricature of authorities and the ridiculing of adversities and inappropriate behavior. A recurring character, who can be said to epitomize the Gaude Jagar, is *goraśer,* a figure that stands out by its conspicuous headgear and oscillates in identity between villain, trickster, and clown.

That the Jagar has become a hallmark of Gaude culture and is celebrated today in about twenty to thirty Gaude villages, most of them located in the Tiswadi and Ponda districts, again has to do with the curious history of the ceremony and its practitioners. Historically, the festival became popular among the Gaude who converted to Catholicism in the sixteenth and seventeenth centuries. There are indications that consciously Catholicized versions of existing popular forms of Hindu religiosity, such as the Jagar, were used by Jesuit missionaries to induce conversion and familiarize new converts with Catholic traditions. As mentioned earlier, this Jesuit policy of *accommodatio* or assimilation was later abandoned, however, and the erstwhile incentive for conversion was now considered a "pagan reminiscence" and banned under severe penalty. As among most of Goa's Catholic *render* population, the Zagor would have been eradicated among the Catholic Gaude except for the fact that, in the early twentieth century, a considerable number of Catholic Gaude decided to convert again, joining, in a spectacular *śuddhi* or purification ceremony, the Hindu tradition. Two consequences of the late-colonial Gaude conversion to Hinduism, which activists of Hindu nationalism like to call a "reconversion" today, are especially noteworthy. First, it stopped the systematic eradication of the Zagor tradition, since, similar to what had happened in Siolim, it was now performed by Hindus and thus removed from the direct control of the local Catholic church. Another implication of the conversion was that, for reasons to be discussed in more detail later, for the Gaude, becoming Hindu did not mean they simply forgot or abandoned their Catholic heritage. Instead, they continued and continue to pay homage in their *nomana* to the Christian principles and Catholic saints that their parents and grandparents had venerated, thereby turning the Jagar into a distinctly syncretistic ceremony. It is the rule for the celebrants to start the ceremonies by invoking the Christian Trinity—*Deu Bapa, Deu Putra ani Ispirita Santa*—followed by invocations of Saibini Mai, the Virgin Mary, and a long list of Catholic patron saints, only to change over at some point to invocations of Ganesha, Maha Dev, Lakshmi, and other pan-Indian Hindu gods and goddesses, followed by Sateri and Shanta Durga, the prominent local incarnations of Hindu female divinity, and finally an equally long list of Hindu *ganvdevāta*. Given the peculiar history of the Gaude Jagar/Zagor and its practitioners, it is not surprising that the linguistic and literary parts of the ceremony also show hybrid features today. Hence the prayers and songs recited during the ceremonies make use of Konkani and pidginized Portuguese, and its literary themes vary, with plots and stories from both the Hindu-Indian and the Luso-Catholic world.

In discussing primarily the Gaude Jagar, I want to address above all the question of why and how it is possible that its practitioners both ritually appreciate the Catholic legacy of their ancestors and reassert the distinctiveness of their Hindu identity today. This seemingly paradoxical attitude comes to the fore not only in their major religious festival. Gaude also explicitly honor the Catholic allegiance of their ancestors in their day-to-day lives. They display and venerate icons of Catholic saints in their homes, care for and pay homage to crosses and Catholic shrines in their villages, and regularly pilgrimage to the feasts of St. Francis Xavier or other Catholic saints. At the same time, Gaude self-consciously assert that they are Hindus, pay great attention to the observance of Hindu life-cycle rituals and holidays, give their children Hindu names, and strive for Hindu temples and shrines in their villages. In fact, as mentioned before, in some villages, the political self-assertion of Hindus in recent years has even initiated a kind of "Hinduization" of the Jagar itself, something that implies the gradual removal of Catholic elements from the ceremonies, changing for instance its association with Catholic feast days to an the association with Hindu holidays, or inserting references to Hindu deities and epics into texts and skits that, so far, have predominantly dealt with Catholic saints and stories.

In order to account for these ambiguous attitudes, it is important to note that Gaude culture and existence have always been precarious and exposed to the historical vicissitudes of shifting power relations and limited economic resources. Traditionally, Gaude gained their livelihood from *kumeri*, that is, shifting cultivation producing millet and pulses complemented by the collecting of wood, honey, wild fruits, and other forest products. But their modes of production often conflicted with ruling forces and developments, and their living space was subjected to serious encroachment. Extension of protected forest areas during Portuguese colonialism, postcolonial expansion of the mining industry, the legal prohibition of *kumeri* for ecological reasons in 1956 and 1962, and, lately, large land conversions for urban expansion and tourism kept and keep curtailing Gaude living space and resources. As a consequence, the tribal community was repeatedly forced to shift its traditional homesteads and turned to other sources of income such as agricultural labor, fishing, wage labor, and, increasingly in recent years, labor migration to the Arabian Gulf states. Although access to economic resources and educational facilities has thus always been precarious and limited for Gaude, it was only in 2004 that, together with Kunbi, Velip, and Dhangar, they were officially recognized as one of Goa's Scheduled Tribes. Even after that, social neglect and political oppression continues, most tragically in May 2011, when a demonstration of the United Tribal Association Alliance was attacked by a violent mob of caste Hindus and two of their young leaders were burned to death in an act of unbelievable cruelty (Narayan 2011).

Today, Gaude can be said to constitute an urban tribal community. That means they are still rooted in kinship relationships that are typical for Indian tribal societies, such as cross-cousin marriage; engage in economic activities such as small farming and fishing; and follow ancient religious traditions such as earth goddess veneration. At the same time, most Gaude are finding themselves in urban environments and acting in modern fashion. They settle in or within the vicinity of cities, take on wage employment or run small businesses in the service sector, and strive to participate in a rapidly modernizing India by seeking a moderately consumptive lifestyle, education for their children, and political recognition as a marginal minority group. The precariousness of Gaude existence comes to the fore in their social and religious life. Gaude identify themselves as *ādivāsi*, that is, aboriginal population, and claim to descend from the first or ancient settlers of the Konkan Coast. This claim is buttressed by the fact that many Gaude clans living in the territories of the New Conquests, where the Portuguese impact was weaker, are named Ganvnkar, which translates as "villager" and marked the status of genuine settlers in the ancient village system *ganvkārī*. As mentioned before, Gaude clans also hold *mān* or ritual honors in many local temple associations, something that underscores their seniority among local castes and communities (Pereira 1978). This situation notwithstanding, Gaude were always related to castes and communities of the lowest social ranking whose living conditions and ritual rights deteriorated during colonial times. Marginalized among both Hindus and Catholics, they were especially exposed to proselytizing campaigns and were among the first whom Jesuit missionaries converted to Christianity in the mid-sixteenth century. These conversions, though, were conducted rather carelessly, involving little if any religious education and often changed the religious allegiance of entire villages in one mass baptism. Legally witnessed by just one Portuguese godfather, these anonymous mass conversions often had the effect that entire village communities were baptized in the name of one Fernandes, De Souza, or Da Silva. Educational and social neglect continued through the centuries and predestined Gaude to become the target of another proselytizing campaign organized by Hindu activists who, in the early twentieth century, succeeded in converting a considerable part of the Catholic Gaude community to Hinduism. As a consequence the tribal group is today divided into three religious communities: the Hindu Gaude who never converted to Christianity, the Catholic Gaude who had converted to Christianity in the sixteenth century and are Christians to this day, and the so-called Nava-Hindu Gaude whose ancestors had converted to Christianity in the sixteenth century but converted back to Hinduism in 1928. None of these three sections entertain marriage or even social relations with any other today.

Given these historical circumstances, Gaude religious allegiance, historical memory, and cultural survival always were and, to this day, are closely related. In particular, two different models by which Gaude remember their past and, by implication, relate to the historically changing religious allegiances of their ancestors help to explain why and how it is indeed not only possible but a matter of cultural survival for them to combine syncretism and religious self-assertion. Following the specifications of historians and literary critics, I call the first model "narrative memory" because it organizes the past as a linear succession of events that is organized by a plot or story (Ricoeur 1980; White 1980). This model represents the paradigm of modern time reckoning and is essentially political in developing around the political history of Goa and, by extension, the Indian nation state. Elaborating this narrative memory in the first section of this chapter, I reconstruct the story of the historical transformation and conversion of the Jagar and its practitioners from a form of ludic religiosity that was practiced—perhaps by specified occupational castes—during Hindu temple festivals in precolonial times, to a part of the Catholic liturgy celebrated by converted Catholics during local church feasts in the colonial period, to, finally, the syncretistic village festival of today that emerged from its practitioners' second conversion to Hinduism and played a role in Goa's Liberation Movement in the late-colonial period.

Following the traditions of anthropologists and scholars of ritual studies (Staal 1979; Tambiah 1979; Humphrey and Laidlaw 1994; Bell 1992; Asad 1993), I call the second model of Gaude's historical consciousness "ritual memory" because it remembers the past through material and iconic media, genealogical, and mimetic modes that gain their strongest significance in and through rituals. I elaborate Gaude's ritual memory in the second section of the chapter by analyzing the performative sequence and significance of the *nomana* or invocation and *songe* or dramatic play of the Jagar in the village of Kakra (Tiswadi). Ritual concerns for memory, neighborhood, and practice stand out here in organizing time in the form of a palimpsest that renders the changing Hindu and Catholic allegiances and manifestations of the past coeval in the ritual presence of today.

Narrative Memory

The earliest archival evidence of Jagar ceremonies can be found in a *foral*, that is, Portuguese tax list for the southern province of Salcete that was valid from 1567 to 1585. The brief bureaucratic entry determines taxes for the village Benaulim as follows: "*Pa[ra] se fazerem dous autos q[ue] se fazem de noite q[ue] se chama zagor en todo o anno pagavã doze t[an]gas br[an]cas*" (*Foral de Salcete [1567–1585]* 1990: 61).[3] In translation, the sum of twelve "white Tangas," a currency common in the early-modern Estado da Índia, was raised as an annual tax levy from the village community for the "nocturnal performance of two acts of what is called zagor." Interestingly, this entry comes immediately after another tax levy that was raised "*por cantarem no pagode q[ue] se chama aoijagar*" (ibid.), that is, for "singing in a temple called Aoijagar." The assumption that the Jagar was a nocturnal ceremony performed in precolonial times in and around Hindu temples is supported by the Goan historian Pandurang Pissurlencar who describes the Jagar as "a Hindu theatre which is usually performed in certain religious festivities in Goa" (1962: 44). Interestingly, though not specified, his note also says that "already in 1526, the Goan poet Crisnada Xamã had mentioned the *nattadhara*, that is, actors of this theatre" (ibid.). An entrance in the *Vocabulario das lingues canarim* of 1620, which was compiled by the Jesuit Diogo Ribeiro, points in the same direction, specifying the *zagaru* as an *auto dos gentios,* a theatrical "act of heathens" (Ribeiro 1620: 668). That a Jagar tradition existed already in precolonial Goa is also the assumption of Teotonio de Souza. Likewise based on a tax list that refers to a village named Karbely (possibly Caramboli/Tiswadi) in 1600, the Goan historian concludes in his *Medieval Goa,* "It was in the temple premises that children were educated and where adults organized their cultural activities, particularly their zagor or dramatic performances" (De Souza 1979: 91).[4]

After the mid-seventeenth century, archival sources become silent on the Jagar for more than a century, taking up the subject again only in 1777. From the bureaucratic attention that the ludic genre gained thereafter, we learn first of all that, in the meantime, the Zagor and some other Indian customs such as the *fama* (discussed below) had become part of the Catholic liturgy in the territories of the Old Conquests. More precisely, the sources indicate that the missionaries, after thoroughly replacing the invocation of Hindu deities with the invocation of the Christian Trinity and Catholic saints and substituting all literary references to Hindu ideas with Catholic one, had made the Zagor a regular part of the church festivals that were celebrated every year in honor of the local patron saints. To this day, most Gaude Jagar are therefore associated with the dates of local church feasts, even though all other organizational connections with the churches have been abandoned. Archival and ethnographic evidence further indicates that, notwithstanding its later dismissal by the church, the Zagor became a popular spectacle and was performed in dozens of Catholic *comunidades* in each of the districts of the Old Conquests: Tiswadi, Bardez, and Salcete. Historically, the early-modern creation of the Catholic Zagor was most probably part of the Jesuit policy of *accommodatio,* the assimilation of Indian customs and literary styles in Catholic liturgy and culture, which, in Goa, found its literary masterpiece in Thomas Stephens's 1619 *Kristapurana.* In fact, there are good reasons to argue that the *Kristapurana* served as a literary model for the traditional *nomana* hymns in the Catholic Zagor. This assumption is supported by the fact that the literary style and language of the Catholic *nomana* closely resembles the "Old Marathi" language style, which linguistic specialists describe for the *Kristapurana* (Van Skyhawk 1999; Priolkar 1958), and also largely replicates the *ovi* or quatrain meter that Stephens had borrowed from contemporary Hindu *bhakti* literature. Moreover, the Catholic Zagor repeats the narrative structure of the *Kristapurana,* particularly the second part that opens with the *nomana* of God the Father, God the Son, and God the Holy Spirit, and then tells the story of the New Testament and life of Jesus, including the story of the Virgin Mary, Jesus's teachings to the Twelve Apostles, his death on the cross and eventual resurrection and ascendance into heaven. While we cannot establish a certified link between the archived copies of the ancient text of the *Kristapurana* and the oral traditions on which the *nomana* of the contemporary Gaude Jagar are based, there is no doubt that the *nomana* hymns are very old texts handed down from originals dating back to the times when the Christian missionaries transformed, as it were, the Hindu Jagar into the Catholic Zagor. Their word-for-word recitations mark one of the indispensable elements of the ritual performance to this day, even though the historical vicissitudes that the ceremony and its practitioners have experienced through the centuries left their marks on the ancient text. Thus, many parts of the *nomana*—and also the old texts recited in the ludic part today—show considerable orthographic uncertainties, semantic gaps, and syntactical muddles that make it difficult, if not impossible, to fully decode and reconstruct their meanings. In fact, this holds true even for the practitioners themselves, so that the singers recite a good part of the hymns and songs primarily using a phonetic memory that utters the words and articulates the sounds without fully understanding their meaning. All these textual uncertainties notwithstanding, it may not be mere historical contingency that the most competent help in deciphering and translating the cryptic passages of the *nomana* came from religious laymen in Arambol (Pernem) who, to this day, at certain occasions such as the night vigil for a deceased family member, recite passages from the *Kristapurana*. Although many passages of the Jagar *nomana* remained unclear even to them, it was they who drew my attention to the literary resemblance with the *Kristapurana* and, more precisely, directed me to Joseph L. Saldanha's vocabulary in the appendix to the 1907 edition of the *Kristapurana,* which was of great help in translating the *nomana.*

While the literary style of the Catholic Zagor thus reveals the missionary hand that was involved in its early-modern creation, the reappearance of the ludic genre in the clerical sources in the eighteenth century indicates a dramatic shift in missionary policy. Obviously, the dismissal of the Jesuit *accommodatio* policy in the mid-seventeenth century effected the Zagor as well as the custom called *fama,* whose Catholicized continuation once was thought to be an incentive for the local people to convert to Christianity. Both were now abolished and condemned as "superstitious, immoral and pagan practices." A pastoral letter written by the archbishop in Goa in 1784 gives an indication of this change in policy. The letter categorically states,

> It is condemned the practice [*auto*], celebrated with much noise and hype, which the Christians call *fama* and the pagans [*gentios*] call *olly,* as well as the amusement [*divertimento*] called Zagor; it is deplored to try to entice people into the church by these means: firstly, it is renewed the threat of punishment of excommunication, issued in the archiepiscopal decree of November 14th, 1777, for those who support the *fama* and Zagor and the priests are authorized to fine and warn the one or the other; secondly, the priests who come to know that a *fama* will be celebrated shall tell the people that the feast will not be held that will give opportunity for this *fama* or Zagor. (Nazareth [1873] 1894: 36)

The custom called *fama* mentioned here helps to demonstrate the implications and complications that the *accommodatio* policy and its abolition meant for Goan Catholics and even Portuguese clerics. In 1663, Manuel Godinho, a Jesuit traveling through Portuguese India, reported that the *fama* marked the beginning of the *novenas,* that is, the nine days of prayers that preceded the annual feast days of the local patron saints. As part of processions, during which people put on funny costumes and performed frolic dances in the streets, the ritual apex of the *fama* was the planting of a decorated pole (*maḍḍi*) on the tip of which the image of the local saint was displayed (Dalgado [1918] 1988: 1:386). This ritual of *fama* had such a close resemblance to the ceremonies of the so-called *olly,* that is, the Hindu Holi festival, which is celebrated every year in February-March and during which people also planted ritual poles and displayed religious icons, that the name *fama* became a synonym for both ceremonies. Accordingly, *fama*'s origins from the Hindu or Catholic world, however, are still debated (ibid.: 1:385ff., 2:121; Xavier 1861: 126). Hence, the Portuguese Indologist Sebastião Rudolpho Dalgado notes about the *fama,* "It seems that this custom comes from Hinduism, which has an identical ceremony, although I am assured that a similar practice is enacted in parts of Portugal which, however, may have been imported from India" (Dalgado [1918] 1988: 1:386). These uncertainties about the Hindu or Catholic origin and content of the *fama* were so intricate that discussions about its compatibility with the Catholic doctrine and liturgy lasted among Catholic scholars well into the twentieth century. Hence, Manuel de Albuquerque, the compiler of the Goan church decrees, accused his predecessor Casimiro Christovão de Nazareth in 1922 of "confusing the forbidden *fama* with the *fama* that precedes the solemn festivities before the *novenas,* which has nothing barbaric and superstitious to it, . . . nor should [the ritual] be confused with the immoral popular amusement of *fama* and *zagor* and other ludic performances that are usually practiced during the feasts and the *novenas*" (Albuquerque 1922: 3n1).

While these uncertainties explain to some extent why the suppression of the popular ceremonies of the *fama* and Zagor became drawn-out affairs and never fully succeeded, there can be no doubt that the church authorities and, at a later stage, the colonial government pursued their prohibition tenaciously. Thus, after the 1777 and 1784 decrees, the bans on the Zagor and *fama* were repeated by the archbishop and the vicar general in 1791, 1812, 1897, and 1905 (Xavier 1861: 126; Albuquerque 1922: 41, 66, 223, 240). The main concern behind the ban was that the indicted practices were suspected of being a *reminiscencia pagã,* that is, a "reminiscence of pagan beliefs and practices" (Albuquerque 1922: 241). Accordingly, breaches of the Zagor ban were punished severely: perpetrators and their helpers threatened with excommunication, and festivities and processions in the villages in which the ceremony was performed were prohibited for an entire year. This situation notwithstanding, the repeated renewal of the ban also indicates that people complied only very reluctantly with these laws, and the performance of the Zagor, in private or in open rebellion, became a routine subversive practice. The categorical ban of the Zagor was renewed once again in a church decree of 1905, which stated,

> We reconfirm all that had been ordered earlier regarding the superstitious and immoral entertainment of the so-called Zagor and we keep up the prohibition, issued likewise by our predecessors, to show the Most Sacred Sacrament and to perform processions in those communities in which it took place. And knowing that this ceremony is of pagan origin, the priests shall be neither reluctant nor hesitant to ask the worldly authorities for its suppression and to enforce ecclesiastical punishments against the excuses and deceptions used by some persons not to have the measures applied that prohibit this [ceremony]. The hidden and almost dark spot at which the Zagor is performed at late hours, the gathering of people of both sexes and all generations for so many hours during the night, suffices, apart from anything else, to prohibit this barbaric entertainment. (Albuquerque 1922: 249)

Archival sources show that, in the first decade of the twentieth century, the combined forces of the Portuguese state and the Catholic Church started a major offensive against the Zagor targeting above all Gaude villages. Between 1900 and 1905, no less than nine villages—Taligao, Curca, Verna, Corlim, Assolna, Naushe, Bambolim, Naroa, and Merces—all of which are located in Tiswadi and have a considerable Gaude population, were sanctioned by the archbishop *"por causa de zagor,"* that is, because of the Zagor (Martins 1912: 43, 190, 222). The impression that, by this time, the Zagor had become a thorn in the side not only of the Catholic Church but also the Portuguese government in Goa is supported by ethnographic evidence. Older Zagor activists remember that the ceremonies became a voice of subaltern resistance, articulating social grievances and criticizing colonial authorities, as continues to this day in the ridiculing of "tax collectors," "Portuguese soldiers," and "Firanghis" in the Jagar play. More serious forms of political subversion developed when people began to use the Zagor as a platform for the dissemination and propagation of the ideas and activities of the emerging independence movement in British India, known as the Liberation Movement in Goa. Quite a few Zagor practitioners from the Perni, *render/mundkār,* and Gaude communities were active "liberation fighters" and struggle, to this day, with the Goan government for political recognition and economic compensation for time spent in Portuguese prisons. Historically, the Portuguese introduced special task forces to try to censor, if not stop, the Zagor performances in order to prevent the propagation of anticolonial sentiments and comments in support of the independence movement in British India. Nevertheless, people remember to this day with a degree of satisfaction that the Zagor practitioners and their audiences found ways to undermine this control and avoid the censorship. For instance, simply wearing a certain style of *dhoti,* that is, a loincloth, on the Zagor stage would suffice to bring Mahatma Gandhi alive, and showing a type of *topi* or headdress could easily stand for Jawaharlal Nehru, reminding people of the leaders of the Satyagraha Movement. To convey their ideas, Zagor activists also used a specially camouflaged form of Konkani that was understood by Goan villagers but not the Portuguese police.

These subversive activities notwithstanding, the complete suppression of the Catholic Zagor would have occurred eventually, had it not ironically been for the re-strengthening of Hinduism in Goa. Two developments, in particular, supported the revival of Hindu culture in Goa. This was, first, the gradual re-population of the predominantly Catholic areas of the Old Conquests by Hindus. This development had its background in the, albeit gradual and drawn-out, liberalization of the politics of religion, which, in the late eighteenth century, led to the recognition of religious freedom for Hindus in the newly acquired territories of the New Conquests, then, around the middle of the nineteenth century, also allowed the practice of Hinduism in the territories of the Old Conquests, thereby encouraging Hindus from the New Conquests to "return" to the core of Portuguese Goa. The gradual repopulation of the Old Conquests by Hindus was reinforced by economic factors. Beginning in the nineteenth and culminating in the early twentieth century, economic degradation in the Portuguese colony triggered an increasing emigration of Goans seeking work and better living conditions in British India or elsewhere in the world. "By 1921," Michael Pearson notes, "when Goa's population was 469.000, it was estimated that up to 200.000 Goans lived outside—in British India, Burma, East Africa and Mesopotamia of whom about one-quarter were in Bombay Presidency. In the 1950s the total population of Goa was 547.000 with another 180.000 outside. Of these 100.000 were in India, . . . 30.000 in Pakistan, another 30.000 in Kenya and Uganda, and 20.000 in the Persian Gulf" (1987: 155ff.). A closer inspection reveals that the vast majority of these emigrants were Catholics from the Old Conquests (Henn 2003: 140) whose gradual replacement by Hindus from the New Conquests and other parts of India changed the political power relations between the two religious communities in such a way that—as we have seen in Siolim (Bardez)—Hindus could now become part of the Zagor/Jagar and thus prevent its eradication by the Catholic Church.

Another development that indirectly facilitated the survival of the Jagar came from Hindu reform movements that began to establish themselves in British India in the nineteenth century and played an important role in the emerging Indian independence and nationalist movement. More precisely, the impulse came from the Arya Samaj reform movement, which was the first to initiate campaigns for what was called *śuddhi,* that is, "purification ceremonies" meant to bring people whose ancestors had once converted to Islam or Christianity "back" into the fold of Hinduism (Jaffrelot 1994; Clémentine-Ojha 1994). The idea to perform a *śuddhi* ceremony in Goa was first raised in 1917 in a journal called *Kesari*, published in Poona and Bombay by Lokmanya Tilak (1856–1920), a militant leader of the anticolonial movement in Maharashtra (Kamat 1957). Most likely due to theological frictions, it took another ten years, though, before high-ranking Hindus in Goa agreed to take up the idea and assigned its implementation to Vinayak Masurkar, the abbot of a Vaishnavaite *matha* or temple school in Satari in Goa. From its very beginning, the campaign was set to focus exclusively on Goa's tribal population Gaude. Masurkar and a group of Brahmanical priests thus traveled for weeks through Gaude villages, singing Hindu hymns, performing Hindu rituals, and distributing the then technical novelty of photographic images of Hindu gods among Catholic Gaude (Kakodkar 1988: 250). Religious instruction was complemented by promises of bureaucratic and religious support for those who would agree to convert. Hence, Gaude were assured that birth, death, and marriage registers would be established and that they would be protected from the expected harassment by Portuguese officials. Moreover, Gaude were assured that *purohit,* that is, Hindu priests, would care for their religious education and make sure that they would receive access to the local temples, something that was not at all uncontested among high-caste Hindus in the region (Kamat 1957). When a large number of Gaude agreed to convert, preparations for the *śuddhi* ceremony started in early 1928. An office was established in Santa Cruz/Calapur (Tiswadi) where Hindu lawyers issued affidavits for Gaude declaring their willingness to convert. High-ranking members of the Hindu Mahasabha in Bombay and Delhi, and influential local Hindu families, such as Dempe in Santa Cruz/Calapur and Vaidya in Ponda, assured their political support. The actual *śuddhi* ceremonies started on 25 February 1928 in the village of Chimbel (Tiswadi) with 350 Catholic Gaude publicly declaring their conversion to Hinduism. It was repeated in more than fifty villages through the end of May and resulted in a total of 7,815 converts (Kakodkar 1988: 261). As expected, the event, which was publicized in local Hindu newspapers and received congratulatory telegrams from Hindu leaders and communities all over India, did not find approval with the Portuguese and Catholic officials in Goa. A couple of priests managed to immediately reconvert some Gaude to Catholicism, allegedly threatening them with severe worldly and spiritual sanctions, only to activate *śuddhi* activists who again nullified the reconversion. A number of *śuddhi* activists were arrested, but a large crowd of the newly constituted Nawa Hindu Gaude courageously marched in front of the Portuguese governor's residence, thereby effecting the speedy release of the detainees. The movement also had the support of high-ranking Hindu political leaders from British India, among them B. R. Ambedkar, who later became the political spokesman of India's Dalits, so that the Portuguese-Catholic powers in Goa *nolens volens* had to tolerate it.

Only a few old Gaude still remember the *śuddhi* affair of 1928 today, and even fewer people are probably aware of the historical details of the much earlier conversion of their ancestors to Christianity. Nonetheless, Gaude do account for their religious identity today in terms of the narrative memory that tells the story of the contingencies, that is, conversions, re-conversions, and subversions, that the historical encounter between Hindu and Catholic forces have inscribed into their culture, society, and Self. The religious ceremony that marks their most important ethnic and cultural expression today, the Jagar, as we have seen, was itself subject to a dual transformation, first to Catholic, then to Hindu expressions and values, and reasserts this narrative memory by connecting it with the collective memory of Goa and the Indian nation at large. This memory claims leading authority today in India's media, education, and public discourse, and portrays the historically shifting power relations between Hindus and Catholics in Goa as part of a larger story that talks about "origins" and "ancient cultures," "invasions" and "colonial domination," "political resistance" and "independence." Religious differences are connected here with historical circumstances and incidences: the religion of ancient India, the rule of Islam, the colonial hegemony of Portuguese and British Christians, the national assertion of Hinduism and other Indic religions, all inscribing themselves into Goa's and India's cultures and people as an irreversible course of events into time. Much like the modern consciousness that the Today can never be the same as the Yesterday, and the Tomorrow, by definition, is different from the Today (Koselleck 1984), it is for Gaude a matter of fact thus that the doctrines and identities of Hindus and Catholics are different. One can always only belong to one or the other, and conversions or changes between the two require radical and complete transformations of mind, body, and cultural habitus. Therefore, Nawa Hindu Gaude have no doubt in asserting their identity as Hindus and see themselves as different from Catholics.

Ritual Memory

Arguably, though, the narrative memory that marks modern historical consciousness is not the only way that Gaude remember the past and relate to the historically changing religious allegiances and ritual practices of their ancestors. Instead, Gaude see the historical manifestations of the divine and saintly as agents of time themselves and, therefore, do not consider them as mere symbols of a bygone past, but as icons of an ongoing ritual presence. In order to describe and analyze what I therefore call ritual memory, I rely above all on the performative aspects of the Jagar ceremony in the village of Kakra (Tiswadi), which I repeatedly saw, recorded, and studied during my fieldwork between 1993 and 2010.[5] I can say that I had the opportunity of studying the Kakra ceremonies very intensely not only because the people of this village allowed me in 1994 and 2010 to take part in the rehearsal of their Jagar play, which took place twice a week for about a month in the yard of the house of the *zolmi*, that is, the community leader. As a form of reciprocity for helping me in my research and cooperating with me in the audio- and video-recording of their ceremony,[6] the people of

Kakra also insisted that I should perform one character in their Jagar play. It was agreed that I should dance the part of a *Soldade Portugalre,* something that they laughingly described as adding a *mūl paklo,* that is, a "genuine foreigner," to their Jagar. For the people, my participation in the play was above all a matter of fun and perhaps also a way to embellish and increase the attractiveness of their ludic program, in order to bring in more visitors, since the thirty or so Gaude communities performing the Jagar in the 1990s engaged in a committed competition among each other. For me, my participation turned out to provide tremendous instruction and insight because, as mentioned earlier, it helped me to understand that the gravity of this ceremony did not only lie in the *meanings* of its textual and narrative content, which I put great effort into recording, transcribing, and translating, but also in the *significance* of the bodily enactment and the material embodiment of the dances and spiritual icons involved.

Kakra is a small independent village that, officially, is part of the town of Santa Cruz/Calapur (Tiswadi). Separated from Santa Cruz/Calapur by a hill on which, since the 1980s, the buildings of Goa University, All India Radio, and a couple of multistory residences have built up, the village has about 400 inhabitants, roughly 350 of whom were Nawa Hindu Gaude and about 50 were Catholic *render.* Still reflecting its former Catholic orientation, the Kakra Jagar is calendrically associated with the feast day of the Santa Cruz/Calapur church, which falls every year on the first Sunday after 3 May. Except for one family who, due to a conflict, boycotted the Jagar for a couple of years, male members of all Gaude families of Kakra, led by the *zolmi* family, actively participated in the ceremonies. These were preceded by a number of ritual and practical activities, such as the rehearsals of the skits and, about three days before the festival, the building of the *matto,* that is, the temporary ceremonial house. After ritually placing its first Tulsi-garlanded pole, the people built this *matto* from the trunks and leaves of palm trees on the central village plaza, near the great village well and next to a *khuris,* a shrine housing a white stone cross framed on three sides by a low wall and covered by a simple metal-sheet roof. The ceremonial house gave room for the ten-by-ten-meter large *mand,* which was open at three sides and, on one side, had a stage-background canvas showing a forest scene behind which stood a small backstage area in which the dancers put on their costumes and had their faces painted by a hired makeup artist. Demarcated by light bamboo galleries and two brass oil lamps from the area in which spectators sit on hired plastic chairs, the *mand* is itself divided into two zones. In one sits the chorus of male village dignitaries on the ground, facing another oil lamp while singing and playing the drums and cymbals; the other zone is the sandy ground on which the performers, individually and in groups, present their dances and songs. The entire ceremonial house is covered by a decorative canopy of cloth and equipped with colorful fairy lights and a powerful loudspeaker system.

Another ritual that preceded the actual ceremony is notable because a small group of Kakra's Catholic *render* played a brief role in it. This ritual is known as the *Ladhain,* literally "Latin," and indeed consists of a short Latin prayer that a group of male Catholic *render* recite in front of the *khuris* on behalf of the Hindu Jagar practitioners. For this ceremony, which took place on the morning of the Jagar, the men from the Hindu *zolmi* family acted as the *yajamān* or trustees of the *khuris,* meaning they decorated the cross with flowers and burning candles and shielded the candles from the blowing wind while the Catholic *render* recited the following prayer:

> *Kyrie eleison*
> *Christe eleison*
> *Kyrie eleison*
> *Christe, audi nos*
> *Christe, exaudi nos*
> *Pater de Coelis Deus, miserere nobis*
> *Fili Redemptor mundi Deus, miserere nobis*
> *Spiritus Sancte Deus, miserere nobis*
> *Sancta trinitas unus Deus, miserere nobis*
> *Agnus Dei, qui tollis peccata mundis, pace nobis Domine*
> *Agnus Dei, qui tollis peccata mundis, exaude nos Domine*
> *Agnus Dei, qui tollis peccata mundis, miserer nobis.*

After the prayer, each of the Catholic men received a glass of coconut liquor and a handful of boiled chickpeas from the Hindu *zolmi* family, and thereafter left for his own home.

During the day and evening, the village gradually filled with visitors from outside, many of whom were relatives and in-laws of the Kakra people and were invited guests who received a festive diner before the ceremony. The actual Jagar started in the house of the *zolmi* family, which displayed an interesting collection of devotional objects. In the space right opposite the entrance, a small shrine, high on the wall, held a small plastic crucifix framed by the icons of St. Sebastian and Our Lady of Vailankanni, all decorated by burning candles. Inside, in a windowless room known as the *devace kudh,* that is, "room of the gods," in a hole in the wall, soot-blackened from burning oil lamps, two coconuts represented the *zolmi* ancestors surrounded by images of Krishna, Lakshmi, Sai Baba, and a number of local Hindu village gods. In this room, the Jagar ceremony was officially started around midnight with a prayer in front of the ancestral shrine. Due to the fact that only a year ago the *zolmi* family head had died, the prayer was spoken by his aged widow assisted by her eldest son. Densely crowded into the room, the dignitaries of the village and performers of the Jagar, some already dressed in their costumes, attended the prayer spoken by the old lady:

Devu, we ask you, *Ganv Mai,* we ask you, *Khuris,* we ask you, *Bautis,* we ask
   you;
Here is our *[V]odil,* we ask you and pray to you, guide us well [to the
   ceremonial house] and bring us back well;
Guide them [the performers] well and bring them back well, without all
   obstacles;
This is your ceremony, you created it; let it be well;
If we have committed mistakes, forgive us;
And we ask you too, *Fatorpekarin,* with folded hands,
And *Sateri* and *Ravalnath* and *Vetal Devu,* that all these men may return well
   and the ceremony may work well;
Here at your feet, the whole *dhājān* [literally the "ten person," that is, the
   village council] has gathered; they too shall come back well.

At this point, the son interrupted the prayer, saying, "Pray also to this god," upon
which the old lady asked, "What is his name?" The son answered, "Jhariveilo,"
that is, "The-One-from-the-Spring." The old woman continued,

We have prayed. If we have forgotten you, forgive us;
We are ignorant, you are knowledgeable;
What you once did, we are doing now;
You have planted the *maddi* [ritual pole], you made the *mand;*
Like this it shall happen also now.

The prayer reviews some of the gods, saints, and tutelary beings that are addressed in the Kakra Jagar. *Devu* is the Konkani word for God and resonates as
much with the Sanskrit *deva* as with the Latin *deus. Ganv Mai,* literally "village
mother," is the village goddess who has no special manifestation in Kakra but is
generally associated with the village space and soil. *Khuris,* the creolized Portuguese *cruz,* refers to the patron saint of the nearby town of Santa Cruz, who is
manifested in Kakra by the large stone cross at the village plaza. *Bautis* is St. John
the Baptist whose precise association with the *zolmi* family and Kakra is unknown but may originate from the time before 1928 when the people from Kakra
were still Catholics. *Odil,* actually *vodil,* stands for the "ancestor" or "ancestors"
of the *zolmi* family, and *Fatorpekarin* is the family goddess of the *zolmi* clan,
whose temple is in the South Goan town of Fatorpa, from where the Gaude claim
descent and from whose name also derives their family name, Fatorpekar. *Sateri*
is the most widespread Hindu female deity in Goa and, in this case, the *ganvdevi*
of Santa Cruz. It is said that her temple was destroyed during the early period of
Christianization and rebuilt in the nineteenth century. *Ravalnath* and *Vetal* are
two Hindu village gods who once had temples in Santa Cruz, which were also
destroyed. Nonetheless, Ravalnath is regularly remembered when the annual
procession through Santa Cruz carrying the icon of Sateri stops for prayers at

the presumed site of his former temple. Jhariveilo, finally, is the most important "tutelary god" in Kakra, whose name "The-One-from-the-Spring," indicates the location of his shrine near a natural spring that also marks the boundary between *rān,* the wilderness, and *vāḍo,* the village territory.[7]

After the prayer, the ceremony continued with a solemn procession of dignitaries, neighbors, and guests to the ceremonial house. This procession was headed by the oldest brother of the *zolmi* family carrying the sacred oil lamp, followed by his younger brothers and performers from other families carrying the big wooden drum (*dhol*) and the smaller earthen drums (*ghumat*), as well as the colorful headgear of Gorashed, the central character of the Jagar play. The procession passed the shrine of Jhariveilo, the protector of the spring and village boundary, and a Tulsi Vrindhavan that was said to mark the site of a house of one of the village's ancestors. At both places offerings of flowers and incense were made, firecrackers shot in the air, and short prayers recited. Arriving at the ceremonial house, which by then was filled with hundreds of men, women, and children, the oil lamp was placed in the middle of the *mand,* where the dignitaries took their place starting to sing the *nomana:*

> *Ādīvana Dev Bappā Satīvantā;* repeat.
> In the Beginning, God Father, the Holiness; rpt.
> *Bappā āṇī Putrā, Ispirita Santa;* rpt.
> God Father, Son [and] Holy Spirit; rpt.
> *Tiguy meḷūn ekuc Satīvantā;* rpt.
> Three persons in One Holiness; rpt.
> *Krupā dīgā Bappā, ādir chandālla;* rpt.
> Have Mercy Father, [with us] original sinners;[8] rpt.
> *Khurisā Jesu, nomana, noman;* rpt.
> Jesus's Cross, *nomana, noman;* rpt.
> *Nomana majhe, Mogāḷḷā Māte;* rpt.
> My *nomana* to the Loving Mother;[9] rpt.
> *Kīristanv jāṇāga tujhā sate;* rpt.
> Christians know your Truth; rpt.
> *Khurisā Jesu, nomana, noman;* rpt.
> Jesus's Cross, *nomana, noman;* rpt.
> *Khurisā Jesu, nomana, noman;* rpt.
> Jesus's Cross, *nomana, noman;* rpt.
> *Nomana majhe, Dev Surgāratā;* rpt.
> My *nomana* to the Splendid God;[10] rpt.
> *Yāde kar yāḍe, carana lāgatā;* rpt.
> In remembrance, [we] touch your feet [?]; rpt.
> *Nijyā putra bāḷā mukī darīlā;* rpt.
> . . . [?]
> *Khurisā Jesu, nomana, noman;* rpt.

Jesus's Cross, *nomana, noman;* rpt.
Nomana majhe, Māndoyā Guru; rpt.
My *nomana* to the honored teacher; rpt.
Tane śikoylā barana avatar; rpt.
He taught the good avatar [?]; rpt.
Tane dovrīlā sarvoyāce mūl; rpt.
He gave the origin to all; rpt.
Tajhe ūpkār Dev bāpuḍe; rpt.
. . . [?]
Khurisā Jesu, nomana, noman; rpt.
Jesus's Cross, *nomana, noman;* rpt.
Nomana majhe, ādī samestān; rpt.
My *nomana* to the ancient assembly; rpt.
Jesukiristanvje Bāraī Bhagata; rpt.
Jesus Christ's Twelve Followers; rpt.
Bāraī Bhagata, Bhagevantā; rpt.
Twelve Followers [and] Saints; rpt.
Khurisā Jesu, nomana, noman; rpt.
Jesus's Cross, *nomana, noman;* rpt.
Santa Iruginīce, Kāraṇā Aī; rpt.
Holy . . . [?], . . . [?] Mother; rpt.
Dev surgārīla, Jesu khursāru; rpt.
Heavenly God . . . , Jesus was crucified; rpt.
Khurisā ārāmīlā āpule ghor; rpt.
. . . [?]
Khurisā Jesu, nomana, noman; rpt.
Jesus's Cross, *nomana, noman;* rpt.

As discussed before, the *nomana* hymn is obviously a legacy from the time when the Kakra Jagar was part of the Catholic liturgy of the Santa Cruz church's feast and thus starts with the invocation of the Christian Trinity, Jesus Christ, and the Virgin Mary. Interestingly, this Catholic invocation is interrupted though at one point by an invocation of Ganesha, the elephant-headed Hindu god. This passage is especially cryptic and says: *Varnea vrate Gajanan jhāla, sānt ānī bhagevanta,* something that can only approximately be translated as "Doing worship, Ganesha comes, the Holy One and Saintly One." Thereafter, the text of the *nomana* is fragmentary and pays homage once again to the Christian Trinity, to *Devu Jīvantā,* the Living God, to *Bom Jesus,* the Good Jesus who is said to "hold Goa in his hand," and to *Igroj,* the Church, "whose teaching all Christians should learn to reach the paradise in heaven." The passage that refers to Ganesha, it is important to note, has obviously been inserted into the Catholic text in recent years only. I will come back to it later in this chapter in order to reflect on the particular circumstances of this change.

After the *nomana,* the ludic part of the ceremony, which presented more than fifty *songe* or characters embedded in about twenty independent sketches, began. Unlike Siolim, where Jagoryo, an especially named Jagar God, makes his appearance on stage, Kakra and the Gaude Jagar in general do not have any central mimetic embodiment of the divine. Nonetheless, a number of semidivine beings appear in the sketches. A case in point is the story of Gairama, an unspecified female tutelary being opening the series of sketches, who visits various *templas,* a word that is used here for both Hindu temples and Catholic churches, in neighboring villages where she meets with well-known local Catholic saints and Hindu gods:

> Gairama comes to the temple [*templā*] of Bidar,
> Oh Gairama, there stands St. John [*Sanjāo Saibu*], the Lord.
> Gairama comes to the temple of Kakra,
> Oh Gairama, there stands Sateri Mai.
> Gairama comes to the temple of Calapur,
> Oh Gairama, there stands *Santa Khursa.*
> Gairama comes to the temple of Bambolim,
> Oh Gairama, there stands St. Hieronymus [*Sanjerun*].
> Gairama comes to the temple of Taligao,
> Oh Gairama, there stands St. Michael [*Sanmigelu*].
> Bhūmi Mai . . . we pray to you for health [*saude*],
> Oh Mother, we pray to you for health.
> . . . [?]
> Our song [*garane*] is sung for you.
> Mother of the Rosary [*Rusari Mai*] with your golden eyes [*bhangaraco ḍoḷe*],
> Have your merciful gaze on us sinners [*pāpayank*].
> On the rock, where the well is made, is the church forever,
> Oh women who are fetching the water, do you know the saint's name.
> His name is *Santa Khuris* and he holds the village Calapur together,
> His name is famed in his village.

Other characters representing the realm between the divine and the human are Lakshmi Kansatli Nar, the Hindu "Rice Lady," who "protects the patty fields of the village"; Semotri, who is also called Shambu and whose name, costume, and wild dance alludes to the great Shiva; and Ānā, "the bearded Wandering Ascetic" leading a group of dancing boys. A particularly enigmatic, yet prominent character is *goraśer,* who wears the most outstanding costume and, above all, a large crownlike headpiece made of flowers swinging during the dance. Epitomizing in many regards the Gaude Jagar, *goraśer* can be seen on photographs from the 1910s and 1920s in the Panjim museum showing the "Gaude Zagor." In today's performances, *goraśer* appears in numerous sketches and represents a dazzling figure that oscillates between clown, trickster, and villain.

Figure 5.2. Gaude Jagar, Kakra, Goa. Photograph by Gabriele Henn.

An especially large and manifold category of characters represent occupational and caste figures such as *mhār ānī mhārīn,* the Dalit and his wife; *maloṇī,* the gardeners, *moḍvaḷ ānī moḍvaḷīn,* the washerman and his wife; *pernī,* the pearl vendor; *vaḍār,* the stonemason; *sambārī,* the spice vendor; *govḷī,* the milkman; *mhālo,* the barber; *poder,* the baker; *cāpekār,* the flower vendor; and *gosāvī,* the beggar and fortune teller. Typically, the sketches show the encounter of people from different ethnicities, classes, gender, or occupational groups, and deal with certain dilemmas, misbehavior, or adversities. A case in point is the story of *Jujhep ānī Macep,* that is, Josepha, the Catholic girl, who is dressed in a typical Catholic outfit with blouse, skirt, and parasol, and Macep, standing for two Portuguese soldiers wearing khaki uniforms and carrying guns. This sketch is also notable for its many creolized Portuguese words:

> *Josepha*
> Josepha is my name and I come from Calapur. My name is known [*famad*] in
>   Panjim too. Josepha is my name and I call Macep.
> *Soldiers*
> Let's promenade [*vamso pasoyāre amī*] to the *Kanāri* [old form for "Konkan"]
>   market. Let's buy *mogri* flowers there, *mogri* flowers for the dance. Let's
>   promenade to the *Kanāri* market.
> *Chorus*

Once, we had been noble sons [*kūnvar vhaḍā vhaḍā gele*], but then we lost
    [*perdiz*] everything and thus they gave us to the soldiers [*amkā soldad
    dile*].
Soldiers
Portuguese soldiers [*Soldad Portugalre*] are we and we want to marry [*ker
    kasār*] Josepha.
Chorus
Once, we had been noble sons, but then we lost everything and thus they
    humiliated us [*amkā disgras dile*].
Soldiers
Portuguese soldiers are we and we want to marry Josepha.
Chorus
Once, we had been noble sons, but then we lost everything and thus. . . .
    [*amkā pātśāk dile*] [?].
Soldiers
Viva Annemarie Satesh and viva Maria!
Chorus
Once we were wearing socks and shoes [*meu ānī motce*] but now we have to
    go barefooted.
Soldiers
Oh my captain of Goa, oh my captain of Goa!
Chorus
Once we were wearing uniforms [*fat*], but now we walk around naked.
Soldiers
Oh my captain of Goa, oh my captain of Goa!
Chorus
Once we were wearing bonnets [*kepe*], but now we walk around bareheaded.
Soldiers
Oh my captain of Goa, oh my captain of Goa!

At this point *mhālo,* the barber, enters the stage holding a razor blade and bowl
in his hands:

Pandu Barber is my name; Saturday I go round the town; Sunday I cut Macep's
beard. But today I let his stinking beard, because my blade is blunt and my
shoe is lost.

Poder, the baker, enters the stage holding a bread basket in his hand:

Mahesh Poder is my name; Kakra is where I was born. And my name is known
in Panjim, and I sell my bread in Calapur.

Capekār, the flower seller, comes on stage:

Ramchandra Capekar is my name and I sell my *cāfi* flowers in Panjim.

The theme of inappropriate relationships between men and women varies in different versions. Thus, *Tendlī ānī Dadlo* tells in many metaphors and allusions of "mangoes" and "sticks" the story of an erotic affair between a local women and a male visitor, which ends with a dialogue between the women and her sisters:

> *Sisters*
> Oh sister, you come from the garden, what happened to you?
> How did your braid [*māthyācī vīṇī*] become so deranged?
> How did your flowers [*fūlā*] become so deranged?
> How did your sari [*sāṛī*] become so deranged?
> How did your blouse [*coḷī*] become so deranged?
> How did your necklace [*mūṇī*] become so deranged?
> How did your forehead mark [*tiḷā*] become so deranged?
> *Tendlī*
> Oh sisters, I met a man on my way, he gave me flowers, and he seduced
>   [*buloile*] me.

In a similar way, *Tayākāsa*, whose title combines the Konkani word *tayā* for "lake" with the Portuguese word *caça* for "hunt," tells the story of two *Istudantes* that are after the *borebore* (fine-looking), *goregore* (fair-tainted) *Marie Bejel*. Stories like this are especially critical where "foreigners" are involved, as in *Polkis*, the story of two *moṭmoṭele*, that is, "fat foreigners," who come on the steamboat from Daman to Goa in order to look for *malfiriad bāyl*, prostitutes.

Skits dealing with "strangers" mark another recurring theme in the Gaude Jagar play. Hence, Firanghī, "the Frank," who has become synonymous with the historical European; Paklo, the historical Portuguese; Hapshi, "the Abyssinian African"; Kapro, "the Black African"; Khan Saib, "the Muslim"; and even Hindustan Dadlo ānī Hindustan Bāyl, "the Indian Man and the Indian Woman," all represent "foreigners" or "strangers." The topic of the Foreign is also variously invoked when *goraśer* is associated with strange imaginative lands such as *Bablater* or *Minglater*. Among the various characters representing officials or authorities, Nikandār, the historical Havaldār, that is, "Chief and Tax collector," and Porpotī, the historical "Village Barker," are the most conspicuous in the Gaude Jagar, if only for the fact that they come along on stilts. Like the various stories presenting Portuguese Soldiers, their appearance shows a certain aloofness that borders on ridiculousness, especially when the songs in some villages report how villagers cheat on Nikandār by hiding the chicken and grain that he has come to confiscate. In Kakra, the story goes like this:

> *Nikandār*
> *Namaskār, namaskār, Santa Khuris, namaskār.*
> I came along and saw the *Kapre* and *Firanghi* fighting.
> *Chorus*
> Baba Nikandār, you are the biggest chief [*havaldār*].

Nikandār
I came from Sukur where they slaughtered a pig [*dukor*] which had no arms
  and legs and genitalia [*hātnā pītnā gāṇīn pokoḷ*].
Chorus
Baba Nikandār, you are the biggest guardian [*rākhaṇḍār*].
Nikandār
I came to Codna, and a coconut was my pillow on which I slept when girls
  played dirty games in an old house. . . .
Chorus
Baba Nikandār, god's blessing be with you.

Occasionally, the stories allude to classical Hindu mythology such as Harichandra, "the Hindu King," who has his entrance with Karamati, his wife; Rohidas, his son; and Vishvamitra, his "Counselor." The serious topic of Indian widowhood is raised in *Māmā ānī Batco*, "the (Maternal) Uncle and His Nephew," whose story tells how the uncle instructs his nephew in using a gun, upon which the nephew—whether accidently or purposely remains unclear—shoots the uncle. Thereafter, Māmī, the aunt, asks in a long lamentation who will now protect *kaplāco tilā*, the decorative mark on her forehead; *māthyāci fūlān*, the flowers in her hair; *hātāci kānṇā*, the bangles on her arms; and *galyāco mūṇī*, the attire around her neck, all of which stand as symbols of her femininity. The sketch ends with the macabre dance of the *bhūtā* or ghosts who carry the dead uncle away.

Eventually, at daybreak, the ceremonies ended with a final *nomana* hymn that declares the village as "peaceful" and "cool" and once again recites a list of those honored and invoked:

We play this tune [*rumbat*] for all these gods;
We play for Sateri Mai;
We play for Ravalnath;
We play for Ganv Mai;
We play for the sacred oil lamp [*javtā dipa*];
We play for The-One-of-the-Place [*Jāgyācyā Deva*];
Jesus was born in Bethlehem [*Belyātu*], in the Virgin Mary's arms, he rests;
Jesus was born in Bethlehem city [*Belyā nagārun*], joy is there, in Bethlehem
  city.

Three lines of invocation that are standard in the concluding part of most Gaude Jagar are especially important to note because they indicate with particular clarity the rationale of the ritual:

baslele sabhek, "all sitting in the assembly";
tihthis koti devā, the proverbial "33 million gods," living in India; and, finally,
cuklya maklya devā, "all other deities," whom one might possibly have
  forgotten.

What comes to the fore here is the concern of the celebrants not to leave anybody out in the long list of gods, saints, ancestors, and tutelary beings that are associated with the village and, therefore, must be acknowledged and honored in the annual ceremony. This concern is not uncommon in popular religiosity and is usually associated with the idea that only regular ritual acknowledgment of divine and saintly beings guarantees their readiness to respond to their devotees and grant protection or perform miracles. In fact, in Hindu belief, gods, ancestors, and tutelary beings who are ritually neglected may be feared as they are likely to turn resentful and inflict on people precisely those harms and risks from which they otherwise shield or cure. To prevent such negative consequences, people take special precautionary measures if the extraordinary circumstances occur that make it impossible to perform the Jagar. For instance, if the Jagar cannot be performed in one year because of the pollution affecting some of its prominent practitioners through the recent death of family members, people perform a short ritual called *jāgoratco dīs* or *bogaval,* which, in very brief form and without ceremony, calls and appeases all major gods, saints, ancestors, and tutelary beings of the village. What is interesting to see here are that the three major ritual concerns dealing with aspects of time, space, and performance still guide the ritual and are critical for its success.

The ritual concern regarding time and history has been mentioned already and applies above all to the necessity to perform the ritual or, as we have seen, at least a token of it, every year. The date of the annual Jagar is predetermined, and in most villages reflects its Catholic legacy by being connected with the annual feast of the local patron saint. While this connection with the Catholic calendar has become problematic for the predominantly Hindu practitioners in some villages, and has sometimes been changed to a date significant in the Hindu calendar, these changes are rare and nowhere taken lightly because they are associated with ritual risks and may bring harm to the village and its people. The apex of the ritual concern with time is the *praesentia,* that is, the ritual presence of all gods, saints, ancestors, tutelary beings, and men that are constitutive and relevant for the village at the moment and time of the Jagar. It is therefore of greatest importance that from every family of the village at least one male member participates in the ceremony and is part of the *sabhā,* the assembly of village dignitaries that sits on the *mand.* The absence of male representation of an important family of the village, which sometimes happens as an expression of protest or conflict, or simply because all its men have left the village to work abroad, can trigger great concern and efforts at appeasement or correction. Ideally, the temporal bonds between the divine, saintly, and human beings of the village are genealogical or through family relationships. The most important agents to be invoked and honored in the ceremonies are the *purvoj* or *vodil,* that is, ancestors of the important village clans, some of whom are deified and embodied in iconic tokens such as coconuts, or are represented by shrines in the village territory. As for the gods and saints, ideally, the ritual presence of all those who have been of relevance for the village in the past and are of relevance in the present is required, regardless of their religious connection. The Hindu Gaude appreciate the Catholic "origins" of their festival by invoking the Christian Trinity, the Catholic Mother of God, and the authority of the Church in their *nomana,* and honor *Bautis,* that is, St. John the Baptist, and other Catholic saints as patrons of their Catholic ancestors. Likewise, the long list of Hindu gods invoked in the ceremony indicates historic flexibility and inclusivity, when ancient gods such as Sateri, Ravalnath, and Vetal can be found next to Fatorpekarin, the goddess of the village Fatorpa, and Ganesha, who have been incorporated only in more recent times.

Finally, the dramatic characters and skits of the Jagar play are part of the ritual presence, albeit in a more ephemeral and playful way. Showing historical, social, and imaginative characters, the presentation of these skits demonstrates the greatest openness for change and modernity. Occasionally, one can see totally new figures such as *hippie,* the prototype of the contemporary tourist, making their appearance on the Jagar stage, and young performers introduce popular melodies from Hindi film songs and new forms of disco dancing in the traditional repertoire and styles of the Jagar play. Showing thus a certain responsiveness to a changing social and cultural environment, the malleability of the play is still subject to restrictions. Its lyrics and performative styles are seen as part of what is called *kaido,* or "tradition," and changes are considered critical and, in fact, even potentially dangerous for the outcome of the ritual. Accordingly, people are reluctant to change anything, and if they nevertheless do so, take special precautions not to disrupt the entire setting. I observed an illustrative example of such moderated change in the play of the Kakra Jagar in 1994. The change was related to the then-ongoing first American Gulf War, which was of particular concern to the villagers because some of them were migrant laborers and were anxious about returning to their working places in Kuwait and other parts of the Arabian Gulf. Accordingly, some performers decided to make a reference to the situation in the Middle East in a traditional song telling the story of *Kaṇsātlī Nār,* the female "guardian of the rice fields," who comes out on the *mand* with two *sipoy,* soldiers, armed with rifles and guns. The traditional song narrates how the bellicose trio guards the rice fields against a type of parrot known in Konkani as *kir.* "*Kirak marun pistol hatla,*" one line of the song goes, something that translates as, "To kill the parrots pistols are brought." Obviously, the villagers were inspired by the fact that the linguistic accusative for the Konkani word *kir* is *kirak,* which sounds similar to the word "Iraq." That means the text lent itself to a very striking semantic change by a simple twist of the tongue effected by changing it to "*Irak marun pistol Israyelche hatla,*" which now says, "To fight Iraq pistols are brought from Israel." The textual transformation was completed by inserting the words *getan* for "air jet" and *munval* for "warship" at some other passages and out came a new song that now dealt with the critical war scenario in the Middle East without changing the sound, rhyme structure, narrative framework, or main characters of the old song.

Although a singular episode, the case reveals something axiomatic about the relationship of the Jagar to history and change. The Jagar play may represent manifold social and cultural perspectives and reflect myriad influences and transformations to which Gaude culture has been and currently is exposed. Nonetheless, it cannot simply be reduced to a theatrical kaleidoscope or artistic representation of Gaude history and presence, but is obviously obliged to the ritual concept of *praesentia*, which curtails its openness for change. This restriction becomes even more critical where the liturgical parts of the ritual are at stake, as with the insertion of the invocation of Ganesha into the otherwise completely Catholic content of the initial *nomana*. Notably, this insertion, which should be seen in the context of the growing significance of Hinduism for the Gaude community, was made in recent years and reflects a particular concern for the unbroken ritual integrity of the ceremony. Hence, a comparison with the Jagar of a neighboring village shows that the traditional text passage was "*Varnea vrate Igrojan jhāla, sānt ānī bhagevanta,*" something that translates as, "In order to worship, come into the Church, the Holy One and Saintly One." This was then changed to "*Varnea vrate Gajanan jhāla, sānt ānī bhagevanta,*" something that is not grammatically consistent but can approximately be translated as, "In order to worship Ganesha comes, the Holy One and Saintly One." Where changes are made to the liturgical content, this example demonstrates once again, they very consciously keep with the stylistic and performative structures of the text, thereby, by default, keeping with the syncretistic nature of the ritual at large.

Another major ritual concern regards space and neighborhood and applies, first of all, to the necessity of performing the ritual within the village territory. The epitomic embodiment of the ritual concern for space is the *mand*, that is, the demarcated ritual space in which all gods, saints, ancestors, tutelary beings, men, and dramatic characters relevant for the village come together during the Jagar ceremony. Corresponding with the constitutive function of Hindu gods and Catholic saints, whose iconic bodies are equated with the soil of the village and Goa at large, Sateri, Bhumika, and St. Francis Xavier are honored in all Goan Jagar. All other gods and saints invoked in the ceremonies are specified by their respective territorial associations. In this case, the village gods and patron saints of Kakra and Santa Cruz/Calapur are obviously most important. Next come gods and saints of neighboring villages such as Bambolim and Taligao with whom the people are related through kinship and social relationships. Fatorpekarin, the goddess of the village Fatorpa, is honored because she marks the place from which the *zolmi* family of Kakra claims its descent. Tutelary beings marking special spots and locations in the village, such as the spring, the *khuris,* the well, the border, and so on, are also honored. Moreover, many of the stories of the ludic part have distinctly spatial connotations and refer to real or imaginative places, contrast home and foreign lands, or describe allegoric journeys undertaken by dramatic characters such as *Gairamā, Kaṇsātlī Nār,* or *Goraśer* to reach the Jagar *mand.*

It is this strict association of the ritual with the village territory that triggers serious debate when, for instance, somebody whose ancestral home is not located on the village land wants to perform a function in the ritual. More serious concern is caused by the request to perform some part or dramatic characters of the Jagar outside the village territory. Such requests have occurred increasingly in recent years, because cultural institutions, and public and private agents of the tourist industry see the colorful performances of the Jagar as ideal representations of Goan culture and powerful attractions for Goan tourism. Their requests are often resolved by the local village communities only after consulting the oracles of their village gods.

The concerns for the ritual presence and the ritual space gain their common apex in the significance of the sacred oil lamp that is placed in the middle of the *mand.* This oil lamp is considered the site at which all gods, saints, ancestors, and tutelary beings invoked in the ritual manifest their *praesentia* during the ceremony. All dancers and singers, therefore, always face the oil lamp during their performances, thereby turning their backs on the human audience most of the time. In the strictest sense, the songs, dances, and sketches undertaken during the Jagar are thus not performed for the human but for the divine audience that is represented by the oil lamp.

Finally, the ritual is guided by a performative concern, which, like the concerns regarding time and space, is considered critical for its efficacy and success. This performative concern reveals an intricate interrelationship between the human and the divine agents in what is the central and name-giving purpose of the ritual, that is, to be *jāgṛit* or awake. As mentioned earlier, the quality of Hindu gods to be *jāgṛit,* which in many ways resembles the quality of Catholic Saints to work miracles, is widely appreciated but also considered precarious. Special activities are needed therefore to evoke and perpetuate this quality of which the Jagar ceremony is one. In fact, one can say that, among all the rituals performed in the village in the course of the year, the Jagar generates the *jāgṛ* or wakefulness of the gods, saints, ancestors, and tutelary beings most effectively because it enacts a peculiar mimetic interaction between the divine and the human agents of the ritual. In other words, the ritual essence of the Jagar is based on the idea that it is the villagers' determination to stay awake for a full night and beat the drums, dance the dances, and sing the songs that triggers and guarantees the readiness of the gods, saints, ancestors, and tutelary beings to stay awake, on their part, and protect the village and be responsive to the villagers' needs and requests for a full year.

It is this emphasis on the mimetic activity of the ritual, rather than its communicative meaning, that becomes most important for the ritual efficacy. "As performative praxis, which wants to help to come into being what it says and does," Bourdieu writes, elaborating on the general principle, "ritual is most often but a practical mimesis of the natural process that it advances" (Bourdieu 1993: 168). Strictly speaking, the meaning of the sketches and stories presented in the Jagar play and even the identity and doctrinal belonging of the gods and saints evoked in the *nomana* are therefore irrelevant or, at least, secondary vis-à-vis the primary purpose of the ritual—to keep the divine and human agents awake and alert. In a certain perspective, the Jagar is thus nothing more than a practical technique for keeping its divine and human agents awake. Theories stating that rituals have their ontic purpose strongly or even exclusively in their activity have been widely discussed in recent years (Henn 2008). Communicative meanings of rituals, it is argued, are either generally secondary (Staal 1979; Michaels 2006; Tambiah 1979), or specific only for certain types of ritual (Humphrey and Laidlaw 1994; Schieffelin 1985), or part of distinct historical or "semiotic ideologies" (Asad 1993; Keane 2004, 2007). While confirming the general emphasis of the performative, rather than communicative, purpose of the ritual, the Goan Jagar marks an interesting case in this discussion because it reveals that, even where ritual can be said to be "pure activity" (Staal 1979: 9), it still relies on cultural models that embody such kinds of activities. Thus, the Konkani and, by extension, Indian-language equivalent of the Western term for ritual, which is *devukār,* combines the terms *devu,* god, and *kār,* to do, thereby designating ritual as something like "doing in the name of god" or ontic activity.

More specifically, the tautological quality of the action performed in the Jagar refers to the subtleties of the Hindu theology that is associated with the concept of *līlā,* that is, the playful nature of god. The earliest archival evidence of *līlā,* Indologist Norvin Hein (1995) notes, is the Vedanta Sutra, an ancient Hindu text ascribed to the third century BCE, in which the author defends the belief in a divine creator. This belief is challenged by the objection that, given the prevailing axiom of god being radically all-embracing, any notion of the activity of god and in particular of his or her creation of the world, is nonsensical because it implicates the existence of and desire for something that does not exist. The author rejects this objection by arguing that the activity and creativity implicated in the idea of a divine creator does not presume any ontic lacunae or desire, but simply marks an absolutely purposeless, playful action that is free from all *kāma,* that is, desire, and all *karma,* that is, consequences. Such a tautological action for action's sake is called *līlā,* the play of the gods. Realized in manifold ways in Hindu mythology, iconography, theater, and arguably also in the Goan Jagar, *līlā* marks an ambiguous view of the gods and the world. On the one hand, it shows the unreliability and unpredictability of the gods and, by extension, the world at large, which suggests that the Jagar is nothing but play and, at worst, imagination, deception, and chaos. On the other hand, *līlā* and the Jagar are the ultimate divine activity through which the world keeps going, continuously renewing itself, and, in mimetic interaction between gods and humans, is protected from misfortune and evil. Therefore, at the cost of disaster and annihilation, the Jagar simply cannot not be done but also, as the Goan scholar Mário Cabral e Sá (1997: 131) cogently says, mirrors the obvious necessity that "it takes all kinds to make this world."

Religion, Memory, and Survival

In conclusion, Gaude religious allegiance, that is, avowing themselves to the community and doctrines of Hindus or to the community and doctrines of Catholics, always was a political issue connected to their cultural survival. Variously in history, we have seen, a large part of the population of this marginalized community felt the necessity to adjust to the shifting power relations between Hindus and Catholics in Goa, and collectively changed their religious identity and belonging. While these conversions invariably effected radical changes in their cultural habitus and social relationships, serious limitations in educational support and social acknowledgment made it neither possible nor wise for the Gaude to fully implement these changes. Instead, holding on, at least partially, to the values and legacies of their respective previous religious communities and doctrines was as essential for their social life and cultural survival as changing their religious allegiances and identities from one to the other.

Furthermore, the always critical and contested question of whether Gaude should ritually acknowledge the shifting religious allegiances of their ancestors, or strictly assert the distinctness and exclusivity of their actual religious identity, was a political question that depended on power relations and was part of strategic considerations. What needs also to be noted here is, however, that the question of syncretism and religious self-assertion never was only a political question; it never could be solely reduced to the politics of religious identity and difference between Hindus and Catholics. In fact, what prevented Gaude from becoming a mere political plaything in and between the shifting power relations of Hindus and Catholics, and what—despite acknowledging their subaltern status—always also empowered them to resist, to some extent, the exigencies of the respective religious hegemonies, was that, to them, religion had and has a dimension that does not fully resolve itself in the values and politics that govern the interplay between the forces of Hinduism and Catholicism. This dimension of religion comes to the fore in the various ritual concerns and commitments that culminate in a form of ritual memory that celebrates and remembers the divine and saintly as iconic embodiments manifested in time and space. In doing this, the ritual memory takes care that, ideally, none of the gods, saints, ancestors, or tutelary beings who ever has been of relevance for the village in the past, nor anyone who ever manifested him- or herself in the territory that is relevant for the village now, is left out of the annual honoring and invocation. Such ritual reference to history and space is not uncommon, and the scholarship on "cultural memory" (Assmann 1988) has long ago shown that material and iconic media along with genealogical and mimetic modes of remembering play an important role in it. Likewise, the *chronotopos,* that is, the representation and remembering of time in space, for instance in the "ritual journey," is a concept and practice common to literary studies as well as the anthropology of religion (Bachtin 2008; Taussig 1993). What is notable though in Gaude's ritual memory is that it invalidates their otherwise validated narrative memory by not appreciating and replicating the constitutive paradigm of modern historical consciousness, that is, the paradigm of linear time. Unlike the Hegelian appreciation of Chronos, whose mythological emasculation of his own father epitomizes the modern idea that the Posterior always radically transforms, if not annihilates, the Anterior, Gaude's ritual memory thus appreciates the palimpsest, the historical inscription that never fully eradicates what has been written before.

6 Crossroads of Religion

Shrines and Urban Mobility

In this final chapter I want to briefly explore Hindu and Catholic wayside shrines in Goa's cities. The reason for paying attention to these shrines is that they are especially popular in the urban milieu and, although it is impossible to give exact figures, outnumber temples and churches by a large margin. Their popularity seems especially striking because the shrines are generally quite simple structures, many of which seem to be stylistically at odds with the aesthetics of the urban architecture, or are placed at locations where they seem to founder in the midst of modern structures or be overrun by the heavy traffic. These circumstances notwithstanding, the shrines persist in the rapidly changing urban environment and continue to grow in numbers. Some of them—such as the Catholic Holy Cross Shrine on the outskirts of Panjim and the Shri Dev Bodgeshvar Shrine in Mapusa—have gained a degree of popularity in recent years that exceeds even the local temples and churches in terms of their architectural visibility and numbers of regular devotees.

Notably, though, wayside shrines are neither exclusively urban nor modern phenomena but are instead rooted in the ancient form of religiosity that is based on Hindu village gods, Catholic patron saints, and tutelary beings, and that is believed to embody and protect the spaces and precarious localities of villages and towns. Trying, then, to account for the outstanding popularity that these shrines enjoy today, I argue that the religious devotion dedicated to them successfully negotiates the old structures of Hindu village gods and Catholic patron saints with the needs and concerns of people facing rapid sociocultural change and mobility. In particular, I show that the shrines respond to three forms of mobility that occur more markedly in the urban environment: cultural mobility, that is, the diversification and fluctuation of religious ideas and practices across the formal divisions of Hindu and Catholic doctrines; social mobility, that is, the diversification and fluctuation of people coming from different castes, social classes, and geographical regions; and, finally, physical mobility, that is, the movement of and around increasingly dense and complex flows of motorized traffic.[1]

Cultural Mobility

One of the features contributing to the special appeal that wayside shrines have in urban spaces is their openness to devotional diversity. The shrines not only relate to the veneration of a multitude of major and minor, local and translocal Hindu gods and Catholic saints, but many of them also represent Hindu deities and Catholic saints in close contiguity or in one and the same shrine, thereby inviting lateral or even syncretistic worship. Prominent though not unique examples of shrines located in close proximity are those representing the Hindu Shri Dev Bodgeshvar and the Catholic Lady of Vailankanni in the heart of the market of Mapusa. Located back to back to a tree, both these shrines actually claim one and the same spot. More commonly, hybrid shrines shelter Hindu and Christian icons in the same shrine or under one roof. A prominent example of this type is the shrine of, again, Our Lady of Vailankanni located at the central plaza of Margao, which also hosts an image of Shri Dev Damodar, the Hindu village god of the city.

There is instead strong evidence that multireligious shrines were facilitated as early as the sixteenth and seventeenth centuries by the iconoclastic nature of the Portuguese-Catholic conquest discussed in chapter 2. The conquerors not only destroyed the Hindu monuments but systematically replaced them with Christian churches, chapels, and crosses, thereby producing, although unintentionally, an exact Catholic replica of the spatial order of Hindu monuments and sites. Thus, when Hindus in the late nineteenth and throughout the twentieth centuries reinstated their claim on the Goan landscape by (re)building temples and shrines, if not in the very same places, at least following the old pattern of the spatial distribution of religious sites, this led to a close contiguity of Hindu and Catholic monuments. Such shrines enjoy a particular appeal today to the diversifying and fluctuating population of Goa's urban dwellers, businesspeople, and tourists, especially flourishing at locations where public and private forms of worship intersect, as is often the case in urban contexts. Two patterns of this type of intersection are worth explaining in greater detail. First, in service and business locations, such as offices, markets, shops, and workshops, the display of images, icons, and tokens of gods, saints, tutelary figures, and religious scenes from various religious traditions is especially frequent and appealing because the staff, employees, customers, and visitors of these places also belong to diverse religions. Especially conspicuous are the shrines at urban hospitals and taxi stands that, obviously reflecting the physically critical nature of their services, are usually very elaborate and multireligious, commonly displaying images of Hindu gods, Christian saints, and often also a picture of the Muslim Kaaba.

Another common pattern of syncretistic urban devotion can be seen in public shrines displaying images of sacred beings that have become popular with Goans for personal and individual reasons, rather than due to the traditional village or family associations. These sacred beings, whose images may be found at individual shrines or together with images of local village gods and patron saints, vary from local figures such as the Catholic Father Agnello or the Hindu holy man Arjudh Anand, both of whom gained fame in Goa in the early twentieth century due to their miraculous healing powers, to figures of supra-local, national, and even international reputation. Most popular among the latter in Goa today are Shirdi Sai Baba and Our Lady of Vailankanni, two saints who, at first glance, seem to embody quite different characters. Shirdi Sai Baba was born in 1872 in Shirdi, a town in central Maharashtra, where he lived the life of a religious ascetic and became recognized and worshipped as a saint for his *siddhis* or supernatural powers. Our Lady of Vailankanni, also known as Our Lady of Good Health, represents an incorporation of the Christian Mary who, according to legend, manifested herself in a series of apparitions and miracles in the sixteenth and seventeenth centuries in Vailankanni, a coastal town close to Chennai in Tamil Nadu. A closer look, though, reveals certain similarities between these two saints, which supports the hypothesis that urban shrines gain their special popularity in part by allowing for devotional fluidity and diversity. First of all, both saints have a distinctly charismatic appeal, that is, a reputation for miraculous power that radiates beyond their respective home regions. In other words, they are predestined to become autonomous spiritual patrons functioning independently from the traditional territorial associations and social rootedness characteristic of established Hindu village gods and Catholic patron saints. Shirdi Sai Baba is worshipped in countless public and private shrines in Goa and other parts of India and, interestingly, even in a series of devotional centers in the United States, Canada, Cuba, and other international locations.[2] Likewise, Our Lady of Vailankanni is popular in Goan shrines and draws millions of pilgrims from all over India to worship her at her home basilica in Vailankanni every year. Another significant commonality between the two saints is their distinct cross-religious origin and appeal. Shirdi Sai Baba was born a Hindu Brahman, yet, orphaned as a child, was brought up by a pious Muslim and, in his later teaching and practice, combined elements of Hindu *bhakti* and Muslim Sufi devotion that made him popular among Hindus as well as Muslims (White 1972; Babb, 1991). Vailankanni, who unifies in her person numerous characteristics of the Virgin Mary and the Hindu Devi, and is worshipped in a distinctly "Indic" way that combines Catholic and Hindu iconographies and practices, not surprisingly has become famous for attracting Catholic as well as Hindu devotees (Newman 2001; Meibohm 2002, 2004). Finally, both saints are embedded in hagiographic narratives that, while stereotypical in their respective Hindu or Catholic contexts,

Figure 6.1. Urban Shrine I, Panjim, Goa. Photograph by Gabriele Henn.

address a particular sociological audience common to both saints. Hence, while Shirdi Sai Baba embodies the familiar Hindu evolution from *sādhu* to *avatār*, that is, ascetic to holy man, Vailankanni, also known as the Lourdes of the East, represents the typical Catholic apparition to the shepherd boy. Both saints manifest their powers outside established Brahmanical or clerical frameworks, thereby becoming particularly appealing to the proverbial "ordinary people." In sum, the two saints most frequently worshipped in urban wayside shrines in Goa demonstrate the shrines' devotional diversity in three ways: first, they exhibit a distinctly charismatic, that is, independent and personal authority; second, they refer to distinctly hybrid, Hindu-Muslim and Hindu-Catholic origins or traditions; and third, they work outside established Brahmanical and clerical frameworks.

Social Mobility

Due to their tentatively autonomous status in the old village system, the shrines are accessible and attractive to worshippers belonging to diverse castes and classes, and also to people whose social status changes due to shifting socioeconomic conditions. The shrines are also open to worshippers from different geographical regions. Two urban shrines that have experienced an extraordinary evolution in Goan cities in postcolonial times illustrate this diversity and fluidity of shrine worshippers in an exemplary way. The first is the shrine (now temple) of Shri Dev Bodgeshvar in the city of Mapusa. This shrine originated in the mid-1930s, when people started to pay ritual homage to a tree on the outskirts of the city. Judging from its location, paraphernalia, and mythology, this old shrine was associated with a sacred being belonging to the category of either *śīmeveiḷe*, that is, border guardians, or holy men, that is, sanctified Hindu ascetics. In the following years and in particular after Goa's independence from Portuguese domination in 1961, the shrine continued to grow in popularity and size until, by 1966, it had evolved into a small temple that was officially recognized and registered in Mapusa. By the end of the 1970s, the *Gazetteer of the Union Territory: Goa, Daman, and Diu* notably mentions Bodgeshvar's temple under "places of interest" in Mapusa, presumably because its annual festival in December-January has become "one of the biggest fairs in Goa" (Government of India 1979: 787). In 1993, the construction work was finally completed that replaced the small temple with a large and sumptuous temple, showing now a life-sized anthropomorphic icon of Bodgeshvar, who by then had been theologically ennobled and was now called Shri Dev Bodgeshvar. As I have described in greater detail elsewhere (Henn 2006), the extraordinary evolution of this shrine was, and to this day is, closely related to the demographic growth and socioeconomic prosperity that Mapusa, like other cities in Goa, has experienced since the end of Portuguese rule. More precisely, the shrine appeals to and is supported by the highly dynamic, socioeconomically mobile, and ethnically diversifying urban population of Mapusa. Unlike the other temples in the city, whose trustees are either Gaud Saraswat Brahmans, belonging to Goa's largest caste of Brahmans, or Vani, belonging to a long-established merchant caste of Mapusa, Bodgeshvar's trustees represent a mixed group of people belonging to Vani, Maratha, and Bandhari castes. Thus, Bodgeshvar's trustees not only constitute a heterogeneous caste group, some of which belong to the subaltern rank of Sudra, but also owe their positions to recent professional and business success and socioeconomic prosperity, rather than longstanding establishment and social anchorage in the city. Not surprisingly, therefore, and obviously facilitated by the fact that his iconography and mythology oscillates between a local god and a mendicant monk, Bodgeshvar also enjoys great popularity among Mapusa's growing migrant labor force from Karnataka and other Indian regions.

Another wayside shrine that has experienced an extraordinary evolution in recent years is the shrine of the Holy Cross of Bambolim, also known as *Fulancho Khuris,* the "Flower Cross," on the outskirts of Goa's capital, Panjim. Memories of this shrine go back to the 1940s, when people started to pay homage to a small white stone cross located next to the mud road that was eventually to become India's National Highway 17, connecting Panjim with Mangalore and Mumbai. Legends explaining what transformed this particular cross, as distinct from the thousands of crosses scattered all over Goa's landscape and settlements, into a prominent religious landmark vary in detail, but they all refer to the miraculous interventions by which the cross is said to have protected people from danger and accidents or cured them of illnesses. Among those reporting early miracles of the Bambolim Cross were miners working in nearby quarries, farmhands harvesting cashew fruits in the surrounding forests, construction workers building the highway, and one Cassiano Afonso from the nearby village of Siridao, whose wife was miraculously cured of cancer. These stories recur down the decades and document, above all, the ever-growing and changing population worshipping what later became known as *Milangrinco Khuris,* the "Miraculous Cross." Regular devotees included, in particular, the communities of Gaude from the nearby villages of Bambolim and Siridao, who once formed part of Goa's tribal population, although today, for various reasons, they constitute a rather diverse group. They earn their living today partly from agricultural labor and fishing, partly from employment in the service sector and small businesses, and partly as migrant labor in Europe and the Persian Gulf. The popularity of the Bambolim Cross was further increased by still more diversified and changing groups of worshippers, such as soldiers from a nearby military camp and colony, who reportedly adorned it with a metal canopy and marble tiles in 1969; the patients, visitors, and staff of the nearby Goa Medical College and Hospital; and last but not least, the innumerable crowd of drivers and passengers of private cars, two-wheelers, taxis, buses, and trucks stopping on their way in and out of Panjim to pay homage. Eventually, the committee of the Bambolim Cross, which was formed by an enterprising priest of Siridao and a couple of lawyers and businessmen from Panjim, successfully cleared the legal ground and raised the money necessary to make the small cross into a church in 1996. The intangible and material support that made the transformation of an inconspicuous cross into an impressive church possible, as the resultant souvenir shows (Shrine of [the] Holy Cross of Bambolim 1996), came to a large extent from private people and businesses in Panjim and, to a remarkable extent, also from the Gaude population from nearby villages working and living today in the Persian Gulf.

Traveling and Traffic

The appeal of wayside shrines to urban populations ultimately is built on their relationship with traveling and traffic. At first glance, this relationship seems awkward, given the fact that many shrines are obviously at odds with their urban environment. Many old shrines are literally in the way of the expanding construction of urban roads, almost foundering amid the heavy traffic surrounding them, and sometimes even creating dangerous traffic hazards and bottlenecks. Similarly, old shrines can be found next to modern houses, business centers, and shopping malls, where their archaic outlook starkly contrasts with the modern style of the architectural environment. Conspicuously, however, these technical and stylistic oddities usually do not lead to the demolition of shrines but rather to their integration into the new urban design. A particular case in point occurred in 1993, when the small chapel of St. Anthony in the village of Soccorro (Bardes) was set to be demolished in order to give way to the widening of National Highway 17 leading to Mapusa. The plan triggered a vociferous public protest that filled the local newspapers for weeks, and was settled only when the local traffic department agreed not to demolish the chapel but to carefully dismantle it and exactly rebuild it alongside the widened highway (Dias 1993; Mahambre 1993). A similar case involving another chapel located at the highway entrance into Margao (Salcete) has been pending for years. No agreement has been reached so far, with the result that the chapel, still located at its original spot, now encroaches onto the highway space and seriously impedes the flow of traffic. Another very common sight are old wayside shrines, crosses, and chapels located right in the middle of busy crossroads with heavy traffic flowing around them. In the heart of Goa's modern cities, the uneasy integration of the shrines into the urban architecture is evidenced in some odd views and perspectives. Not only does the integration of old shrines into late-modern architecture create the impression of an anachronistic blend, but, in some spots, new or remodeled shrines that adapt to the modernist architectural style of their modern environment curiously stand out from the common, traditional shapes of shrines.

The odd location and appearance of wayside shrines, and their tenacious persistence in the urban space, is arguably due to their traditional functions. The

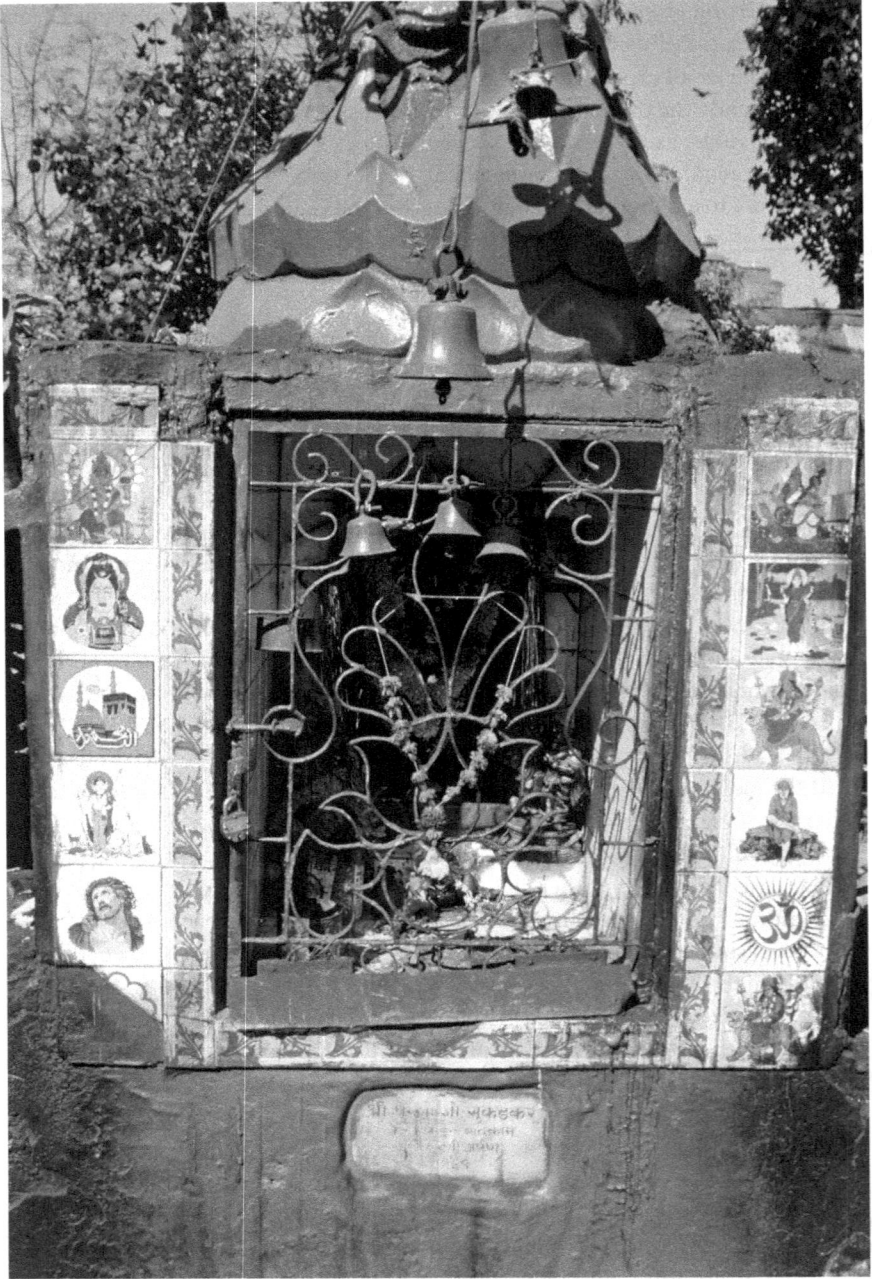

Figure 6.2. Urban Shrine II, Margao, Goa. Photograph by Gabriele Henn.

shrines represent local village gods, patron saints, and tutelary beings, and are located at significant locations in and around villages and cities. Since central and liminal locations such as plazas and marketplaces, borders, bridges, and crossroads are traditionally predestined for wayside shrines, their present-day locations at critical traffic points is inevitable. The people commonly believe that the sacred beings protect the inhabitants and the people living nearby or passing by the territories and locations with which they are associated. Traditionally, the protection related to the shrines ranged from natural calamities, such as storms and floods, to social disharmony and human maliciousness, to illnesses and accidents. Protection while moving and traveling, be it on roads, by sea, or nowadays by air always was a special function attributed to territorial patrons. Both Hindus and Catholics have particular spiritual patrons who are famed for their protection of travelers. For Catholics this is, for instance, *Nossa Senhora de Boa Viajem*, Our Lady of Safe Travel; for Hindus, the entire class of little deities known as *rakhne* or "guardians" are said to protect people walking or traveling *their* territories and roads. Another way in which the territorial patrons are associated with protection while moving and traveling is through their location at liminal sites such as boundaries, bridges, and crossroads. While here concerns used to focus on ritually relevant transgressions of village boundaries, for instance when marrying across them or changing one's residence, in modern times, the physical dangers and risks when traveling in or through the cities has become a more important issue for the shrine's protective appeal.

These shifting concerns reflect the fact that, during the last three decades of the twentieth century, motorized traffic underwent a dramatic increase in Goa and throughout India. From just 35,205 vehicles in operation in Goa in 1981 (Government of Goa, Daman, and Diu 1981: 77), the number increased to 125,965 in 1991 (Government of Goa 1991) and 333,666 in 2001 (Government of Goa 2001: 101). This increase in motorized traffic not only intensified the concerns of Goans relating to injury or death caused by traffic accidents, but also increased their appreciation of deities and saints known for protecting them from precisely these dangers. It is no surprise, therefore, that the shrines of tutelary beings located at crucial points in the city traffic, such as access and exit roads, bypasses, crossroads, central plazas, and marketplaces, are the most frequently worshipped of all shrines today. In addition, many places that are related to travel and traffic, such as taxi stands, bus and railway stations, landing docks for boats and ships, and travel agencies, have sumptuous and often multireligious shrines. Hence, the images, idols, and signatures of protecting patrons can also be found in or on most private cars and two-wheelers, boats and ships, and taxicabs, rickshaws, and buses. Especially noteworthy is the Panjim office of Indian Airlines, which provides spiritual protection for its clientele by displaying a life-sized statue of St. Francis Xavier.

Urban Shrines and Late-Modern Religiosity

The religiosity dedicated to wayside shrines in Goa's cities has modified and transformed the centuries-old religious devotion dedicated to Hindu village gods and Catholic patron saints to fit the conditions of late-modern city life. In particular, a culturally diversifying, socially changing, and geographically fluctuating population engages with a variety of personalized deities and saints whose charismatic authority is not only quite independent from formalized local social hierarchies, but also often cuts across the orthodox divisions among religious traditions. Moreover, the shrines, and the tutelary beings believed to reside in them, have become sites for the articulation of concerns emerging from the increasing hazards of urban motorized traffic and provide some reassurance against them. The shrines express and enact a form of religiosity that proves to be especially apt for cities in which cultural, social, and motorized mobility mutually enhance each other in a rapidly changing modern world. Refuting earlier modernist and Marxist theories, the urban shrines also supply evidence that religion stands its ground publicly in modernity. Notably, this evidence does not, however, add to the concerned, if not alarmist, report of a late-modern increase in religious intolerance, conflict, and violence (Juergensmeyer 2000), but rather reveals the less dramatic and therefore often missed qualities of a religiosity that mediates and reconciles cultural and social difference and appeases rapid change (Mayaram 2005). These qualities have gained distinctly modern features by simultaneously narrowing and widening traditional community-based religious orientations. The religiosity dedicated to the shrines, on the one hand, widens the local hierarchies and orthodox boundaries among castes, classes, and people belonging to different religious communities by allowing the social and cultural diversification of both the worshipping communities and the worshipped beings. More generally, this religiosity shows a flexibility that lives up to late-modern urban conditions and concerns. On the other hand, it narrows the community-based interaction between worshippers and worshipped by tending to reduce it to an interaction between individualized worshippers and personalized gods and saints. This also reflects a tendency not only in Goa but worldwide. The Goan case therefore suggests that late-modern urban religiosity realizes individual approaches to global conditions and concerns.

Conclusion

Religion and Religions: Syncretism Reconsidered

Religion is not a native category.

—(Smith 1998: 269)

It is a mistake to imply that religious pluralism is found only in modern contexts.

—(Cannell 2010: 96)

In the sixteenth and seventeenth centuries, a new, modern understanding of religion was blazing its trail in Christian Europe. This modernizing perspective was facilitated by both internal and external processes that, starting in the sixteenth century, were challenging the exclusivist and undivided Christian claim for Truth and propagating the existence of a plurality of religions. The processes involved were, on the one hand, the violent strife of the Reformation that brought about the division of Catholicism and Protestantism in Europe and triggered a profound Catholic renewal, and, on the other hand, the Portuguese and Spanish encounters with sophisticated yet largely unknown religious cultures of so-called gentiles or idolaters at the colonial frontiers in Asia and America. These internal and external religious divisions and encounters were both fostered and moderated by a fundamental transformation of the concept of religion that combined the philosophically argued singular of Religion with the culturally experienced plural of religions. The philosophies of humanism and Enlightenment, in other words, increasingly conceptualized religion as a universal human quality or "natural religion" for that matter, while anthropological experience revealed ever more culturally diverse religions around the globe. Not without a certain tautology, the modern Western concept of Religion thus became both in this process: the philosophical presupposition for the experience and the theoretical paradigm for the integration of the global religious plurality. This correlation of modern perspectives and experiences in the recognition of religious diversity had its equivalent in the field of history. There it was the paradigm of "Progress," as Reinhart Koselleck (1984) cogently showed, that allowed for the recognition of the historicity of all local, tribal, and dynastic histories by integrating them into one linear temporality or Universal History.

Specific evidence for the emergence of this modern perspective on religion in Europe comes from books published in the early seventeenth century, which for the first time employed the plural term "religions" in their titles. An exemplary case is the widely read *Purchas His Pilgrimage; or, Relations of the World and the Religions Observed in Al[l] Ages and Places Discovered, from the Creation to This Present,* which was first published in London in 1613. The opening of the European Christian perspective for other religions was further consolidated by scholarly compendia that, in numerous variations from the early seventeenth to the mid-nineteenth century, described and classified four different categories of religion—Christianity, Judaism, "Mohammedanism," and "idolatry" (Masuzawa 2005). For Guy Stroumsa, this new schema represented an "intellectual revolution" alluding to nothing less than "A New Science," that is, the comparative study of religion that promised the self-critical overcoming of biases and a growing tolerance toward the recognition of the religious plurality around the globe.

> In earlier times religion had remained a binary concept, centered on the Augustinian opposition between *vera* and *falsa religio.* Together with the devaluation of Christianity . . . [in post-Reformation Europe], the discovery of so many and so different forms of religion [at the colonial frontier] permitted, paradoxically, the development of a singular concept of religion. Henceforth, religion would be perceived, primarily, as a central aspect of any society, endowed with a different function in each. Religion had become part of humankind's collective identity, and the study of religions would see, gradually, intellectual curiosity overtake polemical animus. (Stroumsa 2010: 7)

The historical material from Portugal and Goa discussed in this book support this view to some extent. Vasco da Gama's initiation of a lasting and intensive encounter between European Christians and the so-far largely unknown cultures of those who eventually became known as Hindus, Buddhists, and Jains did, in the long run, indeed change the Christian and European perspective on religion. In fact, the encounter between Iberian Christianity and Indian Hinduism played an especially crucial role in this process because both religious traditions and both cultural regions were involved in particularly strong multicultural dynamism in the early-modern period. With regard to Hinduism, I suggest that its formation was owed to a protracted and complex historical process which contained mechanisms of both integration and encounter, incorporation and division among a large multitude of devotional, philosophical, and ritual traditions both native and imported to South Asia. This process was old and had entailed, at an earlier stage already, Buddhist, Christian, Jain, Muslim, Parsi, Sikh, and other traditions that were to become "world religions" in the nineteenth century. It arguably gained a major boost in the sixteenth century when, in relatively short sequence, the central Indian Hindu kingdom of Vijayanagara fell to the Muslim forces of the Bahmani Sultanate, which, sometime later, was confronted and curtailed on its part by the Portuguese-Christian forces conquering or controlling considerable parts of western and southern India (De Silva 1994).

In early-modern Iberia, the situation was comparable insofar as here the coming together of reconquistadorial, reformatory, imperial, and colonial dynamics created an atmosphere of intense encounters of diverse religious communities and traditions. Old (Catholic, Orthodox, Eastern) and new (Protestant, Muslim- and Jewish-converted) Christians, local and foreign Muslims, and Jews met in Spain and Portugal with the news about recently "discovered" pagans or gentiles in Asia and America. Despite the threatening surveillance of the Inquisition, the cohabitation of Catholics, Protestants, Moriscos (converted Muslims), Marranos (converted Jews), Moors and Mohammetans or Maghrebian, Middle Eastern and Central Asian Muslims, and Jews from Spain, Portugal, and various other European and Middle Eastern countries was a common thing in early-modern Iberia, which, as Bernand and Gruzinski point out, was *"presque aussi juive et musulman, que chretienne"* (almost as much Jewish and Musulman as Christian; Bernand and Gruzinski 1988: 18). The reach of the Spanish empire under Charles V made the influences of Erasmus's humanism and Martin Luther's Protestantism felt in the southern European peninsula especially through its Spanish extensions into Dutch and Flanders. The Portuguese expansion to Asia renewed and intensified the encounter with Orthodox and Eastern Christians. In fact, Ottoman's far-reaching control over the Christian territories in the Middle East and Central Asia had fostered Western interests in Eastern Christians above all in the hope of a reunification of Christian forces in the face of Muslim supremacy. Unfortunately, though, hopes and realities proved to be quite irreconcilable. Vasco da Gama's messianic dream of finding the legendary Christian kingdom of Prester John in India burst and subsequent Portuguese-Catholic encounters with small groups of "Armenian," "Georgian," "Chaldean," "Abyssinian," "Sabinian," "Greek," "St. Thomas," and "St. John" Christians in India and Goa turned out to become rather issues of the theological "errors" of these "foreign Christians," that is, recognizing or rectifying their theological differences, than winning them over for the envisioned grand Christian reunification (Wicki 1969: 18, 23; Rogers 1962).

Spanish and Portuguese Christians were also in the forefront of the colonial encounter at the American and Asian frontiers, and with the incoming news about the religious cultures in Mexico, Japan, China, and India, European views about "pagans" and "idolaters" gradually began to change. This became visible initially in the work of early missionary humanists like the Spanish Dominican Bartolomé de las Casas (1484–1566), who was the first to protest against the atrocities the Spanish committed in the conquest of Mexico and, thereafter, argued in the celebrated Debate of Valladolid in 1550 that the American Indians were fully human and their enslavement an unjustifiable crime. More importantly, De las Casas's intellectual engagement with the rationalizing influence of Aristotelian and Thomasian thought brought him close to acknowledging the existence of an independent Indian religion in Mexico. "All humans," he argued, "by their cognition are inclined to search for and to worship God . . . [and] all humans have some, if although sometimes distorted, knowledge of God" (Bernand and Gruzinski 1988: 44). Therefore, he continues, "all nations of the world, . . . some more, others less, . . . have religious rites [*cultes*] [and] no human can live without some God, be it a false or the true one" (ibid.: 46). If any one of the early-modern Portuguese writers came close to De las Casas in the genuineness and intensity of his interest in the unknown religious cultures encountered at the colonial frontier in India, it was Diogo do Couto. Although nowhere reaching the humanist fervor and philosophical vision of De las Casas, Couto undertook serious efforts to learn about the culture of the so-called gentiles, engaged in earnest conversations with their Brahmans and scholars, and developed a systematic view about their cosmological perspectives and theological principles. All of this enabled him to the remarkable act of, at least sporadically and in passing, acknowledging that their views and practices are a *religião*, that is, a religion. In general, it is reasonable therefore to argue that the roughly coeval events of the early-modern Protestant-Catholic division of Christianity and the European encounter with unknown religions in Asia and America facilitated in Christian Europe the gradual acknowledgment of a plurality of religions around the globe. In particular, this perspective can claim to have supported the modern conceptualization of Hinduism and Christianity, albeit with the notable qualification that, in the case of Hinduism, this involved, above all, the gradual "syndication" (Thapar 1997), that is, integration of a multitude of devotional, philosophical, and ritual traditions, while in the case of Christianity, the matter was more about "confessionalization" (MacCulloch 2005), that is, the acknowledgment of internal divisions and the fact of being just one among many religions in the world.

The part played by Portuguese colonialism in the formation of Hinduism may of course be considered small, given Portugal's relatively short historical heyday and limited geographical reach in India. On the other hand, it is worth considering that Portuguese colonialism, as part of its early-modern impetus and legacy, pursued an explicitly religious and aggressive proselytizing mission. While seemingly paradoxical in light of its aggressive and iconoclastic course of action, Portuguese colonialism and Catholic hegemony also profoundly engaged in the adoption and assimilation of Hindu forms of expression and practice in Catholic life and liturgy, thereby arguably effecting in its territories a much stronger cultural impact on Indian life and culture than the British in their territories. Regarding this argument, one largely unexplored circumstance is that not only did the society of Catholic converts in Portuguese-controlled India adopt the Hindu caste system. The Portuguese colonial society at large, including the Portuguese, Indians, and so-called *mestiços* living in India, were stratified in a hierarchy that in its principles of racial purity and regulated physical contact, and its complexity of ranks, was very similar to the Hindu system of castes (Pearson 1987: 95; Boxer [1969] 1991: 250; De Silva 1994: 306). Not coincidentally, the Hindu notion of *varnā* therefore owes its European-language designation to the Portuguese term *casta*. If, therefore, the formation of "modern Hindu identity" was facilitated *inter alia* by the emergence of a complex sociocultural hierarchy, which organized religious differences in a system of stratified castes, as leading scholars argue today, then the encounter with the Portuguese-Catholic racial stratification may at least not have been an impediment and more likely was a stimulus to the hierarchical consolidation of Hinduism.

On the part of the Christians, a closer look reveals of course that the recognition of the modern philosophical axiom of Religion/religions was, at best, nascent in the sixteenth century, and European Christian agents were still riddled with serious theological, epistemological, and practical problems in accepting it. Indicative here is that the term "religion" was only gradually and with distinct restrictions used in the early-modern colonial discourse. "Religion," Jonathan Z. Smith notes with regard to early-modern Spanish writings about America, "is not a native category. . . . It is a category imposed from the outside on some aspect of native culture." Moreover, he continues, when applied to the foreign nations, religion does not refer to any sort of inner belief or piety but distinctly focuses on the description of outward appearances, religious objects, agents, and practices and is used as an equivalent of "ceremony," "deed," "custom," "superstition," "rite," "feast," "sacrifice," and, above all, "idolatry" (Smith 1998: 269, 270). Restrictions in the use of the term "religion" can also be found in the *Livro do Pai dos Cristãos* (Wicki 1969), the historical compendium of royal and clerical ordinances and laws issued between 1534 and 1842 for the legal surveillance and protection of the newly converted Christians in the Portuguese Estado da Índia. In the chronological order of this compendium, the term *religião* notably appears for the first time only in the year 1714, in a letter written by King Dom João V and, then, only in the phrasing *nossa relligião* [sic], "our religion," in reference to the Christian Self (ibid.: 327). Before that, the terms used as equivalents for, or in contrast to, what we call religion today were *fé*, "faith," or, more commonly and in acknowledgment of the iconic status of the word, *nossa santa fé*, "our holy faith," used exclusively for Christians; *seita*, "sect," used especially for Jews and Muslims; *gentilismo*, a generic term for all concepts, objects, and practices of the so-called gentiles whose designation changed to "Brahmanismo" and eventually "Hinduismo" only in the nineteenth century; *idolatria,* "idolatry," used as a general equivalent for pagan; and finally *demônio,* "demonism," used for allegedly diabolic concepts, objects, and practices in the Judeo-Christian context and for certain Hindu gods and practices (ibid.: *passim*).

The work of the Goan linguist Mhadavi Sardessai (2012) reveals further details of the protracted and complicated process that concepts like Hindu and its regional, that is, Konkan specification "Konkno" or "Konkanno" had to undergo, until they eventually were recognized as equivalents of "religion." The seventeenth-century *Vocabulario da lingoa Canarim* composed by the Jesuit Diogo Ribeiro, Sardessai shows, listed the term "Hindu" but with a distinctly nonreligious meaning, that is, *gente da India* or "people of India" (ibid.: 3). The term "Konkanno" was translated as *home desta Concaõ tomando entre nos por gentio,* "a man of the Konkan whom we consider a gentile," and thus had a certain religious connotation, even though the term *gentio,* as we have seen, was ambiguous in itself. Religious connotation becomes more evident in Thomas Stephens's *Doutrina Christá em Lingua Bramana-Canarim,* published in 1622, which contrasts the term *Concannapanna*—that equates the term *Conconni Ponni* of the Library Purana discussed in chapter 3—with *Christãuapanna* or "Christendom," associating it, among other things, with *ghaddipanna,* "witchcraft," and *zoisipanna,* "fortune telling" (ibid.: 2). Sardessai further illustrates the ambivalent process by reference to another contemporary source, Miguel de Almeida's *Vonvalleancho Mallo,* or *Jardim dos Pastores,* which was published in Goa in 1658. Almeida deals with the subject by making use of the Konkani terms *bhâuvartu* for "faith" or "believer," and *anabhâuvartu* for "nonfaith" or "infidel," thereafter qualifying both Konkanne and Hindu as *anabhâuvartu* and contrasting them with the linguistic parallelism *fe-bhâuvartu,* "Christian Faith" (ibid.: 4). The protracted and reluctant semantic career that the concepts Konkno and Hindu passed through, first from designating ethnic and geographical identities then to labeling a status of distinct nonfaith before finally becoming designations of an independent religion was completed only in the nineteenth century, Sardessai cogently shows, when the Italian Jesuit Angelus Francisco Maffei in his bilingual *English-Konkani Dictionary* published in Mangalore in 1883 listed "Konkano" as "Konkani-speaking Hindu" (ibid.: 5). For Goan Hindus, the linguistic and practical recognition of religious diversity was not an easy thing either. Historically, European Christians were invariably called *Firanghi.* While this term, which derives from the medieval encounter with Carolingian Francs, actually articulates an ethnic designation, Hindus took special ritual precautions when dealing with European Christians, as we have seen from Diogo do Couto's report. With regard to converted local Christians, who were and occasionally are to this day referred to by Goan Hindus as *batlele,* literally "polluted," these biases are clearly reflected in the designation itself. Accordingly, ritual precautions in dealing with Christians, as noted by Damodar Kosambi, were common for pious Hindus until the twentieth century. "My grandfather was so strict in his observances," he reports, "that even after talking with any of his numerous Christian friends, he would go home and take the ritual bath of purification" (Kosambi [1962] 1992: 11).

That the early-modern classification of Christianity, Judaism, "Mohammedanism," and "idolatry"—or gentility, paganism, or *Conconni Ponni,* for that matter—remained ambiguous for a long time, expressing as much a step toward a "new language of pluralism and diversity," as merely another instance of the "old discourse of Christian supremacy," is also the view of Tomoko Masuzawa. She notes,

> On the one hand we might say that according to the early-modern system, there were four clear categories—that is, three individually distinct religions [Christianity, Judaism, Islam] and one generic type [idolatry], under which all the rest were subsumed. . . . On the other hand it can be reasonably suggested that in the last analysis, only one religion—the true one [Christianity]—was recognized; alongside it were two forms of deviance [Judaism and Islam]; as for the rest [idolatry], they were nations bereft of religion altogether. (2005: 60)

Interestingly, the material from Goa and Portugal suggests that the complications and delay in acknowledging the existence of a plurality of equally valued religions were not caused by the fact that the early-modern colonial discourse polarized Indian gentiles as distinct Others, but rather that it absorbed, assimilated, and integrated them as, albeit allegedly derivative, corrupted, or even forged, parts of the Christian Self. It is here that we realize that Vasco da Gama's celebrated error of mistaking Hindus for Christians can neither be reduced to a short-lived "gaffe" nor a "liberal attitude" on the part of the early-modern explorer, nor even a genuine first-contact hermeneutic deficiency. Instead, it marks an epitomic expression of the complexity inhering the notion of religion at the historical beginning of colonialism and modernity. Alleged similarities between the expressions and practices of Hindus and Christians, we have seen, were crucial for this role and had not only prompted Da Gama's error but occupied Portuguese and European explorers, chroniclers, and missionaries writing about and working in India intensely over a long period. These alleged similarities revived old mythologies about "lost Eastern Christians," inspired ideas of the corruption or distortion of the Christian Truth effected by the detrimental impact of Muslims, if not the devil himself, and elicited debates about possible theological affinities or genealogical relationships between Christians and gentiles. More than that, the category of "similarity" also became critical by raising questions and reviving debates about the use of religious images and, in general, the mechanisms for representing the divine and the Truth.

In Goa and those parts of India that were under Portuguese control, the revival of these debates was nothing less than dramatic. The Portuguese-Catholic regime launched a violent attack against Hindu culture in the mid-sixteenth century that, in little more than a decade, led to the destruction of literally all Hindu temples, shrines, and images, and ruthlessly suppressed all Hindu expressions and practices in its core colony of Goa. Justification for this massive cultural onslaught was that the gentiles allegedly were adhering to the utterly condemned practice of idolatry. A closer inspection reveals that violent animosities against images was not new in Judeo-Christian theology and praxis, and had triggered iconoclastic attacks by the forces of Roman Catholicism against Eastern Christians in the Byzantine empire as early as the eighth century. Its modern revival though arguably gained a distinctly new quality. Technically, this came to the fore in the striking synchronicity of the iconoclasm executed by Protestant activists against Catholic images in central Europe and the iconoclasm executed by Catholic missionaries against religious images in India and America, indicating that the conflict had gained a truly global dimension. Theoretically, the new quality reveals that the definition of the offense moved beyond a strict theological criteria, thus Catholics could be defendants in Europe and persecutors in India, and gave the accusation a concise scientific explanation. The original definition of idolatry in the first of the Ten Commandments was distinctly unspecific in prohibiting not only the worship of "graven images" but also of "other gods." Moreover, the ancient source left open all sorts of theological, moral, and scholarly arguments against the use of religious images, which were discussed and applied in the legal praxis of the late medieval period, such as the argument of the nondepictability of God, moral standards of decency of the body, theories about the relationship between human artifice and nature, and even ideas about the deceptive activity of the devil. The revival of the image debate and iconoclastic violence in early modernity was based then on scholarly theories and legal specifications brought forward by Protestant reformers and re-enacted by Catholic renovators who made it clear that the offense was now above all a matter of semiotic principles. Idolatry, it was argued and decreed, was based on the ignorance and disregard of the ontological division of image and prototype and theologically articulated in the accusation that idolaters worship the image instead of what it represents.

Notably, the strict enforcement of the distinction of image and prototype brought about much more than the militant reconstitution of the division between Christians and "idolaters." It was part of fundamental changes in the system of knowledge and signification, which substituted premodern ideas of an iconic, that is, reified, affinity between sign and signified, knower and known, by modern ideas of the autonomy of knower and knowledge and a symbolic, that is, neutral, and arbitrary code connecting the sign and the signified, knowledge and meaning (Foucault [1966] 1980; Todorov 1985; Blumenberg 1986). In the religious field, the changes effected increasing control and suppression of the use of images, rituals, and bodily practices, favoring instead the significance of text, education, and personal creed. Although gradually and with notable regional and confessional nuances, the modern European Christian concept of religion thus transformed from the idea of revealed, embodied, and enacted Truth to the idea of interiorized, acquired, and expressive faith (Stroumsa 2010; Smith 1998; Asad 1993).

Syncretism Reconsidered

The transition from the premodern to the modern era was thus a dramatic and protracted process of cultural encounters, religious upheavals, and epistemic disruptions. In this process, the emerging notion of religion marked a field of notable ambiguity and hybridity that, unlike the later emerging notion of race, cannot be condensed into the generation of polarities and the marking of distances between the Christian Self and the gentile Other. Rather, religion constituted a domain that was ridden by deep and lasting uncertainties, variously expressed in qualms as to whether similarities or differences, hermeneutics or violence, syncretistic mediation or religious self-assertion, should have strategic priority in the proselytizing mission and colonial conquest. The Goan material shows that these complexities still resonate in the religious culture in Goa today; another major question that arises is therefore how, against this historical background, modern anthropological theory should account for the syncretistic practices and expressions of Hindus and Catholics in Goa.

When addressing this question, it should be mentioned first that anthropological theory has long been reluctant to deal with the phenomenon of syncretism, or hybridity for that matter. Apart from singular and rather isolated approaches such as Melville Herskovitz's analysis of African and Native American "acculturation" in the United States ([1941] 1958), the so-called mixing of cultural traits or religious beliefs from different origins was either considered something not worth studying or was looked down upon as detrimental for the scholarly appreciated "purity" or "genuineness" of cultures. Notably, this analytical neglect of cultural hybridization was intrinsic to modern anthropology, since it was related to one of the discipline's most essential theoretical axioms, the theory of cultural relativism. Whether couched in the romantic image of the *Volksgeist,* the scientist paradigm of the "organism," the philosophico-linguistic idea of "structure" and "system," or the hermeneutic analogy of the "text," modern anthropological theory systematically undermined the analysis of inter- or cross-cultural processes, and effectively argued that each culture is unique and self-centered and, therefore, should be studied only by reference to itself. Looking at "Religion as a Cultural System," Clifford Geertz made it clear that this methodological prioritization of the systemic in culture also led to a rather uncritical scholarly privileging of established religions as, supposedly, opposed to hybrid religiosity, when he quotes George Santayana at the beginning of his seminal article to the effect that it is simply impossible "to have a religion that shall be no religion in particular" (1973: 87).

In the wake of postmodern theory, syncretism was taken up in anthropological books such as Charles Stewart's and Rosalind Shaw's *Syncretism/Anti-Syncretism* (1994b) only with distinct and explicit precaution. The "contentious term," it was said, needed a critical revision and correction, setting right, at least, three major shortcomings in its earlier use (Stewart and Shaw 1994a). In brief, these shortcomings are highlighted as (1) the need to free syncretism from the pejorative meanings it had acquired in nineteenth-century theological discourse in which it was often used to indicate a "contamination" of supposedly "pure" forms of belief, something that in German scholarship was also discredited as *Religionsmischerei* (Colpe 1974: 218); (2) the need to end the scholarly aporia into which earlier anthropological and religious studies' attempts had run when trying to define syncretism and ascertain rather mechanical conditions and temporary stages of syncretism (Colpe 1974, 1975; Rudolph 1979); and, most importantly, (3) the need to circumvent the critique of postmodern constructivism arguing that no culture or religion can be reduced to any "essence" that exists outside the historicity and political conditionality of human existence, so that the notion of syncretism too is misguided, because its allusion to synthesis and fusion logically presupposes precisely the assumption of such preexisting essences (Stewart and Shaw 1994a). A major strategy to escape these predicaments of the scholarly legacy of the term was to reconceptualize its use in the analysis of the "Politics of Religious Synthesis," as Stewart and Shaw (1994b) subtitle their groundbreaking volume on the subject. In other words, syncretism was now, in a well-known modernist division of secular and religious domains, seen as a form of religiosity or a religious process whose actors are primarily acting under political auspices. More precisely, many anthropologists associate syncretism today with conditions and processes that are typical for the operating of religious pluralism in the modern polity.

In order to substantiate this position and highlight its limitations in the face of the Goan ethnography, I will briefly look at two essays, both of which appeared in Stewart's and Shaw's book and deal with syncretism in contemporary Indian contexts. The first essay is written by Peter van der Veer who, from the outset, agrees with the editors in that syncretism's political significance, if not the concept itself, originates in the historical contexts of the European Reformation and humanism.[1] More precisely, Van der Veer elaborates two modern philosophical and political achievements as substantial presuppositions for syncretism. One refers to early British deism and in particular to Lord Edward Herbert's (1583–1643) proclamation of a universal definition of religion encapsulated in what he called "natural religion." According to Van der Veer, ". . . the emergence of the notion of natural religion as *a belief in and worship of a supreme power which is found among all human beings* is related to the emergence of the notion of syncretism" (Van der Veer 1994: 197; emphasis mine). Another presupposition of syncretism, he argues, emerged in the recognition of the plurality of religions resulting from the Protestant challenge to the Catholic claim of universal Truth. "Initially this caused large-scale civic strife, based on religious differences. One answer to this war of all against all was the rise of the absolutist state and its successor *the secular nation state. . . . combined [with] notions of syncretism and religious tolerance*" (ibid: 198; emphasis mine).

The anthropologist then turns to the virulent conflicts between Hindus and Muslims in contemporary India, where he suggests syncretism played an ambiguous role. While acknowledging the occasional reconciling power of religion, inspired by ideas and principles that had been propagated by celebrated Indian philosophers and religious leaders such as Vivekananda, Mahatma Gandhi, and Sarvepalli Radhakrishnan (ibid.: 200ff.), he rejects the assumption of an "essentially tolerant and pluralistic character of Indian civilization" that was brought up in 1990 by the Indian scholar Ashis Nandy (ibid.: 202). The allegedly pluralistic "spirit of India," Van der Veer interjects, is often effectively Hindu, that is, it "denies that Muslims have a religion which is different from that of the Hindus" (ibid.: 203). Syncretism, he argues, therefore often does not so much reconcile or integrate religious differences as it politically absorbs and subdues the respective, weaker Other. A case in point is taken from his fieldwork among Muslim Rifa'i brotherhoods in Surat, whose annual saints' celebrations regularly draw crowds of Hindus worshipping the tombs and icons of Muslim saints. What looks like an expression of tolerance and harmony, as the anthropologist demystifies the event, is rather a case of what Stewart and Shaw (1994a: 22) call "hierarchical encompassment," since high-caste Hindus interpret the happening just "as a lower, impure practice in a Hindu worldview" (Van der Veer 1994: 207).

Van der Veer can certainly not be blamed for romanticizing syncretism. What nevertheless proves frustrating in his approach is that he tends to confine the subject to the political arena, and, by implication, philosophical ethos of the modern Western polity. Even if syncretism in praxis is often perverted in processes of political encompassment and submission, we are given to understand that this happens under the auspices of the secular nation state that facilitates the political mediation of religious differences. Not only does the anthropologist thus tentatively exclude any other than modern political circumstances from the practice of syncretism. His initial emphasis of the constitutive role played in the formation of syncretism by "the belief in and worship of a supreme power found among all human beings" also leaves little room for religious practices and philosophical worldviews that favor the existence of many and diverse gods, saints, and divine agencies over the Western philosophical imagination of a universal nature of religion on the basis of a monotheistic concept of the divine (ibid.: 197).

Another chapter in Stewart's and Shaw's book that deserves our attention is David Mosse's analysis of the syncretistic interaction between Hindus and Catholics in Tamil Nadu (1994). "Religious forms" of Hindus and Catholics may be different, Mosse argues, but they nevertheless participate in "shared meanings" by being part of the social system of castes. Catholic iconography, such as the image of the local patron saint St. James, can therefore take on the meaning of a divine warrior that has its model in a deified Hindu king fulfilling his caste *dharma* (duty) of protecting the village; and ancient Hindu rituals, such as presenting betel nuts to local caste dignitaries during village festivals, can become part of Catholic church feasts, because "caste [is] viewed as a matter of 'worldly honors'" (ibid.: 92).

In historicizing his view, Mosse refers to Roberto Nobili, thereby indirectly buttressing the interpretations of historians such as Guy G. Stroumsa and Ines Županov who argue that the association of the "discovery of civil religion" and the "emergence of religious pluralism" originates with the distinction that early-modern Jesuit missionaries in China and India made between religious practice and social custom, something that arguably anticipated, if not initiated, the modern division of the secular and the religious (Stroumsa 2010: 44; Županov 2001). What makes the anthropologist's recollection of the historical encounter of Hindus and Catholics important here is that he brings to the fore that this was not only the distinction of social from religious customs generating a secular ground on which the mediation of religious differences was arguably more feasible. More critically, Mosse makes us aware that this was the moment—which, to this day, is perhaps best theorized in Émile Durkheim's *Formes élémentaires de la vie religieuse* ([1912] 1971)—in which the distinction of the sacred and the profane transformed religion into a symbolic, as opposed to a literal articulation of the Truth or reality for that matter. In other words, Nobili's *accommodatio* was part of a dramatic disruption of a Hindu (as well as Catholic) worldview for which religious expressions did not merely have the metaphoric status of symbols, nor could they be detached from their social embeddedness and cultural embodiment.[2]

Accordingly, the previous chapters of this book have shown that the historical encounter between Hindus and Catholics was not only a religious battle over different theological doctrines filled with forced conversion and inquisitorial oppression, but also a semiotic and epistemological battle over different modes of the cognition and representation of the Truth filled with iconoclastic destruction and replacement of images, icons, books, literary genres, and other forms of signification. To be fair, though he largely sees the symbolic mediation between Hindu and Catholic "meanings" in the light of Nobili's *accommodatio*, David

Mosse also notes that not all was right in the interaction between missionaries and converts. "By distinguishing 'form' from 'content' or 'religion' from 'caste,'" he writes, "missionaries conceived local ritual practice in ways which differed significantly from those of the actors themselves" (Mosse 1994: 91). In particular he mentions that, to this day, local voices object to the policies of "inculturation," that is, the symbolic mediation of Catholic liturgy and Indian modes of expression initiated by the Second Vatican Councils (1962–1965), and that, as he adds, "ironically, . . . often finds its strongest support from among Western members of the churches" (ibid.: 102).

It is at this point that the particularities of ethnography of the Hindu-Catholic encounter in Goa on the other hand become visible. From the outset, these particularities emerge from the complexity of the situation in Goa in which, as we have seen, the transgression of the conventional boundaries between Hindus and Catholics, and the assertion of these boundaries, go literally hand in hand and cannot, at least in practical terms, be separated from each other. Hence, we have seen that it is quite common among Goan Hindus and Catholics of all castes and classes, in the countryside and in the cities, to pay ritual homage and invoke the spiritual help of divine or saintly powers that formally "belong" to the respective other religious tradition and community. At the same time, however, it is the rule that none of the syncretistic expressions and practices is ever understood by its practitioners to challenge or even impact their respective religious identities as Hindus or Catholics. Instead, the people who appreciate syncretistic expressions or engage in syncretistic practices, like anyone else, self-consciously and sometimes even anxiously assert their respective religious identities. In fact, this assertion frequently happens in the very syncretistic contexts themselves. Thus, Hindus and Catholics jointly participating in a festival quite often take care to consciously mark their respective religious identities by, for instance, presenting different offerings, operating in distinct groups, or acting in different spaces or at different times. Even more intriguingly, Hindus and Catholics engaging in syncretistic practices may nourish animosities against each other that precisely allude to their different religious identities. Obviously, such seemingly paradoxical circumstances can prevail only because the people involved do not consider what we perceive as "transgression of boundaries" to have any effect on their respective religious identities, and, conversely, what we perceive as "assertion of boundaries" to have anything to do with their syncretistic practices. It is this complex situation of people who not only assert and transgress religious boundaries and identities but also deny that either one of these attitudes or actions has an impact on, or even relevance for, the respective other attitude or action that characterizes the syncretistic situation and justifies its scholarly distinction.

What looks like a logical paradox finds explanation in the fact that the syncretistic phenomena to a large extent escape the philosophical modalities by which modernity constructs and mediates religious plurality. The Goan phrase

Devu ekutch re, which comments on syncretistic expressions or practices, we have seen, does not endorse the modern axiom that religion is a human universal but resonates with either the Hindu idea of Brahma encompassing all forms or the Christian reference to the Three Persons unified in the one God. Nor does syncretism articulate a particular tolerant attitude. As we have noted with regard to the history and idiosyncrasy of many Hindu-Catholic twin-shrines, what at first looks like tolerance, at second inspection often reveals a sort of competition of two who want to be in the same place. More importantly, the tolerant attitudes that local media, politicians, and public discourse like to read into the Hindu-Catholic syncretism in Goa today stand singularly in their modern novelty and philosophical abstraction in the midst of the manifold longstanding and practically embedded motives and values that are at stake when Goan Hindus and Catholics honor and trust the divine agencies of the respective other religion. In other words, the Goan syncretism cannot be explained by reference to any abstract "third" or mediating ground, such as the modern concept of a secular state, or the notion of a "natural religion" detached from any culture and society. Similarly, the Goan syncretism does not reveal its functioning by reference to a form of arbitrary or neutral signification, such as symbolic representation or translation that has no substantive link with what it represents. Instead, we have seen that the Goan syncretism is based on culturally embodied and socially embedded human concerns whose realization bring together praxis and metaphysics with forms of signification and articulation that entail intrinsic connections with what they represent.

More precisely, the Goan syncretism is based on three particular ritual concerns regarding the constitution, reproduction, and well-being of the *ganv* or village community. These are the concerns for (a) the ritual acknowledgment of spatial commonalities valued as neighborhood, proximity, and origin, as well as commonly appreciated sacred landscapes, locations, and boundaries; (b) the ritual commemoration of shared pasts and interrelated genealogies embodied and celebrated in festive events, mythological histories, and cultural memories, as well as icons and ideas of clanship, motherhood, siblinghood, and the appreciation of gender; and, last but not least, (c) ritual evocation of the protective, therapeutic, and otherwise efficacious qualities of divine or sacred powers celebrated in the iconographies of patrons, guardians, warriors, and mothers, trusted to provide protection, healing, and appeasement.

At the heart of the syncretistic concord that these three existential human concerns can be satisfied by the divine and saintly forces of the Hindu as well as Catholic tradition lies the understanding that the god(s) and saints present themselves in bodily manifestations. The most expressive articulation is here the idea that the body of the patron god or saint itself either embodies or by its presence protects the territory with which he or she is associated from natural, social, and spiritual hazards and dangers. Exemplary cases, we have seen, are Saibini Sateri–Shanta Durga, the archetypical Goan village goddess, whose archaic icon, the sacred anthill, indicates that her body is actually the land of Goa or any Goan village for that matter, and Saiba St. Francis Xavier, the archetypical Goan patron saint, whose mummified body is preserved as a precious relic in the Old Goa Church and venerated as the sacred token for his protection of Goa and, again, any Goan village for that matter. From Saibini and Saiba, the local manifestation of the divine and saintly is broken down in myriad patron gods, saints, ancestors, and tutelary beings that are represented and worshipped in the temples and churches, chapels and shrines, crosses, images, idols, sacred trees, stones, and locations that mark every notable place and village and the landscape of Goa at large.

Goan Hindus and Catholics, we have seen, are willing to have the ritual acknowledgment of the gods and saints that embody the spatial contiguity, genealogical rootedness, and bodily welfare of their village community overrule the belonging to their respective religious tradition and doctrine. The effective principle underlying this trumping of ritual over doctrine is not only the idea that the icon and the prototype, the sign and the signified, are connected by a substantial material similarity or affinity. If under certain circumstances the material manifestation of a god or saint is more important than his or her religious identity, then it is also important that, at times, the performance of tangible rituals gains more weight than the abstract expression of confessional belief. In fact, we have seen that sometimes the ritual activities are performed not to express any meaning at all, but only to mime a significant act. Hence, the primary purpose of the ludic performances of the Jagar ritual is arguably not to present any content but to prevent the ritual practitioners from falling asleep, since only when the men stay awake for a full night and honor the ancestors, gods, and saints, it is said, will the ancestors, gods, and saints for their part stay awake for a full year to protect the village and respond to the villagers' needs and requests. The ritual's ultimate significance is thus its ontic activity and not the expression of any meaning.

Another aspect of ritual is worth recollecting because it marks a type of memory that overrules the narrative of linear time and abrogates the religious changes effected by the various historical shifts of political domination and cultural hegemony that transformed Goa and its people. This happens again in the Jagar ritual, when the village men collectively sit on the *mand* or ritual space and solemnly recite the *nomana* or invocation of the ancestors, gods, and saints associated with the village. This moment marks the *praesentia*, or ritual presence, of all gods and saints that have ever manifested themselves in the course of time in the village realm, irrespective of their religious belonging, as well as all ancestors and living dignitaries of the village, irrespective of the diverse historical conversions and re-conversions that have changed their families' religious identities over time. Effecting thus a kind of palimpsest, in which the Present does not overwrite and overrule the Past, but renders transformation and difference contemporaneous and contiguous, this ritual memory remarkably resists what Chakrabarty (2000) calls the "historicism of modernity."

There can be no doubt finally that syncretism constitutes religion, even if it does not confine itself to any one religion in particular. What is important here is to refute all elitist insinuations that this is only an inferior form of religion, in which people, and especially people of allegedly low class and little education, are suspected to engage only because they do not know better. Providing orientation and belonging in space, remembrance and continuity in time, and protection and health to the body through a complex system of knowledge and signification, praxis and metaphysics clearly constitute the characteristics of religion. Syncretism's peculiarity is however that it relies on forms of knowledge and modes of signification that, to some extent, resist the epistemological revolutions and semiotic upheavals that characterize the transformation from the premodern to the modern era. This, of course, does not mean to romanticize the premodern era as the Garden of Eden of religious pluralism. It is a moot question to ask which era generated more religious violence: the premodern Portuguese-Catholic search for alleged cultural similarities and practical assimilations between Christians and gentiles or the modern aloofness and racial distancing that the British practiced vis-à-vis Hindus and Hinduism. What the Goan syncretism reveals though is that the modern Western philosophical concept of Religion tolerates the cultural plurality of religions around the world only at the cost of a ubiquitous epistemological and semiotic universalism that—like the mythical Procustean bed—curtails or stretches everything that does not fit its own shape.

Notes

Introduction

1. Vasco da Gama's first naval passage between Portugal and India in the years 1497–1499 is seen today as the commencement of Europe's colonial expansion to Asia. Its most important political and economic effect was to circumvent the Muslim Ottoman Empire's control of Europe's land connections with Central and East Asia.

2. Vijayanagara was the largest medieval Hindu kingdom in South India. It originated in 1336 and controlled much of the highland of the Deccan. Long resisting the expansion of the Muslim Bahmani Sultanate in central India, it was eventually in 1632 conquered by an alliance of the Deccan sultanates of Bijapur and Golkonda.

3. How much this composite Hindu-Muslim society was characterized by syncretistic intersections between the two predominant religious traditions in Karnataka is cogently demonstrated in Jackie Assayag's *At the Confluence of Two Rivers: Muslims and Hindus in South India* (2004).

4. *Trimūrti* is a Hindu concept and iconography that brings the three majors gods Brahma, Vishnu, and Shiva together.

5. Devi is a generic Hindu designation for "goddess."

6. *Thīrta* means literally "river ford" and marks the transition or connection between mundane and sacred spheres that typically happens at pilgrimage sites or any holy place. By extension, *thīrta* designates the use of water in Hindu rituals.

7. *Bhakti* or "devotion" characterizes a particular form of Hindu piety that favors an intimate relationship with god expressed especially in devoted prayers and songs.

8. With regard to the Estado da Índia at large, it has been argued that—if one takes seriously the concept of "seizure of land" that resonates in the etymology of the term "colonization"—the early-modern Portuguese expansion in Asia cannot yet really be called colonialism, but rather marks a loosely connected system of maritime trading posts involved in a combination of free trade and coercive tribute-taking operations (Pearson 1987: 77; see also Subrahmanyam 1993; Boxer [1969] 1991; Thomaz 1981–1982). For Goa, the inefficiency of the colonial state is evidenced in particular by the significant economic influence that Hindu merchants, landowners, and middlemen were able to assert throughout the colonial period (Pearson 1973a, 1973b; De Souza 1975).

1. Vasco da Gama's Error

1. Álvaro Velho's authorship of the oldest manuscript of Da Gama's journey is assumed today by most modern historians. See Subrahmanyam 1997a: 81; Rubiés 2000: 165; Rogers 1962: 89.

2. While Ravenstein ([1898] 1998: 54) assumes *quafees* may derive from Arabic *kaz* for "judge," Subrahmanyam (1997a: 133) suggests a derivation from Arabic *kâfir* for "unbeliever."

3. I am using Ravenstein's 1898 English translation (reprinted as a 1998 facsimile) of the sixteenth-century manuscript of Vasco da Gama's first voyage to India. The first modern Portuguese edition of this manuscript, which is ascribed today by most historians to Álvaro Velho, was done by Diogo Köpke and António da Costa Paiva in 1838 (Subrahmanyam 1997a: 80). A modernized version of the Köpke/Paiva edition has been published by Luís de Albuquerque in 1989 under the title *Relação da primeira viagem de Vasco da Gama*.

4. Foucault finds a similar attitude of privileging authoritative text before empirical experience in the *magnum opus* of Miguel Cervantes (1547–1616): "Don Quichotte reads the world to prove the books" (Foucault [1966] 1980: 79).

5. The original of the *Livro das Coisas da Índia* has been lost and survives only through an Italian edition that was published by Giovanni Battista Ramusio around 1550.

6. Peter's vision is part of the tenth chapter of the Acts of Apostles, not the first.

2. Image Wars

1. Mailapur, the township of Madras (Chennai, Tamil Nadu), where the Portuguese had built a church over the claimed tomb of the Apostle St. Thomas, was another site affected by the campaign.

2. During the rule of the Deccan-based dynasties of Chalukyas (600–700 CE) and Silaharas (800–1000 CE), Gopakapattana became the new capital of Goa replacing the ancient Bhoja city of Candrapura (modern Chandor, Salcete). Archaeological remains and Sanskrit inscriptions indicate that Gopakapattana had a temple dedicated to Shiva that also sheltered images of a local deity named Govanatha or Goveshvara. The rule of the Kadamba (1000–1400 CE) brought a significant boost to the regional Hindu culture, which led to the construction of more temples (Mitterwallner 1983a: 23ff.). In particular, there are indications that Kadamba rulers adopted the local deity Saptakotishvara as their family god and built a sumptuous basalt-stone temple for him on the island of Diwar (Tiswadi; Henn 2009; Mitragotri 1999: 159). The rich temple culture of the island is also confirmed by Pereira (1978: 37–61)

3. Boxer made a similar remark regarding the "characteristic improvidence of the Portuguese" (Rabb 1974: 678).

4. As explained in more detail in the next chapter, "power" means that the images and icons are taken to possess and transmit the agency of the divine or sacred forces they embody. While Goan Hindus commonly refer to this power by saying that the images and their prototypes are *jāgṛit,* that is, "awake" and responsive to their devotees' needs and requests, Goan Catholics talk about the miraculous quality of the images or crosses of certain saints. This iconic agency may have positive, that is, protective or therapeutic, or negative, that is, destructive or punitive, effects.

5. For a similar distinction of *vana* and *kṣetra,* settlement and field, in Maharashtra, see Sontheimer 1994.

6. See also Victor and Elizabeth Turner's classic *Image and Pilgrimage in Christian Culture* (1978).

7. Goan Hindus, especially Saraswat Brahmins who had left Goa and resettled further away in North Kanara, Maharashtra, and Bombay also keep memories of their Goan roots through religious knowledge and practices such as mythologies, family deities, and occasional pilgrim visits (Wagle 1974: 231; Conlon 1967: 227).

3. Christian *Purāṇas*

1. One notable exception was Garcia da Orta's *Coloquios dos simples, e drogas, e cousas mediçinaes da India,* a compendium dealing with medicinal plants, published in Goa in 1563.

2. There is a strong indication that Stephens's *magnum opus* was first published under the Portuguese title *Discurso sobre a vinda de Jesu Christo Nosso Salvador ao mundo.* The title *Kristapurana* seems to have become common only with the second edition of 1649 (Cunha Rivara 1858: 84).

3. No copies of these early-modern editions exist today. The *Kristapurana,* however, was re-edited in roman script in 1907 in Mangalore, having been reconstructed from handwritten copies still in liturgical use among the Goan diaspora population in South Kanara. In 1925, a handwritten manuscript in the Devanagari script was found in the School of Oriental Studies archives in London, which Georg Schurhammer dated to the eighteenth century (Falcao 2003: 42). Finally, in 1956 and 1996, modern re-editions in Devanagari appeared in Pune and Mumbai, respectively.

4. Stephens also wrote the *Arte da Lingoa Canarim* (Grammar of Konkani), which was printed after his death in 1640 and is considered the first printed Indian-language grammar.

5. Falcao (2003: 41) mentions that Stephens used about four hundred different "Hindu names" for Jesus Christ in his *Kristapurana.*

6. Falcao's analysis is based on the Marsden manuscript of the *Kristapurana* found in the School of Oriental and Asian Studies archives in London, which is of unknown date and in Devanagari script. As Falcao points out, it may be "more Sanskritized and Indianized" than earlier versions in roman script. The same reservation applies to the 1956 and 1997 Devanagari editions used by Van Skyhawk and Tulpule.

7. Cunha Rivara's perspective must be treated with some caution though, since he was one of the earliest Konkani activists defending Konkani as an independent language against claims that it is a derivate or dialect of Marathi. He therefore had an obvious interest in arguing that there existed an ancient written Konkani literature that was destroyed by the Catholic conquest and inquisition.

8. Cunha Rivara cogently translates *Conconni Ponni* as *Concanismo,* since it combines the adjective "Konkan" with the suffix *-pon* indicating a nominalization (as for instance in *bhurgepon* for "childhood"). *Konkonpon,* to this day, is used in spoken Christian Konkani as a designation for Hinduism. How the term figures in the emerging terminological designation and theological acknowledgment of an independent "religion" of the *gentios* of the Konkan and India in the early-modern Portuguese and Christian discourse is a complex issue that I discuss in the conclusion.

9. Diogo Ribeiro's *Vocabulario das lingues canarim* (1620) confirms that, in the seventeenth century, the Portuguese rendering of the Konkani word *kuḍḍo* and *kuḍḍepon* did indeed stand for both "blind" and "blindness" as well as "false" and "falsehood." This

semantic peculiarity confirms, once again, the ambiguity of the early-modern Christian perception of the gentiles, in the sense that the "falsehood" of gentile religious beliefs was potentially only a cognitive failure or "blindness" and not necessarily the total absence of knowledge or access to the Truth.

4. *Ganv*

1. Traditionally, three subgroups or *jāti* of the Devadasi caste were active in Goa. These were the Kalavant, who were in charge of dancing and music during temple ceremonies, the Bhavani who cleaned and decorated the temples, and the Perni who performed the Jagar play (Sirkar 1983; Shirodkar and Mandal 1993; Cabral e Sá 1997)

2. *Khazān* are saline floodplains along Goa's tidal estuaries and part of a unique agricultural ecosystem. Maintained by a complex system of dykes and sluice gates that regulate the tidal inflow and outflow of waters, *khazān* is a highly productive type of land used for agriculture and pisciculture that, however, is subject to manifold ecological hazards such as flooding and salinization (Noronha et al. 2002).

3. Eight villages are specifically mentioned: Kushasthala (Cortalim), Kelosi (Kelosim), Mathagrama (Madgaon), Varenya (Verem), Loṭali (Lotulim), Kudasthali (Curtorim), and two islands in the Mandovi River, Cudamani (Chorão) and Dipavati (Diwar) (Mitragotri 1999: 48; Wagle 1970: 9).

4. The concept of "sanskrization" was introduced into the Indological discourse in the 1950s by M. N. Srinivas. It circumscribes a process of the ennobling of deities and ritual practices that includes among other things iconographic changes, the adding of name suffixes like *-ishvar,* the change from *bali* or bloody to *nayvedia* or vegetarian offerings, etc. (Srinivas 1989). As Srinivas and other scholars emphasize, these transformations are usually neither linear nor irreversible but, as a rule, initiate oscillations between "great traditions and small traditions," as Robert Redfield and Milton Singer cogently described it in 1954, or processes of "universalization and parochialization," as McKim Marriott called it in 1955, all of which are seen as characteristic to the dynamic and hybrid culture of Hinduism (Fuller 1992: 24; Sontheimer 1989).

5. Temple registration was started by the Portuguese in 1886 under the *Regulamento das Mazanias* act, that is, the "Regulation of the Mazania," the Portuguese rendering of the Konkani notion for "council of *mahājān.*" This regulation stipulated for the official registration of the names of *mahājān,* together with a legal inventory of the movable and immovable property of the temple and possibly also the regulation of usufructs, remunerations of servants, listing of regularly performed ceremonies and festivals, etc. (Pereira 1978: 26ff.).

6. This school also includes Xavier 1903, Pereira 1978, Kosambi (1962) 1992, Thomaz 1981–1982, and Martires Lopes 1996.

7. Arguably the most important interreligious caste alliance in Goa's modern history was the closing of ranks between Hindu and Catholic Brahmins in the celebrated referendum of 1967, which prevented the merger of Goa with Maharashtra (Rubinoff 1998; Fernandes 2003).

8. The paradigm of space, contiguity, and neighborhood may have still other effects on the process of *Gemeinschaft* and syncretism. Hence, Veena Das's expansion of Turner's

notion of *communitas* to interreligious experiences reminds us of the "integrative model of pilgrimage" (1989). Joanne Waghorne speaks of the integrative effect of the "sharing of public space" for Hindus and Catholics in Tamil Nadu whose processions take the same routes (2002).

5. Demotic Ritual

1. Zagor: comical performance in Konkani by illiterate amateurs; crass theater in Goa; Zagor is currently banned by the ecclesiastical authority, under severe penalties, though it was not more immoral than many European theatrical forms.

2. On the subject of the once-respected status of Devadāsī, Goan scholars emphasize that, supported by their *yajamān* or "patrons," a number of Goan Devadāsī women visited renowned music schools in Jaipur, Agra, and Gwalior in the nineteenth and twentieth centuries and became famous Indian artists. The best-known Devadāsī singer from Goa today is Lata Amonkar. A number of old caste names such as *chedvān* (girls), *farjand* (boys), and *band* (bonded) are, however, also taken to indicate the (illegitimate) offspring of the old *yajamān*-Devadāsī relationships (Cabral e Sá 1997; Sirkar 1983; Shirodkar and Mandal 1993).

3. I am especially grateful to Alito Siqueira for alerting me to this document.

4. More references to tax levies paid for Zagor performances in the villages of Palle (Bicholim), Betora (Tiswadi), and Nirankal (Ponda), though most likely only relevant in the nineteenth century, can be found in Pereira 1981: 43 and 136.

5. I did the most intensive fieldwork on the Kakra Jagar in 1994, when I had the opportunity to not only audio- and video-record but also transcribe and translate most of the *nomana* (hymns) and *songe* (songs). Altogether, I have seen the ceremony in Kakra four times, that is, 1993, 1994, 1995, and 2010, something that allows me today to also recognize and compare continuities and changes over the years. Apart from Kakra, I have seen Jagar ceremonies in at least twelve villages: Siolim (Bardez), Baga (Bardez), Naushe (Tiswadi), Bambolim (Tiswadi), Orshel (Tiswadi), Siridao (Tiswadi), Fatorpa (Quepem), Malkarne (Quepem), Keri (Ponda), Apeval (Ponda), Veling (Ponda), Magilvado (Ponda), and Pisgal (Ponda).

6. I produced two video films on the Goan Jagar; one unpublished ninety-minute film on the Kakra Jagar in 1994 for which I owe special thanks to Alito Siqueira, Gauri Patwardhan, and P. Sateesh; and another fifteen-minutes film called *Staying Awake for God: Introducing the Zagor* in 2010, which presents a survey of the Goan Jagar from 1994 to 2010 with clips from ten villages. This film was produced together with Alito Siqueira and Gaspar D'Souza and is available at http://vimeo.com/18668418.

7. The spring protected by Jhariveilo became the issue of a major conflict in the 1980s that exemplified the often difficult relations between the marginalized Gaude community and its rapidly modernizing environment, when the construction work of Goa University seriously damaged and polluted the water supply of the village community.

8. *Chandālla*: a vile, filthy, wicked person, also low caste or a pariah (Stephens 1907: 539).

9. *Mogālla*: affectionate, loving (ibid.: 552).

10. *Suranga*: beautiful, fine, splendid (ibid.: 576).

6. Crossroads of Religion

1. Goa after the end of the Neruhvian planned economy and with India's opening to global markets experienced an extraordinary boom in its cities and tourism industry (Das 2002). Tourist arrivals have increased from 380,000 in 1980 to 1,263,000 in 2000 (Government of Goa, Daman, and Diu 1981: 89; Government of Goa 2001: 115). The number of tourists visiting Goa every year, therefore, roughly equals today its population. More important still, the tourism boom exposes Goa to a dynamic of urbanization that, notwithstanding the comparatively small total figure of its urban population of 668,869 (ibid.: 3), compares with India's metropolitan cities.

2. Sathya Sai Baba (b. 1926), a contemporary Hindu Holy Man figure with a national and international reputation, claims to be an avatar or successor of Shirdi Sai Baba (Urban 2003; Srinivas 2008).

Conclusion

1. Charles Stewart and Rosalind Shaw locate the political relevance of the term "syncretism" in the period of religious wars and civil strife accompanying the Protestant Reformation in central Europe. More precisely, they name humanist George Calixtus (1586–1656) as the leader of a circle of Protestant theologians who debated, in what was called the "syncretistic controversies," the possibilities for a doctrinal and ritual reconciliation of diverse Protestant denominations with Catholicism (Stewart and Shaw 1994a: 4).

2. To make this claim is of course not to say that Hinduism or any other ancient or living religion for that matter was ever free of symbolic representation or interpretation. What is implied, however—and here the historians' emphasis on the significance of the Jesuit distinction of social from religious customs must be acknowledged—is that the period of the Protestant Reformation and European colonialism that is commonly characterized as the beginning of modernity disseminated and enforced the symbolic reading of religious expression and practice like never before.

References

Albuquerque, Luís de. 1989. *Relação da primeira viagem de Vasco da Gama,* texto modernizado. In *Grandes Viagens Marítimas,* vol. 1, edited by Luís de Albuquerque, 7–51. Lisbon: Publicações Alfa.

———, ed. 1994. *Dicionário de história dos descobrimentos Portugueses.* 2 vols. Lisbon: Caminho.

Albuquerque, Manuel J. S. de. 1922. *Sumario cronologico de decretos diocesanos do arcebispado: Desde 1775 até 1922.* Rachol, India: Paroco de Rachol.

Anderson, Benedict. 1991. *Imagined Communities: Reflections on the Origin and Spread of Nationalism.* New York: Verso.

Angle, Prabhakar. 1994. *Goa: Concepts and Misconcepts.* Bombay: Goa Hindu Association.

Appadurai, A., and C. Appadurai Breckenridge. 1976. "The South Indian Temple: Authority, Honor and Redistribution." *Contributions to Indian Sociology* 10 (2): 187–211.

Asad, Talal. 1983. "Anthropological Conceptions of Religion: Reflections on Geertz." *Man* 18: 237–259.

———. 1993. *Genealogies of Religion: Discipline and Reasons of Power in Christianity and Islam.* Baltimore: Johns Hopkins University Press.

———. 2003. *Formations of the Secular: Christianity, Islam, Modernity.* Stanford, Calif.: Stanford University Press.

Assayag, Jackie. 2004. *At the Confluence of Two Rivers: Muslims and Hindus in South India.* New Delhi: Manohar.

Assayag, Jackie, and Gilles Tarabout. 1997. "Présentations." In *Altérité et identité: Islam et Christianisme en Inde,* edited by Jackie Assayag and Gilles Tarabout, 9–24. Paris: École des Hautes Études en Sciences Sociales.

Assmann, Jan. 1988. "Kollektives Gedächtnis und kulturelle Identität." In *Kultur und Gedächtnis,* edited by Jan Assmann and Tonio Hölscher, 9–19. Frankfurt: Suhrkamp.

———. 2010. *The Price of Monotheism.* Translated by Robert Savage. Stanford, Calif.: Stanford University Press.

Ataide de Lobo, Antonio. 1907. *A freguezia de Siolim: Souvenir do benzimento da nova egreja parrochial de S. Antonio.* Nova Goa, India: Typografia da Minerva Indiana.

———. 1931. *A Freguezia de Siolim: Subsidios para su historia.* Mapuca, India: Tipographia Popular.

Aubin, Jean. 1976. "L'ambassade du prêtre Jean a D. Manuel." In *Mare Luso-Indicum études et documents sur l'histoire de l'Ócean Indien et des pays riverains á l'époque de la domination Portugais,* vol. 3, edited by Jean Aubin, 2–56. Geneva: Libraire Minard.

Axelrod, P., and M. A. Fuerch. 1996. "The Flight of the Deities: Hindu Resistance in Portuguese Goa." *Modern Asian Studies* 30 (2): 387–421.

———. 1998. "Portuguese Orientalism and the Making of the Village Communities of Goa." *Ethnohistory* 45 (3): 439–476.

Azevedo, Carmo. 1984. "A Miracle No More." *Goa Today,* November, 11–15.

———. 1985. "The Milagres Church of Mapusa." *Purabhilekh puratatva* 3: 95–104.

Babb, L. 1991. "Sathya Sai Baba's Miracles." In *Religion in India,* edited by T. N. Madan, 277–293. New Delhi: Oxford University Press.

Bachtin, Michail M. 2008. *Chronotopos.* Frankfurt am Main: Suhrkamp.

Baden Powell, B. H. 1900. "The Village of Goa in the Early 16th Century." *Journal of the Royal Asiatik Society* 11: 261–291.

Barbosa, Duarte. (1518) 1918–1921. *The Book of Duarte Barbosa: An Account of the Countries Bordering on the Indian Ocean and Their Inhabitants.* 2 vols. Edited by Mansel Longworth Dames. London: Hakluyt Society.

Barreto Xavier, Ángela. 2008. *A invenção de Goa: Poder imperial e conversões culturais nos séculos XVI e XVII.* Lisbon: Imprensa de Ciências Sociais.

Bayly, Susan. 1989. *Saints, Goddesses and Kings: Muslims and Christians in South Indian Society 1700–1900.* New York: Cambridge University Press.

Bell, Catherine. 1992. *Ritual Theory, Ritual Practice.* Oxford: Oxford University Press.

Belting, Hans. 2000. *Bild und Kult: Eine Geschichte des Bildes vor dem Zeitalter der Kunst.* Munich: Beck.

Bernand, Carmen, and Serge Gruzinski. 1988. *De l'idolâtrie: Une archéologie des sciences religieuses.* Paris: Éditions du Seuil.

Bhabha, Homi. 1994. *The Location of Culture.* London: Routledge.

Biermann, Benno M. 1953. "Der erste Bischof in Ost-Indien." *Neue Zeitschrift für Missionswissenschaften* 11: 81–90.

Blumenberg, Hans. 1986. *Wirklichkeiten in denen wir leben.* Stuttgart: Reclam.

Borghes, Charles. 1993. "Christianization of the Caste System in Goa." In *Goan Society through the Ages,* edited by B. S. Shastry, 48–57. New Delhi: Asian Publication Services.

Bourdieu, Pierre. 1971. "Genèse et structure du champ religieux." *Revue française de sociologie* 12: 295–334.

———. 1993. *Sozialer Sinn: Kritik der theoretischen Vernunft.* Frankfurt am Main: Suhrkamp.

Boxer, Charles R. 1963. *Race Relations in the Portuguese Colonial Empire.* Oxford: Clarendon Press.

———. (1969) 1991. *The Portuguese Seaborne Empire 1415–1825.* London: Carcanet.

Brown, Peter. 1991. *Die Heiligenverehrung: Ihre Entstehung und Funktion in der lateinischen Christenheit.* Leipzig: Benno.

Burghart, Richard. 1989. "Something Lost, Something Gained: Translations of Hinduism." In *Hinduism Reconsidered,* edited by Günther-Dietz Sontheimer and Hermann Kulke, 213–225. New Delhi: Manohar.

Burks, Arthur. 1949. "Icon, Index, and Symbol." *Philosophy and Phenomenological Research* 9 (4): 673–689.

Cabral e Sá, Mário, ed. 1997. *Winds of Fire: The Music and Musicians of Goa.* New Delhi: Promilla.

Camille, Michael. 1989. *The Gothic Idol: Ideology and Image-Making in Medieval Art.* New York: Cambridge University Press.

Camões, Luís de. (1571) 1973. *The Lusiads.* Translated and introduced by William C. Atkinson. Harmondsworth, Eng.: Penguin Books.

Cannell, Fenella. 2010. "The Anthropology of Secularism." *Annual Review of Anthropology* 39: 85–100.

Castanheda, Hernan Lopes de. 1582. *The First Booke of the Histories of the Dicoverie and Conquest of the East Indians.* Translated by N. L. Gentleman. London: Thomas East.

Catholic Encyclopedia. n.d. New Advent. http://www.newadvent.org/cathen/; accessed August 2012.

Chakrabarty, Dipesh. 2000. *Provincializing Europe: Postcolonial Thought and Historical Difference.* Princeton, N.J.: Princeton University Press.

Chandeigne, Michel, ed. 1996. *Goa 1510–1685: L'Inde portugaise, apostolique et commercial.* Paris: Éditions Autrement.

Chatterji, Partha. 1993. *The Nation and Its Fragments: Colonial and Post-Colonial Histories.* Princeton, N.J.: Princeton University Press.

Christian, William, Jr. 1989. *Local Religion in Sixteenth Century Spain.* Princeton, N.J.: Princeton University Press.

Clémentin-Ojha, Catherine. 1994. "La Suddhi de l'Arya Samaj ou l'invention d'un rituel de (re)conversion a l'Hinduisme." *Archives de sciences sociales des religions* 87: 99–114.

Clifford, James. 1988. *The Predicament of Culture: Twentieth-Century Ethnography, Literature, and Art.* Cambridge, Mass.: Harvard University Press.

Cohn, Bernard S. 1996. *Colonialism and Its Forms of Knowledge: The British in India.* Princeton, N.J.: Princeton University Press.

Cohn, Bernard S., and Nicholas Dirks. 1988. "Beyond the Fringe: The Nation State, Colonialism, and the Technologies of Power." *Journal of Historical Sociology* 2: 224–230.

Colpe, Carsten. 1974. "Syncretism." In *The Encyclopedia of Religions,* vol. 14, edited by Mircea Eliade, 218–227. New York: Macmillan.

———. 1975. "Synkretismus, Renaissance, Säkularisation und Neubildung von Religionen in der Gegenwart." In *Handbuch der Religionsgeschichte,* vol. 3, edited by J. P. Asmussen, J. Laessoe, and C. Colpe, 441–523. Göttingen: Vandenhoeck and Ruprecht.

Comaroff, John L., and Jean Comaroff. 1991. *Of Revelation and Revolution: Christianity, Colonialism, and Consciousness in South Africa,* vol. 1. Chicago: University of Chicago Press.

Congresso Provincial da India Portuguesa (7°). 1927. *Memorias Secção VI: Emigracão.* Nova Goa, India: Tipographia R. M. Rau and Irmãos.

Conlon, Frank. 1967. *A Caste in a Changing World: Chitapur Saraswat Brahmins 1700–1955.* New Delhi: Thomson Press.

———. 1974. "Caste by Association: The Gauda Sarasvata Brahmana Unification Movement." *Journal of Asian Studies* 33 (3): 351–365.

Couto, Aurora. 2010. "The Composite Culture of Goa." In *Water: Culture, Politics and Management,* edited by India International Center, 82–91. New Delhi: Pearson Education.

Couto, Dejanirah. 1996. "'Goa Dourada,' la ville dorée." In *Goa 1510–1685: L'Inde portugaise, apostolique et commercial,* edited by Michel Chandeigne, 40–73. Paris: Éditions Autrement.

Couto, Diogo do. 1937. *Década quinta da Ásia.* Edited by Marcus de Jong. Coimbra, Portugal: Biblioteca da Universidade.

Cunha, J. Gerson Da, ed. 1877. *The Sahyadri Khanda of the Skanda Purana: A Mythological, Historical, and Geographical Account of Western India.* Bombay: Thaker, Vining and Company.

Cunha, T. B. n.d. *Denationalisation of Goans.* Panaji, India: Goa Gazetteer Department.

Cunha Rivara, Joachim Heliodoro da. 1858. *Ensaio historico da lingua concani.* Nova Goa, India: Imprensa Nacional.

———, ed. (1862) 1992. *Arquivo Portuguez oriental,* vol. 4, *Os Concílios de Goa e o Synodo de Diamper.* New Delhi: Asian Educational Services.

Dalgado, Sebastião Rudolpho. (1918) 1988. *Glossário Luso-Asiatico.* 2 vols. New Delhi: Asian Educational Services.

Daniel, Valentine E. 1987. *Fluid Signs: Being a Person in the Tamil Way.* Berkeley: University of California Press.

Daniélou, Alain. 1964. *Hindu Polytheism.* London: Routledge and Kegan Paul.

Das, G. 2002. *India Unbound: The Social and Economic Revolution from Independence to the Global Information Age.* New York: Anchor Books.

Das, Veena. 1984. "For a Folk-Theology and a Theological Anthropology of Islam." *Contributions to Indian Sociology* 18: 293–300.

———. 1989. "Difference and Division as Designs for Life." In *Contemporary India: Essays on the Uses of Tradition,* edited by Carla Borden, 45–56. New Delhi: Oxford University Press.

D'Costa, Adelyn. 1977. "Caste Stratification among Roman Catholics of Goa." *Man in India* 57 (4): 283–292.

D'Costa, Anthony. 1962. "The Demolition of the Temples in the Island of Goa in 1540 and the Disposal of Temple Lands." *Nouvelle revue de science missionaire* 18: 161–176.

D'Cruz, Sebastian. 1982. *The Parish and the Village of Siolim: Souvenir of Platinum Jubilee of St. Anthony's Church 1907–1982.* Siolim, India: N.p.

———. 1994. *St. Anthony's Church and the Villages of Siolim and Marna.* Siolim, India: N.p.

Dempsey, Corinne. 1998. "Rivalry, Reliance, and Resemblance: Siblings as Metaphor for Hindu-Christian Relations in Kerala State." *Asian Folklore Studies* 1: 51–70.

De Silva, Chandra Richard. 1994. "Beyond the Cape: The Portuguese Encounters with the People of South Asia." In *Implicit Understandings: Observing, Reporting and Reflecting on the Encounters between Europeans and Other Peoples in the Early Modern Era,* edited by Stuart Schwartz, 295–322. Cambridge: Cambridge University Press.

De Souza, Nora Seco. n.d. "St. Francis Xavier: Goincho Sahib." In *Goa Cradles of My Dreams,* edited by Nora Seco De Souza, 8–14. Pilar, India: Xaverian Press.

De Souza, Robert, and Joel D'Souza. 1987. "Sisters of Harmony." *Goa Today,* June, 32–33.

De Souza, Teotonio. 1975. "Glimpses of Hindu Dominance of Goan Economy in the 17th Century." *Indica* 12: 27–35.

———. 1979. *Medieval Goa: A Socio-Economic History.* New Delhi: Concept.

———, ed. 1985. *Indo-Portuguese History: Old Issues, New Questions.* New Delhi: Concept.

———. 1990. *Goa through the Ages,* vol. 2, *An Economic History.* New Delhi: Concept.

Dias, Elmina. 1993. "No Place for Zealots." *Navhind Times,* 18 October.

Dias, Mariano Jose. 1980. "The Hindu-Christian Society of Goa." *Indica* 17: 109–116.

———. 1995. "Liturgical Books in Devanagri Konkani." *Renovação* 25: 2003–2004.
Dirks, Nicholas D. 1989. "The Invention of Caste: Civil Society in Colonial India." *Social Analysis* 25: 42–53.
———. 1993. *The Hollow Crown: Ethnohistory of an Indian Kingdom.* Ann Arbor: University of Michigan Press.
———. 1995. *Colonialism and Culture.* Ann Arbor: University of Michigan Press.
D'Mello, Ashley. 1994. "A Pilgrim's Progress." *The Times of India,* January, 14, 19.
Doniger, Wendy. 2009. *The Hindus: An Alternative History.* New York: Penguin Books.
Doshi, Saryn, and P. P. Shirodkar. 1983. "Temple Sanctuaries: Expressions of Devotion." In *Goa: Cultural Patterns,* edited by Saryn Doshi, 53–60. Bombay: Marg.
Droogers, A. 1989. "Syncretism: The Problem of Definition, the Definition of the Problem." In *Dialogue and Syncretism: An Interdisciplinary Approach,* edited by H. Gort et al., 7–25. Amsterdam: Eerdmans.
D'Souza, Joel. 1993. "A Common Faith." *Goa Today,* September, 16–20.
Dumont, Louis. 1970. *Homo Hierarchicus: The Caste System and Its Implications.* London: Paladin.
Durkheim, Émile. (1912) 1971. *The Elementary Forms of Religious Life.* Translated by J. W. Swain. London: Allen and Unwin.
Eck, Diana. 1981. *Darsán: Seeing the Divine Image in India.* Chambersburg, Penn.: Anima Books.
Eliade, Mircea. 1986. *Kosmos und Geschichte: Der Mythos der ewigen Wiederkehr.* Frankfurt: Insel.
Erndl, M. Kathleen. 1993. *Victory to the Mother: The Hindu Goddess of Northwest India in Myth, Ritual, and Symbol.* New York: Oxford University Press.
Esteves, Sart. 1986. *Politics and Political Leadership in Goa.* New Delhi: Sterlin.
Falcao, Nelson. 2003. *Kristapurāṇa: A Christian-Hindu Encounter. A Study of Inculturation in the Kristapurāṇa of Thomas Stephens, S.J. (1549–1619).* Anand, India: Gujarat Sahitya Prakash.
Fernandes, Aurelio. 2003. "Goa's Democratic Becoming and the Absence of Mass Political Violence." *Lusotopie:* 331–349.
Figueiredo, Joao Manuel Pacheco de. 1963. "Goa pré-portuguesa." *Studia* 12: 139–259.
Foral de Bardes. (1647) 1712. Vol. 1. Panjim, India: Directorate of Archives, Archaeology, and Museum.
Foral de Salcete (1567–1585). 1990. *Purabhilekh puratatva* 8 (2): 33–71.
Foucault, Michel. (1966) 1980. *Die Ordnung der Dinge.* Frankfurt: Suhrkamp.
———. 1988. *The History of Sexuality.* Translated by Robert Hurley. New York: Vintage Books.
Freedberg, David. 1982. "The Hidden God: Image and Interdiction in the Netherlands in the Sixteenth Century." *Art History* 5: 133–153.
———. 1989. *The Power of Images: Studies in the History and Theory of Response.* Chicago: University of Chicago Press.
Frykenberg, Robert Eric. 2003. "Christians in India: An Historical Overview of Their Complex Origins." In *Christians and Missionaries in India: Cross-Cultural Communication since 1500,* edited by Robert Eric Frykenberg, 1–32. London: Erdmann.
Fuller, Christopher John. 1976. "Kerala Christians and the Caste System." *Man* 11: 53–70.
———. 1992. *The Camphor Flame: Popular Hinduism and Society in India.* Princeton, N.J.: Princeton University Press.

Funkenstein, A. 1986. *Theology and the Scientific Imagination from the Middle Ages.* Princeton, N.J.: Princeton University Press.

Furtado, Luis. 1985. "Mapusa's Lady of the Miracles." *Goa Today,* March, 38.

Gaborieau, Marc. 1975. "La transe rituelle dans l'Himalaya Central: Folie, avatar, meditation." *Purusartha* 2: 147–172.

Gade, Martine. 1996. "Saint François Xavier, l'incorruptible." In *Goa 1510–1685: L'Inde portugaise, apostolique et commercial,* edited by Michel Chandeigne, 92–114. Paris: Éditions Autrement.

Gaitonde, V. D., ed. and transl. 1972. *The Sahyadri Khanda of the Skanda Purana: A Mythological, Historical, and Geographical Account of Western India.* Bombay: Katyayni.

Geertz, Clifford. 1973. *The Interpretation of Cultures.* New York: Basic Books.

General Administration Department of Goa, Daman, and Diu. 1966. "Order." *Boletim oficial do estado da Índia* 3: 428.

Godinho, Manuel. (1665) 1990. *Intrepid Itinerant: Manuel Godinho and His Journey from India to Portugal in 1663.* Edited by J. Correia-Affonso; translated by V. Lobo and J. Correia-Affonso. New Delhi: Oxford University Press.

Góis, Damiao de. (1926) 2001. *Cronica do felicissimo rei D. Manuel, vol. 1 (1566–67).* 4 vols. Edited by D. Lopes. Coimbra, Portugal: Imprensa da Universidade.

Gomes, Bernadette M., and Sunjay Shirodkar. 1991. "Zagor: Rising above Religion." *Gomantak Times,* January, 6.

Gomes, Olivinho J. F. 1987. *Village Goa: A Study of Goan Social Structure and Change.* New Delhi: Chand and Company.

Government of Goa. 1991. *Statistical Pocket Book of Goa 1989–1991.* Panjim, India: Government Printing Press.

———. 2001. *Statistical Handbook of Goa 2001.* Panjim, India: Publication Division.

Government of Goa, Daman, and Diu. 1981. *Statistical Pocket Book of the Union Territory of Goa, Daman, and Diu, 1981.* Panjim, India: Government Printing Press.

Government of India. 1979. *Gazetteer of the Union Territory: Goa, Daman, and Diu (1979),* vol. 1, part 1. Edited by V. T. Gune. Panjim, India: Government of India Press.

———. 2011. Census. http://censusindia.gov.in/Census_Data_2001/Census_data _finder/C_Series/Population_by_religious_communities.htm; accessed August 2012.

Guha, Ranajit. 1989. "Dominance without Hegemony and Its Historiography." In *Subaltern Sudies VI,* edited by Ranajit Guha, 210–309. Oxford: Oxford University Press.

Hall, Maurice. 1992. *Windows on Goa: A History and Guide.* London: Quiller Press.

Hein, Norvin. 1995. "Lila." In *The Gods at Play: Lila in South Asia,* edited by William Sax, 13–20. Oxford: Oxford University Press.

Henn, Alexander. 2000. "The Becoming of Goa: Space and Culture in the Emergence of a Multicultural Lifeworld." *Lusotopie:* 333–339.

———. 2003. *Wachheit der Wesen: Politik, Ritual und Kunst der Akkulturation in Goa.* London: LIT-Verlag.

———. 2006. "The Lord of Mapusa: Genesis of an Urban God in Goa." *Purusartha* 25: 31–47.

———. 2008. "Beyond Norm, Text and Dialectics: Ritual as Social Praxis." In *Rituals in an Unstable World: Contingency—Embodiment—Hybridity,* edited by Alexander Henn and Klaus-Peter Koepping, 9–29. Frankfurt am Main: Peter Lang.

———. 2009. "Hindu Traditions in Goa." In *Encyclopedia of Hinduism,* vol. 1, edited by Knut A. Jacobson, 249–254. Leiden: Brill.

Henn, Alexander, Alito Siqueira, and Gasper D'Souza. 2010. *Staying Awake for God: Introducing the Zagor.* Film. http://vimeo.com/18668418; accessed 14 October 2013.

Heras, Henry. 1933. *The Conversion Policy of the Jesuits in India.* Bombay: Indian Historical Research Institute.

Herskovitz, Melville J. (1941) 1958. *The Myth of the Negro Past.* Boston: Beacon Press.

Hsia, Po-Chia R. 2005. *The World of Catholic Renewal 1540–1770.* Cambridge: Cambridge University Press.

Humphrey, Caroline, and James Laidlaw. 1994. *The Archetypal Actions of Ritual: A Theory of Ritual Illustrated by the Jain Rite of Worship.* Oxford: Clarendon Press.

Ifeka, Caroline. 1985. "The Image of Goa." In *Indo-Portuguese History: Old Issues, New Questions,* edited by Teotonio de Souza, 181–195. New Delhi: Concept.

———. 1989. "Hierarchical Women: Dowry System and Its Implication among Christians in Goa." *Contributions to Indian Sociology* 23 (2): 261–284.

Inden, Ronald. 1986. "Orientalist Constructions of India." *Modern Asian Studies* 20 (3): 401–446.

———. 1990. *Imagining India.* Oxford: Blackwell.

India Portuguesa. 1956. *Repartição central de estatistica e informação: 8. Recenseamento geral da população,* vol. 2. N.p.: Tipographia Aranjo.

Jaffrelot, Christophe. 1994. "Les (re)conversions a l'Hinduisme (1885–1990): Politisation et diffusion d'une 'invention de la tradition'." *Archives de sciences sociales des religions* 87: 73–98.

Jakobson, Roman. 1965. "Quest for the Essence of Language." *Diogenes* 51: 21–37.

Jedin, Hubert. 1935. "Entstehung und Tragweite des Trienter Dekrets über die Bilderverehrung." *Theologische Quartalsschrift* 116: 143–188, 404–429.

Juergensmeyer, M. 2000. *Terror in the Mind of God: The Global Rise of Religious Violence.* Berkeley: University of California Press.

Kakodkar, Archana. 1988. "Shuddhi: Reconversion to Hinduism in Goa." In *Goa: Cultural Trends,* edited by P. P. Shirodkar, 242–263. Panjim, India: Directorate of Archives, Archaeology, and Museum.

Kamat, Jevi. 1957. "Dada vaidya ani shuddhi karan." In *Vaidya Amriti Grantha: In Memoriam Dada Vaidya,* 90–100. Poona, India: S. M. Joshi.

Kamat, Pratima. 2001. "Goa Indo-Portuguesa: The 'Engineering' of Goan Society through Colonial Policies of Coercion and Collaboration." *Portuguese Studies Review* 9 (1–2): 435–466.

Kamath, S. U. 1992. "Origin and Spread of the Gauda Saraswats." *Saraswat* 1: 39–61.

Kaufmann, S. B. 1982. "A Christian Caste in Hindu Society: Religious Leadership and Social Conflict among the Paravas in Southern Tamilnadu." *Modern Asian Studies* 15 (2): 203–245.

Keane, Webb. 2004. "Language and Religion." In *A Companion to Linguistic Anthropology,* edited by A. Duranti, 431–448. Malden, Mass.: Blackwell.

———. 2007. *Christian Moderns: Freedom and Fetish in Mission Encounter.* Berkeley: University of California Press.

Kerkar, Rajendra. 2010. "Sister Act: Faces of Two Feasts." *Times of India, Goa,* 20 April, 2–5.

Khedekar, V. 1983. "Rhythm and Revelry: The Folk Performers." In *Goa: Cultural Patterns,* edited by Saryn Doshi, 133–144. Bombay: Marg.

King, Richard. 1999. *Orientalism and Religion: Postcolonial Theory, India and the "Mythic East."* New Delhi: Oxford University Press.

Kosambi, D. (1962) 1992. *Myth and Reality.* Bombay: Popular Prakashan.

Koselleck, Reinhart. 1984. *Vergangene Zukunft zur Semantik geschichtlicher Zeiten.* Frankfurt: Suhrkamp.

Krengel, Monika. 1999. "Spirit Possession in the Central Himalayas: Jagar-Rituals—An Expression of Custom and Rights." *Purusartha: La possession en Asie du Sud. Parole, Corps* 21: 265–288.

Kulkarni, A. R. 1994. "The Proselytization and Purification Movement in Goa and Konkan." In *Discoveries, Missionary Expansion and Asian Cultures,* edited by Teotonio De Souza, 91–105. New Delhi: Concept.

Lach, Donald. 1994. *Asia in the Making of Europe,* vol. 1, *The Century of Discovery.* Chicago: University of Chicago Press.

Leavitt, John H. 1985. *The Language of the Gods: Discourse and Experience in a Central Himalayan Ritual.* Ph.D. dissertation, University of Chicago.

Levitt, Stephan Hillyer. 1973. *The Patityagramanirnaya: A Puranic History of Degraded Brahman Villages.* Ph.D. dissertation, University of Pennsylvania.

———. 1977. "The Sahyadrikhanda: Some Problems Concerning a Text-Critical Edition of a Puranic Text." *Purana* 19 (1): 1–40.

Lima, Anne. 1996. "Justice et miséricorde." In *Goa 1510–1685: L'Inde portugaise, apostolique et commerciale,* edited by Michel Chandeigne, 135–158. Paris: Éditions Autrement.

MacCulloch, Diarmaid. 2005. *The Reformation.* London: Penguin.

Madan, T. N. 1998. *Modern Myth, Locked Minds: Secularism and Fundamentalism in India.* New Delhi: Oxford University Press.

———. 2005. "Religions of India, Plurality and Pluralism." In *Religious Pluralism in South Asia and Europe,* edited by J. Malik and H. Reifeld, 42–75. New Delhi: Oxford University Press.

Mahambre, U. 1993. "Controversy Raked up over Shifting of Porvorim Chapel." *Navhind Times,* 30 October.

Major, R. H., ed. (1857) 2005. *India in the Fifteenth Century, Being a Collection of Narratives of Voyages to India: The Travels of Nicolò Conti, in the East, in the Early Part of the Fifteenth Century.* Facsimile edition. London: Elibron Classics.

Marriott, McKim. 1955. "Little Communities in an Indigenous Civilization." In *Village India: Studies in the Little Community,* edited by McKim Marriott, 171–222. Chicago: University of Chicago Press.

Martins, T. 1912. *Collecção de decretos diocesanos da archidiocese de Goa.* Nova Goa, India: Tipographia Arthur.

Martires Lopes, Maria Jesus dos. 1996. *Goa setecentista: Tradição e modernidade (1750–1800).* Lisbon: Universidade Católica Portuguesa.

Masuzawa, Tomoko. 2005. *The Invention of World Religions; or, How European Universalism Was Preserved in the Language of Pluralism.* Chicago: University of Chicago Press.

Mayaram, S. 2005. "Living Together Separately: Ajmer as a Paradigm for the (South) Asian City." In *Living Together Separately: Cultural India in History and Politics,* edited by Mushirul Hasan and Asim Roy, 144–170. New Delhi: Oxford University Press.

McGarvey, J. W. 1872. *A Commentary on the Acts of Apostles with a Revised Version of the Text.* Lexington, Ky.: Transylvania Printing. http://www.ccel.org/ccel /mcgarvey/acts.ch10.html; accessed 1 June 2010.

Meibohm, M. 2002. "Past Selves and Present Others: The Ritual Construction of Identity at a Catholic Festival in India." In *Popular Christianity in India: Riting between the Lines,* edited by Selva Raj and C. Dempsey, 61–84. Albany: State University of New York Press.

———. 2004. *Cultural Complexity in South India: Hindu and Catholic in Marian Pilgrimage.* Ph.D. dissertation, University of Pennsylvania.

Mexia, Affonso. (1526) 1992. "Foral de usos e costumes dos gancares, e lavradores desta ilha de Goa e outras aneixas." In *Arquivo Portuguez oriental,* vol. 5, edited by J. H. da Cunha Rivara, 117–133. New Delhi: Asian Educational Services.

Michaels, Axel. 1998. *Der Hinduismus: Geschichte und Gegenwart.* Munich: Beck.

———. 2006. "Ritual and Meaning." In *Theorizing Rituals,* vol. 1, *Issues, Topics, Approaches, Concepts,* edited by Jens Kreinath, Jan Snoek, and Michael Stausberg, 3–14. Leiden: Brill.

Mitragotri, V. R. 1989. "Ravalnath, a Saivite Deity of Goa and Konkan." *Puratar* 14: 49–52.

———. 1999. *Sociocultural History of Goa: From Bhojas to Vijayanagara.* Panaji, India: Institute Menezes Braganza.

Mitragotri, V. R., and K. M. Mathew. 1991. "The Deities of Goa Mentioned in Sahyadrikhand and the Historicity of the Date." Paper presented at the Fifth Seminar on the History of Goa, University of Goa, Panjim, India, 19–20 February.

Mitter, Partha. 1977. *Much Maligned Monsters: History of European Reaction to Indian Art.* Oxford: Clarendon Press.

Mitterwallner, Gritli von. 1981. "The Rock-Cut Cave Temples of Arvalem Goa." In *Madhu: Recent Researches in Indian Archaeology and Art History,* edited by M. S. Nagaraja Rao, 165–174. New Delhi: Agam Kala Prakashan.

———. 1983a. "The Hindu Past: Sculpture and Architecture." In *Goa: Cultural Patterns,* edited by Saryn Doshi, 21–40. Bombay: Marg.

———. 1983b. "Testimonials of Heroism: Memorial Stones and Structures." In *Goa: Cultural Patterns,* edited by Saryn Doshi, 41–49. Bombay: Marg.

Mosse, David. 1994. "The Politics of Religious Synthesis: Roman Catholicism and Hindu Village Society in Tamil Nadu, India." In *Syncretism/Anti-Syncretism: The Politics of Religious Synthesis,* edited by Charles Stewart and Rosalind Shaw, 85–107. London: Routledge.

———. 1997. "Honour, Caste and Conflict: The Ethnohistory of a Catholic Festival in Rural Tamil Nadu (1730–1990)." In *Altérité et identité: Islam et Christianisme en Inde,* edited by J. Assayag and G. Tarabout, 71–120. Paris: Édition Ehess.

Nandy, Ashis. 1990. "The Politics of Secularism and the Recovery of Religious Tolerance." In *Mirrors of Violence,* edited by Veena Das, 69–94. New Delhi: Oxford University Press.

Narayan, Rayan. 2011. "Murder Most Foul." *Goan Observer,* 4 June. http://goanobserver .com/murder-most-foul.html; accessed August 2012.

Nazareth, Casimiro Christovão de. (1873) 1894. *Mitras lusitanas no oriente: Catalogo dos prelados da egreja metropolitana e primacial de Goa e das dioceses suffraganeas com a recopilação por elles emittidas de Goa.* 2nd edition. Lisbon: Imprensa Nacional.

Newman, Robert. 2001. *Of Umbrellas, Goddesses and Dreams: Essays on Goan Culture and Society.* Mapusa: Other India Press.

Noronha, L., et al. 2002. "Goa: Tourism, Migrations and Ecosystem Transformations." *Ambio* 3 (4): 295–302.

Oberhammer, G., ed. 1983. *Inklusivismus: Eine indische Denkform.* Vienna: Institut für Indologie der Universität Wien.

Oliveira Marques, A. H. de. 1971. *Daily Life in Portugal in the Late Middle Ages.* Madison: University of Wisconsin Press.

"Over a Lakh Attend Old Goa Feast." 1990. *Navhind Times,* 4 December.

Pais, F. (1595) 1952. *Tombo da ilha de Goa e das terras de Salcête e Bardês.* Nova Goa, India: Imprensa Nacional.

Patil, Anand. 1999. "Literatures in Portuguese Colonial Goa: The Battle of Puranas." *Govapuri: Bulletin of the Institute Meneses Braganza* 1 (3): 56–84.

Pearson, Michael. 1973a. "Indigenous Dominance in a Colonial Economy: The Goan Rendas 1600–1670." In *Mare Luso-Indicum: Études et documents sur l'histoire de l'Ócean Indien et des pays riverains á l'époque de la domination Portugais,* vol. 2, edited by J. Aubin, 61–73. Paris: Libraire Minard.

———. 1973b. "Wealth and Power: Indian Groups in the Portuguese Indian Economy." *South Asia* 1–3: 36–44.

———. 1987. *The Portuguese in India.* Cambridge: Cambridge University Press.

———. (1984) 2005a. "Goa during the First Century of Portuguese Rule." In *The World of the Indian Ocean 1500–1800: Studies in Economic, Social and Cultural History,* 36–49. Aldershot, Eng.: Ashgate.

———. (1992) 2005b. "The Search for the Similar: Early Contacts between Portuguese and Indians." In *The World of the Indian Ocean 1500–1800: Studies in Economic, Social and Cultural History,* 144–159. Aldershot, Eng.: Ashgate.

Pereira, Clifford. N.d. "Thomas Stephens: An English Jesuit in Goa." http://lists.goanet .org/pipermail/goanet-goanet.org/2004-May/099612.html; accessed 15 October 2013.

Pereira, Rui Gomes de. 1978. *Goa: Hindu Temples and Deities.* Panaji, India: Printwell Press Goa.

———. 1981. *Goa: Gaunkari, The Old Village Associations.* Panjim, India: N.p.

Perez, Rosa Maria. 1997. "Hinduism and Christianity in Goa: The Limits of Caste." In *Stories of Goa,* edited by Rosa Maria Perez, Susana Sardo, and Joaquim Pais de Brito, 107–121. Lisbon: National Museum of Ethnology.

Pires, Tomé. (1944) 1967. *The Suma Oriental: An Account of the East, from the Red Sea to Japan, Written in Malacca and India in 1512–1515.* Translated and edited by Armando Cortesão. Nedeln, Liechtenstein: Kraus Reprint Limited.

Pissurlencar, Pandurang. 1962. *Goa pré-Portuguesa através dos escritores lusitanos dos séculos XVI e XVII.* Bastora, India: Rangel.

Priolkar, Anant Kakba. 1958. *The Printing Press in India: Its Beginnings and Early Development. With an Historical Essay on the Konkani Language by J. H. Cunha Rivara.* Bombay: Marathi Samshodhana Mandala.

———. 1967. *Goa Rediscovered.* Bombay: N.p.

Rabb, Theodore. 1974. "The Expansion of Europe and the Spirit of Capitalism." *The Historical Journal* 17 (4): 675–689.

Rafael, Vicente. 1988. *Contracting Colonialism: Translation and Christian Conversion in Tagalog Society under Early Spanish Rule.* Ithaca, N.Y.: Cornell University Press.

Raman, Shankar. 2001. *Framing India: The Colonial Imaginary in Early Modern Culture.* Stanford, Calif.: Stanford University Press.

Raj, Selva. 2002. "Transgressing Boundaries, Transgressing Turner: The Pilgrimage Tradition at the Shrine of St. John de Britto." In *Popular Christianity in India: Riting between the Lines,* edited by Selva Raj and Corinne Dempsey, 85–113. Albany: State University of New York Press.

Raj, Selva, and Corinne Dempsey, eds. 2002. *Popular Christianity in India: Riting between the Lines.* Albany: State University of New York Press.

Ravenstein, E. G. (1898) 1998. *A Journal of the First Voyage of Vasco Da Gama (1497–1499).* New Delhi: Asian Educational Services.

Redfield, Robert, and Milton Singer. 1954. "The Cultural Role of Cities." *Economic Development and Cultural Change* 3: 53–73.

Ribeiro, Diogo. 1620. *Vocabulário das língues canarim feito pelles padres do Companhia de Jesus.* Goa University Library, Pissurlenkar Collection.

Ricoeur, Paul. 1980. "Narrative Time." *Critical Inquiry* 7 (1): 169–190.

Robinson, Rowena. 1993. "Some Neglected Aspects of the Conversion of Goa: A Socio-Historical Perspective." *Sociological Bulletin* 42: 65–83.

———. 1998. *Conversion, Continuity and Change: Lived Christianity in Southern Goa.* New Delhi: Sage.

———. 2000. "Taboo or Veiled Consent? Goan Inquisitorial Edict of 1736." *Economic and Political Weekly,* 1 July, 2423–2431.

Rodrigues, L. A. 1990. "Glimpses of the Konkani Language at the Turn of the Sixteenth Century." *Boletim do Instituto Menezes Bragança* 163: 43–72.

Rogers, Francis. 1962. *The Quest for Eastern Christians: Travels and Rumors in the Age of Discovery.* Minneapolis: University of Minnesota Press.

———. 1964. "The Attraction of the East and Early Portuguese Discoveries." *Luso-Brazilien Review* 1 (1): 43–59.

Rubiés, Joan-Pau. 2000. *Travel and Ethnology in the Renaissance: South India through European Eyes, 1250–1625.* Cambridge: Cambridge University Press.

Rubinoff, Arthur G. 1998. *The Construction of a Political Community: Integration and Identity in Goa.* New Delhi: Sage.

Rubinoff, Janet Ahner. 1988. "Vangad: The Concept of Lineage in Goan Corporate Village." In *City, Countryside and Society in Maharashtra,* edited by D. W. Atwot, M. Israel, and N. K. Wagle, 191–207. Toronto: University of Toronto Press.

Rudolph, Kurt. 1979. "Synkretismus—Vom Theologischen Scheltwort zum religionswissenschaftlichen Begriff." In *Humanitas Religiosa: Festschrift H. Biezais,* 198–212. Stockholm: Almquist and Wiksell International.

Sahliyeh, E. 1990. "Religious Resurgence and Political Modernization." In *Religious Resurgence and Politics in the Contemporary World,* edited by E. Sahliyeh, 1–16. Albany: State University of New York Press.

Said, Edward. 1985. *Orientalism: Western Conception of the Orient.* London: Penguin.

Saldanha, Antonio de. (1655) 1963. *Santo Antonichi Acharya: The Miracles of St. Antony.* Edited by A. K. Priolkar. Bombay: Marathi Samshodhana Mandala.

Saldanha, J. A. 1908. "The First Englishman in India and His Works, Especially His Christian Puran." *Journal of the Royal Asiatic Society* 22: 209–221.

Saldanha, Mariano. 1912. "O culto Christão entre os Hindus." *O Heraldo,* 24 July, 55–58.

Sardessai, Manohar L. 1980. "Portuguese Influence on the Konkani Language." *Indica* 17: 117–122.

Sardessai, Mhadavi. 2012. "On a Trail with Kōkno." Paper presented at the Twenty-Second European Conference on South Asian Studies, Lisbon, 25–28 July.

Schieffelin, Edward L. 1985. "Performance and the Cultural Construction of Reality." *American Ethnologist* 12: 707–724.

Schrimpf, Robert. 1996. "Le diable et le goupillon." In *Goa 1510–1685: L'Inde portugaise, apostolique et commercial,* edited by Michel Chandeigne, 115–133. Paris: Éditions Autrement.

Seth, Vanita. 2010. *Europe's Indians: Producing Racial Difference, 1500–1900.* Durham, N.C.: Duke University Press.

Shirodkar, P. P. 1988. "Influence of Nath Cult in Goa." In *Goa: Cultural Trends,* edited by P. P. Shirodkar, 8–21. Panjim, India: Directorate of Archives, Archaeology, and Museum.

———. 1991. "Vaishṇavism in Goa." Paper presented at the Fifth Seminar on the History of Goa, Goa University, Goa, India, 19–20 February.

———. 1993. "Naga Worship in Goa." Paper presented at the Indian Council of Social Science Research Workshop on Goan Folklore: Theories, Perspectives, and Methodologies, Goa University, Goa, India, 16–17 April.

Shirodkar, P. P., and H. H. Mandal, eds. 1993. *People of India,* vol. 21, *Goa, Anthropological Survey of India.* Bombay: Popular Prakashan.

Shrine of [the] Holy Cross of Bambolim. 1996. Souvenir. 10 October.

Silva Rego, Antonio da. 1948–1958. *Documentação para a história das missões do padroado Portugues do Oriente,* vols. 1–12, 1499–1582. Lisbon: N.p.

Siqueira, Alito, and Alexander Henn. 2001. "The Ganvpon and the Communidad: Towards an Anthropological Reading for the Social History of Goa." Paper presented at the Maritime Activities of India with Special Reference to the Portuguese: 1500–1800 Conference, Department of History, Goa University, Goa, India, 25–28 April.

Sirkar, Rameshchandra. 1983. "Dedications to the Altar: The Devadasi Tradition." In *Goa: Cultural Patterns,* edited by Saryn Doshi, 145–151. Bombay: Marg.

Smith, Jonathan Z. 1998. "Religion, Religions, Religious." In *Critical Terms for Religious Studies,* edited by M. Taylor, 269–284. Chicago: University of Chicago Press.

Sontheimer, Günther-Dietz. 1989. "Hinduism: The Five Components and Their Interaction." In *Hinduism Reconsidered,* edited by Günther-Dietz Sontheimer and Hermann Kulke, 197–212. New Delhi: Manohar.

———. 1994. "The Vana and the Kṣetra: The Tribal Background of Some Famous Cults." In *Religion and Society in Eastern India: Eschmann Memorial Lectures,* edited by G. C. Tripathi and Hermann Kulke, 116–164. New Delhi: Manohar.

Sontheimer, Günther-Dietz, and Hermann Kulke, eds. 1989. *Hinduism Reconsidered.* New Delhi: Manohar.

Slessarev, Vsevolod. 1959. *Prester John: The Letter and the Legend.* Minneapolis: University of Minnesota Press.

Srinivas, M. N. 1989. *The Cohesive Role of Sanskritization and Other Essays.* New Delhi: Oxford University Press.

Srinivas, S. 2008. *In the Presence of Sai Baba: Body, City and Memory in a Global Religious Movement.* Leiden: Brill.

Srivastava, Harish C. 1990. "Demographic History and Human Resources." In *Goa through the Ages: An Economic History,* vol. 2, edited by T. De Souza, 55–116. New Delhi: Concept.

Srivastava, Sushil. 2001. "Situating the Gentoo in History: European Perceptions of Indians in Early Phase of Colonialism." *Economic and Political Weekly*, 17 February, 576–594.

Staal, J. F. 1979. "The Meaninglessness of Ritual." *Numen* 26 (1): 2–22.

Stein, Burton. 1975. "The State and the Agrarian Order in Medieval South India: A Historical Critique." In *Essays on South Asia*, edited by Burton Stein, 64–91. Honolulu: University of Hawai'i Press.

Stephens, Thomas. 1907. *The Christian Puranna of Father Thomas Stephens of the Society of Jesus*. Edited by Joseph L. Saldanha. Mangalore, India: Simon Alvares.

Stewart, Charles. 1995. "Relocating Syncretism in Social Science Discourse." In *Syncretism and the Commerce of Symbols*, edited by G. Ajmer, 13–37. Göteborg, Sweden: International Arctic Social Sciences Association.

Stewart, Charles, and Rosalind Shaw. 1994a. "Introduction." In *Syncretism/Anti-Syncretism: The Politics of Religious Synthesis*, edited by Charles Stewart and Rosalind Shaw, 1–26. London: Routledge.

———, eds. 1994b. *Syncretism/Anti-Syncretism: The Politics of Religious Synthesis*. London: Routledge.

Stietencron, Heinrich von. 1989. "Hinduism: On the Proper Use of a Deceptive Term." In *Hinduism Reconsidered*, edited by Günther-Dietz Sontheimer and Hermann Kulke, 11–28. New Delhi: Manohar.

Stroumsa, Guy G. 2010. *A New Science: The Discovery of Religion in the Age of Reason*. Cambridge, Mass.: Harvard University Press.

Subrahmanyam, Sanjay. 1993. *The Portuguese Empire 1500–1700: A Political and Economic History*. London: Longman.

———. 1997a. *The Career and Legend of Vasco da Gama*. Cambridge: Cambridge University Press.

———. 1997b. "The Romantic, the Oriental and the Exotic: Notes on the Portuguese in Goa." In *Stories of Goa*, edited by Rosa Maria Perez, Susana Sardo, and Joaquim Pais de Brito, 29–43. Lisbon: National Museum of Ethnology.

———. 2001. *Penumbral Visions: Making Politics in Early Modern South India*. Oxford: Oxford University Press.

Talbot, C. 1995. "Inscribing the Other, Onscribing the Self: Hindu-Muslim Identities in Precolonial India." *Comparative Studies in Society and History* 3 (1): 692–722.

Tambiah, S. J. 1979. "A Performative Approach to Ritual." *Proceedings of the British Academy* 65: 113–167.

———. 1996. *Leveling Crowds: Ethnonationalist Conflicts and Collective Violence in South Asia*. Berkeley: University of California Press.

Taussig, M. T. 1993. *Mimesis and Alterity: A Particular History of the Senses*. London: Routledge.

Thapar, Romila. 1989. "Imagined Religious Communities: Ancient History and the Search for a Hindu Identity." *Modern Asian Studies* 23 (2): 209–231.

———. 1997. "Syndicated Hinduism." In *Hinduism Reconsidered*, 2nd edition, edited by Günther-Dietz Sontheimer and H. Kulke, 54–79. New Delhi: Manohar.

Thiel-Horstmann, Monika. 1985. *Nächtliches Wachen: Eine Form indischen Gottesdienstes*. Bonn: Indica et Tibetica.

Thomaz, Luís Filipe. 1981–1982. "Goa—Une Societé Luso-Indienne." *Bulletin des études portugaises et bresiliennes* 42–43: 15–44.

Todorov, Tzvetan. 1985. *Die Eroberung Amerikas: Das Problem des Anderen.* Translated by Wilfried Böhringer. Frankfurt am Main: Suhrkamp.

Trindade, Freire Paulo de. 1962–1967. *Conquista Espiritual de Oriente.* 3 vols. Edited by F. Felix Lopez. Lisbon: Centro de Estudios Historicaos Ultra Marinos.

Tulpule, Shankar G. 1979. *Classical Marathi Literature.* Wiesbaden, Germany: Otto Harrassowitz.

Turner, R. L. 1966. *A Comparative Dictionary of the Indo-Aryan Language.* Oxford: Oxford University Press.

Turner, Victor, and Edith Turner. 1978. *Image and Pilgrimage in Christian Culture: Anthropological Perspectives.* Oxford: Blackwell.

Urban, H. B. 2003. "Avatar of Our Age: Sathya Sai Baba and the Cultural Contradictions of Late Capitalism." *Religion* 33: 73–93.

Valaulikar, Shenoi Vahman Ragunat Varde, aka Shenoi Goembab. (1945) 1977. *Aine Velar.* Margao, India: Konkani Basha Mandal.

Van der Veer, Peter. 1994. "Syncretism, Multiculturalism and the Discourse of Tolerance." In *Syncretism/Anti-Syncretism: The Politics of Religious Synthesis,* edited by Charles Stewart and Rosalind Shaw, 196–211. London: Routledge.

———. 1995. "Introduction." In *Conversion to Modernities: The Globalization of Christianity,* edited by Peter Van der Veer, 1–21. London: Routledge.

Van Skyhawk, Hugh. 1999. "'. . . In This Bushy Land of Salsette . . .': Father Thomas Stephens and the Kristapurāṇa." In *Studies in Early Modern Indo-Aryan Languages, Literature and Culture,* edited by A. Entwistle et al., 363–378. New Delhi: Manohar.

Veiga Coutinho, Lucia da. 1994. "A Puzzling Epithet: An Exploration of the Rationale behind the 'Goencho Saib' Sobriquet." *Goa Today,* December, 22–25.

Verenkar, Sham. 1991. *Goenchea lokvedacho rupkar.* Panjim, India: Goa Konkani Academy.

Waghorne, Joanne. 2002. "Chariots of the God/s: Riding the Line between Hindu and Christian." In *Popular Christianity in India: Riting between the Lines,* edited by Selva Raj and C. Dempsey, 11–38. Albany: State University of New York Press.

Wagle, N. K. 1970. "The History and Social Organisation of the Gaud Saraswat Brahmans of the West Coast of India." *Journal of Indian History* 142: 7–25.

———. 1974. "The Gaud Saraswat Brahmanas of West Coast India: A Study of Their Matha Institution and Voluntary Associations (1870–1900)." *Journal of the Asiatic Society of Bombay* 26: 228–249.

Wahlen, Clinton. 2005. "Peter's Vision and Conflicting Definitions of Purity." *New Testament Studies* 51: 505–518.

Walker, Benjamin. 1983. *Hindu World: An Encyclopedic Survey of Hinduism.* 2 vols. London: Munshiram Manoharlal.

Weber, M. (1920) 1978. *Economy and Society.* Berkeley: University of California Press.

White, C. S. 1972. "The Sai Baba Movement: Approaches to the Study of Indian Saints." *Journal of Asian Studies* 31 (4): 863–878.

White, Hayden. 1980. "The Value of Narrativity in the Representation of Reality." *Critical Inquiry* 7 (1): 5–27.

Wicki, José, ed. 1969. *O Livro do Pai dos Cristãos: Edição crítica anotada.* Lisbon: Centro de Estudos Históricos Ultramarinos.

Wilfred, Felix. 1998. "Christianity in Hindu Polytheistic Structural Mould: Converts in Southern Tamilnadu Respond to an Alien during the 'Vaco da Gama Epoch.'" *Archives de sciences sociales des religions* 43: 67–87.

Xavier, Felippe Nery. 1852. *Colecçao das leis peculiares das communidades agricolas dos concelhos das Ilhas, Salcete e Bardez.* Panaji, India: Imprensa Nacional.

———. 1861. *Resumo histórico da maravilhosa vida, conversões, e milagres de S. Francisco Xavier, apóstolo, defensor, e patrono das Índias.* Nova Goa, India: Imprensa Nacional.

———. 1903 (vol. 1); 1907 (vol. 2). *Bosquejo histórico das communidades das aldeas dos concelhos das Ilhas, Salcete e Bardes 1801–1901.* 2 vols. Bastora, India: Rangel.

Županov, Ines. 1995. "The Prophetic and the Miraculous in Portuguese Asia: A Hagiographic View of Colonial Culture." *Santa Barbara Portuguese Studies* 2: 135–161.

———. 2001. *Disputed Mission: Jesuit Experiments and Brahmanical Knowledge in Seventeenth-Century India.* New Delhi: Oxford University Press.

Index

ALEXANDER HENN is Associate Professor of Religious Studies at Arizona State University. He is editor (with Klaus-Peter Köpping) of *Rituals in an Unstable World: Contingency, Hybridity, Embodiment.*